Cybersecurity
Handbook for Beginners

A Comprehensive Guide to Safeguarding Digital Assets and Ensuring Data Privacy

Ogee Nwab

Copyright © 2025 **Ogee Nwab**

All Rights Reserved

This book or parts thereof may not be reproduced in any form, stored in any retrieval system, or transmitted in any form by any means—electronic, mechanical, photocopy, recording, or otherwise—without prior written permission of the publisher, except as provided by United States of America copyright law and fair use.

Disclaimer and Terms of Use

The author and publisher of this book and the accompanying materials have used their best efforts in preparing this book. The author and publisher make no representation or warranties with respect to the accuracy, applicability, fitness, or completeness of the contents of this book. The information contained in this book is strictly for informational purposes. Therefore, if you wish to apply the ideas contained in this book, you are taking full responsibility for your actions.

Printed in the United States of America

TABLE OF CONTENTS

TABLE OF CONTENTS III
INTRODUCTION 1
   IMPLEMENTING EFFECTIVE CYBERSECURITY MEASURES 2
CHAPTER ONE 4
GETTING STARTED WITH CYBERSECURITY 4
   OVERVIEW 4
   WHAT IS CYBERSECURITY? 4
   WORKING IN THE FIELD OF CYBERSECURITY 6
      The Value of Transitioning from a Non-Technical Background *8*
   CYBERSECURITY FUNDAMENTALS 9
      Network and Security Concepts *9*
      Authentication *9*
      Authorization *10*
      Non-repudiation *10*
      Confidentiality *10*
      Integrity *11*
      Availability *11*
      Interconnectedness of the CIA Triad *11*
   THE EVOLUTION OF CYBER THREATS: FROM EARLY DAYS TO MODERN WARFARE 11
      The Origins: Viruses and Worms *12*
      An Analysis of the Escalation of Cybercrime: Strategies for Exploitation and Financial Gain *12*
   STATE-SPONSORED CYBER WARFARE: A NEW FRONTIER 13
      The Era of Advanced Persistent Threats: Targeted Attacks and Espionage *13*
      The Future of Cyber Threats: Challenges and Opportunities *14*
   IMPORTANCE OF CYBERSECURITY MEASURES 14
   KEY CONCEPTS AND TERMINOLOGIES 16
   ANALYSIS OF THREATS AND VULNERABILITIES 16
      Analysis of Potential Attack Vectors *17*
      Exploring Defense Mechanisms *17*
   CYBERSECURITY FRAMEWORKS 17
   THE NIST CYBERSECURITY FRAMEWORK 17
   ISO/IEC 27001 17
   CYBERSECURITY THREATS AND TRENDS 18
   RANSOMWARE 18
      Advanced Persistent Threats (APTs) *18*
      • *Internet of Things (IoT) security* *18*
   COMPLIANCE AND REGULATION 18
      The General Data Protection Regulation (GDPR) *18*
   THE HEALTH INSURANCE PORTABILITY AND ACCOUNTABILITY ACT (HIPAA) 19

- Emerging Technologies in Cybersecurity 19
- The World without Cybersecurity 19
- An Exploration of Threats 21
  - Examining the Risks Addressed by Cybersecurity Measures 22
  - The objective of cybersecurity: The CIA Triad 22
- Frequently Asked Questions 24

CHAPTER TWO 25

GETTING TO KNOW COMMON CYBER ATTACKS 25

- Overview 25
- Damage-Dealing Attacks 25
  - Denial-of-service (DoS) attacks 26
- Distributed denial-of-service (DDoS) attacks 26
  - Botnets and zombies 28
  - Data destruction attacks 28
- Phishing 29
- Spear phishing 29
  - CEO fraud 29
  - Smishing 30
  - Vishing 30
  - Pharming 31
- Tampering with Other People's Belongings: A Serious Matter ... 31
  - Interception: Captured in Transit 31
- Man-in-the-middle attacks 32
- Data Theft 32
  - Personal data theft 33
  - Business data theft 34
  - Data exfiltration 35
  - Unauthorized access 35
- Forced policy violations 35
- Malware: Cyber Bombs That Infiltrate Your Devices 36
  - Viruses 36
  - Worms 37
  - Trojans 37
  - Ransomware 37
  - Scareware 38
- Spyware 38
  - Cryptocurrency miners 39
  - Adware 39
  - Blended malware 40
  - Zero-day malware 40
  - Fake malware on computers 40
  - Malicious software targeting mobile devices 41

Phony security subscription renewal notifications 41
ATTACKS ON WEB SERVICES: A DANGEROUS THREAT 41
NETWORK INFRASTRUCTURE POISONING 42
    Malvertising 42
    Drive-by downloads 43
PASSWORD THEFT 43
HIGHLIGHTING MAINTENANCE CHALLENGES 44
    Advanced Attacks 45
    Opportunistic attacks 45
    Targeted attacks 46
    Blended (opportunistic and targeted) attacks 46
VARIOUS TECHNICAL ATTACK TECHNIQUES 47
FREQUENTLY ASKED QUESTIONS 49

CHAPTER THREE 50

CYBERATTACKERS AND THEIR COLORED HATS 50

OVERVIEW 50
CYBERATTACKERS CATEGORIES 50
EXPLORING THE MONETIZATION STRATEGIES OF CYBERCRIMINALS 51
    Direct financial fraud 51
    Indirect financial fraud 52
    Profiting off illegal trading of securities 52
STEALING CREDIT CARDS, DEBIT CARDS, AND OTHER PAYMENT-RELATED INFORMATION 53
    Stealing goods 53
STEALING DATA 54
    Ransomware 54
CRYPTOMINERS 54
DEALING WITH NON-MALICIOUS THREATS: NOT ALL DANGERS COME FROM ATTACKERS 55
HUMAN ERROR 55
THE VULNERABILITY OF CYBERSECURITY LIES IN HUMANS 55
SOCIAL ENGINEERING 56
    External disasters 57
    Natural disasters 57
    Pandemics 57
    Issues caused by human activity in the environment 57
    Cyberwarriors and cyberspies 58
    The ineffective Fair Credit Reporting Act 58
EXPUNGED RECORDS ARE NO LONGER EXPUNGED 59
    Social Security numbers 60
    Social media platforms 60
    Google's highly advanced computers 61
    Tracking the location of mobile devices 61
PROTECTING AGAINST THESE ATTACKERS 62

Frequently Asked Questions 62

CHAPTER FOUR 63

PROTECTION AGAINST CYBER ATTACKS 63

Overview 63

UNDERSTANDING YOUR CURRENT CYBERSECURITY POSTURE 63

THREAT TO COMPUTERS 64

YOUR MOBILE DEVICES 64

YOUR INTERNET OF THINGS (IOT) DEVICES 65

Your networking tool 65

Your work environment 65

Risk Identification 66

UNDERSTANDING ENDPOINTS 66

ENSURING SAFETY FROM POTENTIAL HAZARDS 67

Perimeter defense 67

Firewall/router 68

1. Regularly Update Your Router 68

2. Replace Outdated Routers 68

3. Change the Default Administrative Password 68

4. Choose a Unique SSID (Wi-Fi Network Name) 68

5. Enable Strong Wi-Fi Encryption 69

6. Disable Older Wi-Fi Protocols 69

7. Enable MAC Address Filtering 69

8. Position Your Router Strategically 69

9. Disable Remote Router Access 69

10. Monitor Connected Devices 69

11. Use a Guest Network for Visitors 70

12. Consider Advanced Security Adjustments 70

Conclusion: 70

Security software 70

1. Install Security Software on All Devices 70

2. Use Anti-Spam Software for Email Protection 70

3. Enable Remote Wipe on Mobile Devices 71

4. Set Strong Passwords for Device Access 71

5. Enable Auto-Updates and Keep Devices Updated 71

The physical computer(s) and any other endpoints 71

Backup solutions 72

Detecting 72

Responding 72

Recovering 72

Assessing Your Existing Security Protocols 72

Software and Cybersecurity Considerations 73

Hardware 73

- *Insurance* 74
- *Learning* 74
- *Privacy* 75
- CONSIDER THE CONSEQUENCES BEFORE YOU DECIDE TO SHARE 75
  - *Consider your words before sharing them online* 76
- TIPS FOR MAINTAINING YOUR PRIVACY 77
  - *Ensuring Secure Online Banking* 78
  - *1. Create a Strong, Unique Password* 79
  - *2. Use a Unique PIN for ATM and Phone Authentication* 79
  - *3. Request an ATM-Only Card* 79
  - *4. Understand Fraud Protection* 79
  - *5. Access Online Banking from Trusted Devices* 79
  - *6. Use Secure Networks* 79
  - *7. Access Banking via Official Apps or Browsers* 80
  - *8. Set Up Alerts* 80
  - *9. Enable Multi-Factor Authentication (MFA)* 80
  - *10. Do Not Store Passwords in Your Browser* 80
  - *11. Always Enter Bank URL Manually* 80
  - *12. Use a Separate Computer or Browser for Banking* 80
  - *13. Set Up Browser to Remember Incorrect Passwords* 81
  - *14. Secure Your Devices* 81
  - *15. Monitor Your Accounts for Suspicious Activity* 81
- USING SMART DEVICES WITH SAFETY IN MIND 81
- FREQUENTLY ASKED QUESTIONS 82

CHAPTER FIVE 83

INTRODUCTION TO ENCRYPTION 83

- OVERVIEW 83
- ABOUT ENCRYPTION 83
  - *Encryption Basics* 85
- WHAT EXACTLY IS ENCRYPTION? 85
  - *Exploring the Fundamentals of Encryption* 85
- VARIOUS ENCRYPTION METHODS 86
  - *Uses of Encryption* 86
- CHALLENGES AND CONSIDERATIONS 87
- AN OVERVIEW OF ENCRYPTION ALGORITHMS 88
  - *Various Encryption Algorithms* 89
  - *1. Symmetric Encryption:* 89
  - *2. Asymmetric Encryption:* 89
  - *Advantages and Disadvantages* 90
- APPLICATIONS IN CYBERSECURITY 90
- PUBLIC KEY INFRASTRUCTURE (PKI) 91
  - *PKI Components* 91

- *PKI functions* 92
- *The Significance of PKI in Cybersecurity* 93
- *Challenges and Considerations* 94
- *Anticipated Developments in PKI* 95
- ENCRYPTING DATA AT REST AND IN TRANSIT 96
- METHODS FOR SECURING DATA IN STORAGE 96
  - *Encrypting Data in Transit* 96
- METHODS FOR SECURING DATA DURING TRANSMISSION 96
  - *Challenges and Considerations* 97
- USING SECURE COMMUNICATION PROTOCOLS 97
  - *Secure Communication Protocols Types* 98
- THE IMPORTANCE OF SECURE COMMUNICATION PROTOCOLS IN CYBERSECURITY ... 99
  - *1. Protection of Sensitive Information* 99
  - *2. Prevention of Man-in-the-Middle (MitM) Attacks* 100
  - *3. Enabling Secure Remote Access* 100
  - *4. Securing Online Transactions* 100
  - *5. Enabling Safe Collaboration and Information Sharing* 100
  - *Conclusion:* 101
  - *Challenges and Considerations* 101
- FREQUENTLY ASKED QUESTIONS 102

CHAPTER SIX 104

INCIDENT RESPONSE BASICS 104

- OVERVIEW 104
- INTRODUCTION TO INCIDENT RESPONSE 104
- INCIDENT RESPONSE LIFECYCLE 104
- CHALLENGES AND CONSIDERATIONS 105
- EFFECTIVE STRATEGIES FOR INCIDENT RESPONSE 106
- INCIDENT HANDLING PROCESS 107
  - *1. Preparation* 107
  - *2. Detection and Analysis* 107
  - *3. Containment, Eradication, and Recovery* 108
  - *4. Post-Incident Activities* 108
- ROLES WITHIN THE INCIDENT RESPONSE TEAM 109
  - *1. Incident Commander (IC)* 109
  - *2. Incident Responder* 109
  - *3. Forensic Analyst* 110
  - *4. Communications Coordinator* 110
  - *5. Legal Counsel* 110
- TECHNIQUES FOR DETECTING AND ANALYZING INCIDENTS 111
  - *Advanced Threat Detection Techniques* 111
  - *Intrusion Detection and Prevention Systems (IDS/IPS)* 111
  - *Endpoint Detection and Response (EDR)* 112

- *Security Information and Event Management (SIEM)* 112
- *Integrating Threat Intelligence* 112
- *The Role of Forensic Analysis in Incident Response* 112
- *Effective Incident Response and Mitigation* 113
- IDENTIFYING INDICATORS OF COMPROMISE (IOCS) 113
  - *1. File-based IOCs* 113
  - *2. Network-based IOCs* 113
  - *3. Host-based IOCs* 113
  - *4. Behavioral IOCs* 114
  - *5. Artifact-based IOCs* 114
- IDENTIFYING SIGNS OF COMPROMISE 114
  - *1. Integrating Threat Intelligence* 114
  - *2. Contextual Analysis* 115
  - *3. Behavioral Analytics* 115
  - *4. Endpoint Detection and Response (EDR)* 115
  - *5. Human Expertise* 115
- THE SIGNIFICANCE OF HUMAN INVOLVEMENT 116
  - *1. Flexibility* 116
  - *2. Innovation* 116
  - *3. Critical Thinking* 116
  - *4. Collaboration and Knowledge Sharing* 117
  - *Conclusion* 117
- FREQUENTLY ASKED QUESTIONS 117

CHAPTER SEVEN 118

CYBERSECURITY CONSIDERATIONS WHEN WORKING FROM HOME 118

- OVERVIEW 118
- INTRODUCTION TO CYBERSECURITY CONSIDERATIONS 118
  - *Concerns about Network Security* 119
  - *What are the common security risks associated with remote-worker networks?* 119
  - *What steps can be taken to mitigate these risks?* 120
  - *Concerns About Device Security* 121
- CYBERSECURITY LOCATION 122
- SHOULDER SURFING 122
  - *Eavesdropping* 123
  - *Theft* 123
  - *Human error* 123
- ENSURING CYBERSECURITY IN VIDEO CONFERENCING 123
  - *Ensure that personal items are not visible in the camera frame* 124
- ENSURE THE SECURITY OF YOUR VIDEO CONFERENCES BY PREVENTING UNAUTHORIZED ACCESS 124
- CONCERNS WITH SOCIAL ENGINEERING 125
  - *Regulatory Concerns* 126
- FREQUENTLY ASKED QUESTIONS 126

1. What are the concerns about network security? *126*
2. How do you ensure cybersecurity in video conferencing? *127*
3. What are the concerns with social engineering? *127*

CHAPTER EIGHT **129**

SECURING YOUR ACCOUNTS **129**

OVERVIEW 129
ACCOUNT SAFETY 129
ENSURING THE SAFETY OF YOUR EXTERNAL ACCOUNTS 129
ENSURING THE PROTECTION OF USER ACCOUNT DATA 130
   Use official apps and websites *130*
AVOID INSTALLING SOFTWARE FROM UNTRUSTED SOURCES 131
   Avoid rooting your phone *131*
   Avoid sharing unnecessary sensitive information *131*
   Use payment services that eliminate the need to share credit card numbers *131*
CONSIDER USING ONE-TIME, VIRTUAL CREDIT CARD NUMBERS WHEN IT IS SUITABLE 132
   Keep a close eye on your accounts *133*
   Report any suspicious activity as soon as possible *133*
USE A WELL-THOUGHT-OUT PASSWORD STRATEGY 133
USE MULTI-FACTOR AUTHENTICATION 133
   Remember to log out once you're done *134*
   Use your personal computer or phone *134*
   Lock your PC *135*
USING A SEPARATE, DEDICATED COMPUTER FOR SENSITIVE TASKS 135
   Use a separate browser solely for tasks that require a higher level of security *135*
ENSURE THE SECURITY OF YOUR ACCESS DEVICES 135
   Ensure that your devices are always kept up to date *135*
   Avoid conducting sensitive tasks while connected to public Wi-Fi networks *136*
   Avoid using public Wi-Fi in high-risk locations *136*
   Make sure to access your accounts in secure locations *136*
   Use suitable devices *136*
ESTABLISHING SUITABLE BOUNDARIES 136
   Use alerts *136*
   Regularly monitor access device lists *137*
   Review the most recent login information *137*
   Make sure to respond promptly to any fraud alerts *137*
   Avoid sending sensitive information over an unencrypted connection *137*
   Be cautious of social engineering attacks *137*
SET UP VOICE LOGIN PASSWORDS 138
   Ensure the security of your cell phone number *138*
AVOID CLICKING ON LINKS IN EMAILS OR TEXT MESSAGES 138
   Ensuring the Security of Data Shared with Parties You've Interacted With *138*
   Securing Data at Parties You Haven't Interacted With *139*

Ensuring Data Security by Avoiding Connection with Hardware of Uncertain Origins 140
Frequently Asked Questions 141
   1. How do you ensure the safety of your external accounts? 141
   2. How do you ensure the protection of user account data? 141
   3. How do you secure your accounts generally? 142

CHAPTER NINE 143

COMPUTER SECURITY TECHNOLOGY 143

Overview 143
Computer Security Technology Overview 143
   EtherPeek 143
   QualysGuard 143
   SuperScan 144
WebInspect 144
   LC4 144
   NMAP 144
   Metasploit 144
Burp Suite 145
Angry IP Scanner 145
Frequently Asked Questions 145
   1. What do you understand by computer security technology? 145
   2. What are the different computer security technologies? 145

CHAPTER TEN 147

CYBERSECURITY FOR BUSINESSES AND ORGANIZATIONS 147

Overview 147
Ensuring Effective Leadership 147
Keeping an Eye on Employees 147
Motivate your staff 148
Be cautious about sharing sensitive information 148
   Provide each individual with their own set of login credentials 149
   Limit the access of administrators 149
Restrict access to corporate accounts 149
   Implementing employee policies 150
Implement and uphold social media policies 152
   Keep track of employees 153
   Managing a Remote Workforce 153
Use work devices and separate work networks 153
Establish virtual private networks 154
Develop standardized communication protocols 155
   Use a familiar network 155
   Find out how backups are managed 156
   Remain highly cautious when it comes to social engineering tactics 157

- Exploring Cybersecurity Insurance 157
  - Ensuring the security of employee data 158
- PCI DSS 158
  - The Four PCI Compliance Levels: 159
  - Key Requirements Under PCI DSS: 159
  - Steps to Achieve PCI DSS Compliance: 160
  - Why PCI Compliance Is Important: 160
- Laws regarding the disclosure of breaches 161
  - GDPR 161
  - HIPAA 162
  - Biometric data 162
- Laws regarding the prevention of money laundering 162
  - Global restrictions 163
- Managing Internet Access 163
  - Separate Internet access for personal devices 163
  - Implement policies for employees to bring their own devices (BYOD) 163
  - Ensure efficient management of inbound access 164
- Defend your system from denial-of-service attacks 165
  - Consider using HTTPS 166
  - VPN 166
- Conduct penetration tests 166
- Exercise caution when using IoT devices 166
- Use multiple network segments 167
  - Exercise caution when using payment cards 167
  - Addressing Power Problems 167
- Frequently Asked Questions 167
  - 1. How do you think businesses and organizations should keep off cyber criminals? 167
  - 2. What do you understand by cybersecurity insurance? 168
  - 3. How do you manage internet access in cybersecurity? 169

CHAPTER ELEVEN 170

WIRELESS NETWORK PIRATING 170

- How Wireless Networks Work 170
- Wireless Standards 172
- Wireless Security 173
- Wireless authentication 174
- Wireless Encryption 175
- Wireless Attacks 175
- Rogue Access Points 177
- Disassociation Attacks 179
- Jamming 180
- Setting Up a Wireless Network with Security in Mind 180
- Setting up your access point. 182

- Setting Up Wireless Security 184
- Enabling Filtering 186

CHAPTER TWELVE 189

PURSUING A CYBERSECURITY CAREER 189

- Overview 189
- Cybersecurity Career 189
- Roles in Cybersecurity 189
  - Experienced in the field of security engineering 190
  - Security manager 191
  - Security director 191
  - Chief information security officer (CISO) 191
  - Security analyst 191
  - Security Architect 191
  - Security administrator 192
  - Security auditor 192
  - Cryptographer 192
  - Vulnerability assessment analyst 192
  - Ethical hacker 192
  - Security researcher 193
  - Offensive hacker 193
  - Software security engineer 193
- Software source code security auditor 193
  - Security consultant 193
  - Security expert witness 194
  - Security specialist 194
  - Member of the incident response team 194
  - Expert in forensic analysis 194
  - Cybersecurity regulations expert 194
  - Privacy regulations expert 195
- Exploring Different Career Paths 195
  - Career path: Senior security architect 195
  - Career path: Chief Information Security Officer (CISO) 196
- Getting Started in Information Security 197
- Exploring Popular Certifications 198
  - CISSP 198
  - CISM 199
  - CEH 200
  - Security+ 200
  - GSEC 200
  - Verifiability 201
  - Ethics 201
- Overcoming a Criminal Record 201

  Conquering Bad Credit *202*
 Exploring Alternative Careers with a Focus on Cybersecurity 202
 Frequently Asked Questions 203
  1. What are the job roles in cybersecurity? *203*
  2. What do you understand by information security? *203*
  3. What are the different popular certifications in cybersecurity? *203*
  4. How do you explore alternative careers in cybersecurity? *204*
  5. How do you overcome a criminal record? *205*

CHAPTER THIRTEEN 206

HOW TO DEFEAT BLACK HATS 206

 What's the worst that can happen? 206
 Risks 207
 Threats 209
 Controls 210
 Risk Management Programs 212
 Putting it All Together 213
  Exercise: Conducting a Risk Assessment *215*
 Goodbye, and good luck. 215

CHAPTER FOURTEEN 217

ENHANCING YOUR CYBERSECURITY 217

 Understand that you are a target 217
 Use security software 217
 Encrypt sensitive information 218
 Back-Up Often 219
 Don't share login credentials 219
 Use proper authentication 220
 Use Social Media Wisely 220
 Separate internet access 220
 Use Public Wi-Fi Safely (or Don't Use It!) 221
 Hire a Professional 221

CHAPTER FIFTEEN 222

LESSONS FROM MAJOR CYBERSECURITY BREACHES 222

 Marriott 222
 Target 223
 Sony Pictures 223
 U.S. Office of Personnel Management 224
 Anthem 225
 Colonial Pipeline and JBS SA 225
 JBS 226

CONCLUSION	228
INDEX	**229**

INTRODUCTION

In today's digital world, where technology is deeply woven into nearly every aspect of our daily lives, cybersecurity has become more critical than ever. As technology continues to evolve, it brings both exciting advancements and new risks that were unimaginable just a few decades ago. While these technological improvements have made life more connected and convenient, they also introduce vulnerabilities that, if left unaddressed, can be exploited by malicious actors, leading to severe consequences. This is why cybersecurity plays such a vital role in defending against these growing threats.

Cybersecurity is not merely a technical field; it encompasses a wide range of practices, technologies, and processes designed to protect networks, systems, and sensitive data from unauthorized access and potential harm. It combines advanced technological tools—such as firewalls, encryption, and intrusion detection systems—with human factors like user training, awareness, and adherence to security protocols. Together, these elements form a multi-layered defense strategy that is essential for safeguarding information in today's digital landscape.

The importance of cybersecurity cannot be overstated. Beyond protecting individuals and organizations, it is crucial for national security, economic stability, and public welfare. A cyberattack could have catastrophic effects on critical infrastructure, banking systems, and everyday services that depend on the internet and digital technologies. Cyberattacks can disrupt vital services, steal sensitive data, and result in significant financial losses, often through widespread scams.

As our dependence on digital technologies grows, so does the likelihood of cyber threats. This makes it imperative for individuals, businesses, and governments to prioritize cybersecurity. By doing so, they not only protect themselves from immediate dangers but also contribute to creating a safer, more reliable online environment for everyone. In essence, cybersecurity serves as the backbone of the digital age, enabling us to enjoy the benefits of new technologies while minimizing the risks they bring.

With the rapid pace of technological innovation, the widespread adoption of interconnected devices, and the increasingly sophisticated tactics used by cybercriminals, the threat landscape is constantly evolving. While traditional threats like viruses, malware, and bugs remain prevalent, newer and more deceptive forms of cyberattacks—such as ransomware, phishing, and social engineering—have emerged.

The rise of the Internet of Things (IoT) has further complicated the security landscape. As billions of devices, ranging from smart home appliances to industrial control systems, become interconnected, the potential attack surface expands. This makes robust security measures more critical than ever. The challenges in cybersecurity stem from both technological weaknesses and human factors, including poor security practices and a lack of awareness among users.

The overall risk environment is shaped by a variety of factors, such as vulnerabilities in software and hardware, inadequate security measures, and a lack of user education about potential threats. Moreover, as systems become increasingly interconnected, a breach in one area can have far-reaching effects across entire networks or organizations.

Implementing Effective Cybersecurity Measures

To effectively navigate the constantly evolving landscape of cyber threats, it is crucial to adopt a proactive, multi-layered approach to cybersecurity. The following strategies play a vital role in safeguarding systems and data:

1. **Risk Assessment:** Conducting a thorough risk assessment is a critical first step in developing effective security measures. This process involves identifying potential threats and vulnerabilities within an organization's infrastructure. By understanding these risks, organizations can implement targeted security measures to mitigate them.
2. **Establishing Security Policies and Procedures:** Developing comprehensive security policies and procedures is essential for controlling access, protecting data, responding to incidents, and educating employees. Clear, well-defined guidelines lay the foundation for a strong security posture and ensure that everyone within the organization understands their role in maintaining security.
3. **Technical Controls:** Leveraging technology to enhance security is key in preventing cyberattacks. This includes deploying firewalls, antivirus software, encryption protocols, and intrusion detection systems. By utilizing these technical solutions, organizations can strengthen their defenses against a wide range of threats.
4. **Ongoing Monitoring:** Continuous monitoring of network traffic and system activity is crucial for detecting suspicious behavior or potential security breaches early. This enables prompt responses to emerging threats and helps prevent significant damage.
5. **Incident Response Plan:** Having a well-defined incident response plan is essential for addressing security incidents quickly and efficiently. This proactive strategy helps minimize damage, expedite recovery, and reduce the overall impact of an attack.
6. **Collaboration and Information Sharing:** Given the interconnected nature of the digital world, it is important for organizations, government agencies, and cybersecurity experts to collaborate and share threat intelligence. Exchanging best practices and staying informed about emerging threats strengthens the collective ability to respond to cyber risks.
7. **User Education and Awareness:** Educating users about common cyber threats, safe browsing practices, and the importance of strong passwords is crucial in reducing the risk of human error. Well-informed employees are less likely to fall victim to phishing attacks or other social engineering tactics, significantly improving an organization's overall security posture.

By combining these strategies, organizations can create a robust and adaptable defense system that minimizes risk and ensures a proactive response to evolving cyber threats.

CHAPTER ONE
GETTING STARTED WITH CYBERSECURITY

Overview

Chapter One provides an overview of cybersecurity, explaining its significance in our daily lives and offering a comprehensive introduction to the field. It covers the essential principles and concepts that form the foundation of cybersecurity, including key terms and terminology. In this chapter, you'll gain an understanding of why cybersecurity is crucial for protecting personal information, devices, and online activities, as well as how it impacts individuals, organizations, and society at large. This foundational knowledge sets the stage for deeper exploration into more complex cybersecurity topics.

What Is Cybersecurity?

Cybersecurity is a vital issue for a wide range of stakeholders, including governments, major corporations, small business owners, employees, and individuals in their personal homes.

We are living in an increasingly interconnected world, where more devices are being added to the global network every year. This growing web of connections means that virtually every facet of our lives is now being tracked electronically, creating a digital footprint that spans everything from our health and financial data to our daily activities and personal preferences. Information such as the energy we use, the clothes we wear, our home arrival times, and travel habits is being carefully monitored and stored.

When analyzed, this data can generate profiles so comprehensive that they often reveal more about us than we know about ourselves. This highlights the urgent need for individuals to be aware of the risks and take proactive steps to protect their personal information. Our data is spread across various platforms and systems, making it more fragmented than ever. It's crucial for people to understand where their data is being shared, the potential consequences of that sharing, and what they can do to minimize risks.

For businesses, the stakes are even higher. Cyberattacks are not only becoming more frequent but are also causing greater financial damage. Companies are increasingly aware of the threat and are investing heavily in cybersecurity. In fact, global spending on cybersecurity was expected to surpass $1.7 billion in 2020, marking a 10.7% increase from the previous year. This surge in investment underscores the growing urgency for businesses to address the expanding cyber threat landscape.

A major challenge for companies is the rise of unmanaged and insecure Internet of Things (IoT) devices. These devices are often introduced into corporate environments without proper security protocols, significantly widening the potential attack surface. As IoT devices become more integrated into business operations, the number of potential entry points for cyberattacks increases, making it essential for organizations to adopt comprehensive security strategies.

In this highly connected world, both individuals and businesses must prioritize cybersecurity. For individuals, this means being cautious about where and how personal data is shared, understanding the risks involved, and taking necessary steps to protect themselves. For businesses, it means investing in strong cybersecurity measures, staying ahead of emerging threats, and ensuring that every connected device, especially IoT devices, is properly secured. The benefits of our interconnected world are immense, but they come with an equally significant responsibility to ensure our security.

Cybercriminals and nation-states are increasingly targeting IoT devices, largely because many of these devices lack built-in security features. In fact, incidents like the use of vending machines to steal information have highlighted the vulnerabilities in everyday devices. Data from 2018 showed a staggering 300% rise in IoT-related threats within just a few months. As a result, businesses are recognizing the critical need to invest in cybersecurity training and staff, as the consequences of breaches can be devastating.

Cybersecurity has evolved from being a purely technical issue to an essential part of overall business risk management. The urgency of this shift is clear, given that five million data records are lost or stolen every day worldwide. The impact extends beyond businesses—political stability, peace, and social harmony are increasingly at risk on a global scale. Countries are stealing vast amounts of sensitive data and intellectual property from each other, interfering in elections, and even shaping public discourse. The potential for machines to influence nearly every aspect of society, down to the individual level, underscores the critical importance of addressing security risks in this new era.

Working in the field of cybersecurity

Let's now turn our attention to the field of cybersecurity careers, starting with why this profession is increasingly open to individuals from diverse backgrounds, even those without technical expertise.

Cybersecurity is no longer just for computer scientists or IT professionals; it has evolved into a dynamic, multidisciplinary field that welcomes a broad range of skills and experiences. The growing complexity of cyber threats has made it clear that cybersecurity requires more than just technical knowledge. Professionals with backgrounds in law, policy, business, psychology, communications, and even the arts can contribute valuable perspectives to the industry. For example, those with legal or policy expertise play a crucial role in navigating data privacy regulations and ensuring compliance. People with strong communication skills are needed to help translate complex technical issues into clear, understandable information for executives, clients, and the public. Even those with backgrounds in psychology or behavioral sciences are in demand, as understanding human behavior is key to identifying vulnerabilities in both individuals and organizations.

This diversity of expertise is essential because cybersecurity is about much more than just defending against technical attacks; it also involves understanding the human element, risk management, legal frameworks, and even the ethical implications of new technologies. As cyber threats continue to evolve and affect every part of society, there is a growing need for professionals with a wide variety of perspectives to join the field.

Job Outlook in Cybersecurity

The demand for cybersecurity professionals is stronger than ever. With the constant rise in cyberattacks and the increasing importance of protecting sensitive data, businesses, governments, and organizations across all sectors are actively seeking skilled cybersecurity experts. According to the U.S. Bureau of Labor Statistics, the number of cybersecurity jobs is projected to grow significantly over the next decade, far outpacing the average growth rate for other professions. In fact, some reports predict a shortage of millions of cybersecurity professionals globally in the coming years.

This high demand means that career opportunities in cybersecurity are abundant, with competitive salaries and the potential for career growth across various industries. From financial institutions to healthcare organizations, government agencies to tech companies, virtually every sector requires cybersecurity professionals, making this an exceptionally versatile and secure career path.

Cybersecurity Specialties

One of the great things about a career in cybersecurity is the variety of specialties you can explore. Cybersecurity is a broad field, and professionals can specialize in numerous areas, each offering unique challenges and opportunities. Some of the key specialties in cybersecurity include:

1. **Network Security**: Professionals in this area focus on protecting an organization's computer networks from intrusions, attacks, and unauthorized access. This includes monitoring network traffic, identifying vulnerabilities, and implementing firewalls and other security protocols.
2. **Penetration Testing (Ethical Hacking)**: Penetration testers, also known as ethical hackers, simulate cyberattacks to identify weaknesses in an organization's defenses. This proactive approach helps organizations find and fix vulnerabilities before malicious hackers can exploit them.
3. **Incident Response and Forensics**: This specialty involves responding to security breaches and cyberattacks. Incident response teams work to contain and mitigate damage, while forensics experts analyze digital evidence to understand how a breach occurred and identify the perpetrators.
4. **Security Architecture and Engineering**: Professionals in this field design and build secure systems and infrastructure to prevent attacks. They work closely with IT teams to ensure that security is integrated into every layer of an organization's technology stack.
5. **Compliance and Risk Management**: These professionals focus on ensuring that organizations meet security standards and regulatory requirements (such as GDPR, HIPAA, and others). They also assess risks and help businesses implement strategies to mitigate potential security threats.
6. **Threat Intelligence**: This role involves analyzing and identifying emerging cyber threats. Threat intelligence professionals gather information about cybercriminal tactics, techniques, and procedures (TTPs) to help organizations stay ahead of potential attacks.
7. **Security Awareness Training**: Since human error is often the weakest link in cybersecurity, professionals who specialize in training employees to recognize and respond to threats like phishing and social engineering play a critical role in a company's overall security posture.
8. **Cloud Security**: With more organizations shifting to cloud-based infrastructures, cloud security professionals focus on securing data and applications stored in cloud environments, ensuring compliance with security policies, and protecting against vulnerabilities specific to cloud computing.
9. **Identity and Access Management (IAM)**: IAM specialists focus on ensuring that only authorized individuals have access to an organization's systems and data. They manage user identities, authentication methods, and access controls.

As the digital landscape continues to grow and evolve, cybersecurity remains a dynamic and essential field with a variety of career paths to explore. Whether you're technically inclined or possess expertise in other areas, there is a place for you in this high-demand profession. The key is to find the specialty that aligns with your skills and interests, and then build the necessary knowledge and certifications to succeed.

The Value of Transitioning from a Non-Technical Background

It's a misconception to view security as just one career path. Those passionate about safeguarding our cyber infrastructure have a wide range of roles to choose from within the field of security. The demand for security professionals is rapidly increasing and shows no signs of slowing, offering strong career prospects for those entering the field.

If you believe that a computer science degree and years of technical experience are required to pursue a career in cybersecurity, it's time to reconsider. The field actually requires a diverse set of skills, including expertise in law, psychology, sociology, technology, and organizational sciences to implement effective large-scale security measures. Cybersecurity offers numerous job opportunities for both technical and non-technical individuals. While many people think of roles like crisis response engineers or expert operators as the most prestigious in the field, the reality is that cybersecurity also relies on professionals such as program managers, software developers, marketers, data scientists, and systems analysts. Additionally, security companies have a range of non-technical roles available, including positions in product management, marketing, public relations, and sales.

Having a non-technical background can actually be an advantage, as it allows you to bring a unique perspective and skill set to the table. The cybersecurity industry is made up of people from all walks of life—teachers, journalists, lawyers, control systems experts—and we hire them because we value the diverse perspectives and expertise they bring. Some security professionals focus on policy and law, while others design large, distributed systems, hunt for vulnerabilities, or track down hidden threats. The variety of roles within cybersecurity reflects the broad range of skills needed to keep digital systems safe.

Cybersecurity Fundamentals

Network and Security Concepts

Information Assurance Fundamentals

For maintaining system security, focusing on **confidentiality**, **integrity**, and **availability** is essential. System designers can implement tools such as authentication, authorization, and non-repudiation to protect these critical aspects. Security experts need to understand how these six concepts—authentication, authorization, non-repudiation, confidentiality, integrity, and availability—work together to create secure systems. If any of these elements fail, the entire system could be vulnerable to attacks. To effectively safeguard information systems, professionals must have a clear understanding of these principles, often referred to as the **CIA triad**: confidentiality, integrity, and availability. Additionally, systems must implement identification, authorization, and non-repudiation to ensure secure access and prevent misuse.

This section will explain each of these key concepts and explore their interconnections in the context of cybersecurity. The definitions provided here come from the **National Information Assurance Glossary (NIAG)**, published by the U.S. Committee on National Security Systems.

Authentication

Authentication is a critical aspect of secure systems, ensuring the identity of users and validating the origin of messages. According to the NIAG, authentication is a security process that verifies the legitimacy of a transmission, message, or originator. It also checks the authorization of an individual to access specific information. Authentication typically involves a challenge-response mechanism, where the system requests information that only authenticated users can provide.

There are three main types of authentication factors:

1. **Something you know**: a password or PIN.
2. **Something you have**: a security token or smartphone.
3. **Something you are**: biometric data like fingerprints or facial recognition.

Multi-factor authentication (MFA) enhances security by combining two or more of these factors, making it more difficult for unauthorized individuals to gain access. However, combining two identical factors (like a password and a mother's maiden name) does not constitute MFA, as both belong to the "something you know" category.

For verifying the authenticity of messages (such as network packets or emails), cryptographic techniques like **message authentication codes (MACs)** or **digital signatures** are used. These signatures are created using a hash of the message and a secret key, ensuring that only the intended recipient, who has the key, can validate the message's authenticity.

In summary, authentication is essential for both securing access to systems and ensuring the integrity of digital communications. Using MFA and cryptographic methods can further bolster security, making it difficult for unauthorized entities to interfere with sensitive information.

Authorization

While authentication verifies identity, **authorization** determines the access rights and permissions granted to a user. The NIAG defines authorization as the privileges or permissions given to a user, program, or process. Once a user is authenticated, the system assesses what actions the user can take and what resources they can access. For example, in an online banking system, once a user is authenticated, the system must verify which accounts the user can access and what transactions they are allowed to perform.

Non-repudiation

Non-repudiation ensures that once a transaction or action is completed, neither the sender nor the recipient can deny their involvement. This concept is critical for ensuring accountability in digital communications. For example, in a contract scenario, if Alice agrees to purchase a car from Bob and later denies her involvement, Bob can prove Alice's signature through a notary's verification, preventing Alice from repudiating the transaction.

In the digital world, **asymmetric (public key) cryptography** is often used to establish non-repudiation. In this process, a sender signs a message with their private key, which can later be verified by the recipient using the sender's public key. This ensures that the sender cannot later deny having sent the message, as only their private key could have created the signature.

Confidentiality

Confidentiality ensures that information is not disclosed to unauthorized individuals, processes, or devices. According to the NIAG, confidentiality refers to the assurance that sensitive data remains inaccessible to unauthorized parties. To protect confidentiality, systems must employ strong security measures that limit access to authorized users, as well as identification systems to verify these users. Additionally, sensitive data must be protected during transmission, often through encryption.

For instance, businesses can use **Virtual Private Networks (VPNs)** to securely transmit data over public networks, or encrypt backup tapes when transporting them between locations. Even physical security measures, such as preventing "shoulder surfing" or theft, are important to safeguard confidentiality.

Integrity

Integrity refers to maintaining the accuracy and reliability of data over time. In information security, integrity ensures that data is not modified, destroyed, or tampered with by unauthorized users. The NIAG defines integrity as ensuring that the system's hardware, software, and data structures operate correctly and consistently, without unauthorized alterations.

One of the primary threats to data integrity is **unauthorized modification**, which could be caused by software vulnerabilities or system misconfigurations. For example, an attacker might exploit an **SQL injection** vulnerability to alter or inject malicious data into a database. To prevent this, systems rely on authentication, authorization, and cryptographic methods to ensure data remains intact.

Availability

For an information system to be effective, its data and services must be accessible when needed. The NIAG defines availability as ensuring reliable and timely access to data for authorized users. **Denial of Service (DoS)** attacks, which overwhelm systems with excessive requests, are a primary threat to availability. DoS attacks can exhaust system resources such as CPU, memory, or network bandwidth, rendering the system unavailable to legitimate users. Effective defense mechanisms, such as traffic filtering or load balancing, are essential for maintaining system availability.

Interconnectedness of the CIA Triad

Each element of the **CIA triad** (Confidentiality, Integrity, and Availability) is critical for maintaining overall system security. If one of these elements is compromised, the security of the entire system is at risk. Authentication, authorization, and non-repudiation are techniques that support these principles and ensure that systems remain secure. Security professionals must understand how these concepts work together to protect data and services from various threats. Each pillar contributes to a balanced and effective security strategy.

The Evolution of Cyber Threats: From Early Days to Modern Warfare

In today's rapidly evolving digital landscape, the importance of security has become paramount. As technology advances, so too do the methods and motivations of those seeking to exploit it for malicious purposes. The rise of cyber threats is shaped by a complex mix of factors, including technological progress, geopolitical tensions, and the ever-evolving strategies of adversarial actors. From the earliest computer viruses to the sophisticated cyber warfare tactics employed by nation-states today, the history of cyber threats underscores the ongoing need for vigilance and constant innovation in the field of cybersecurity. This evolution highlights the critical and ever-present demand for adaptive security measures to stay ahead of increasingly advanced and diverse threats.

The Origins: Viruses and Worms

Cyber risks have their origins in the early days of computing. The rise of personal computers in the 1970s and 1980s marked the emergence of malicious software, now commonly referred to as **malware**. One of the earliest known instances of this was the **Creeper virus**, which appeared on ARPANET (the precursor to the modern internet) in 1971. The Creeper virus was a simple program that displayed the message, *"I am the Creeper, endeavor to apprehend me if you are able!"* on infected computers, signaling the start of a new era in cybersecurity.

As personal computers became more widespread in the 1980s, the frequency of viruses and worms also grew. Early forms of malware were typically spread through infected floppy disks and relied on user actions—such as transferring disks between systems—to propagate. One of the most significant malware incidents during this period was the **Morris Worm**, created in 1988 by Robert Tappan Morris. This worm exploited vulnerabilities in **Unix** systems, causing widespread infection and significant disruption across thousands of computers. The Morris Worm is often regarded as one of the first major examples of a worm attack and remains a key moment in the history of cybersecurity.

An Analysis of the Escalation of Cybercrime: Strategies for Exploitation and Financial Gain

As the internet became more widespread in the 1990s, opportunities for cybercriminals expanded significantly. The growth of **e-commerce** and **online banking** created a ripe environment for exploitation, as malicious actors sought to take advantage of vulnerabilities in online systems. One of the most notable developments during this period was the rise of **phishing** attacks, where cybercriminals tricked users into divulging sensitive information, such as passwords and credit card numbers.

In the late 1990s and early 2000s, cybercrime surged, largely due to the increasing interconnectedness of digital systems. The widespread distribution of **malware** became a major concern, with high-profile incidents like the **ILOVEYOU worm** and the **Code Red** and **Nimda** worms drawing attention to the growing risks of rapidly spreading malicious software on the internet. These attacks wreaked havoc on global systems, causing billions of dollars in financial losses. The scale and impact of these incidents underscored the urgent need for stronger cybersecurity measures and a more comprehensive approach to safeguarding digital infrastructure.

State-Sponsored Cyber Warfare: A New Frontier

In recent years, the rise of **state-sponsored cyber warfare** has dramatically reshaped the landscape of cyber threats. Nation-states are increasingly leveraging cyberspace as a tool to further their strategic objectives, engaging in activities such as **espionage**, **sabotage**, and **cyber warfare**. One of the most notable examples of state-backed cyber operations is the **Stuxnet** worm, discovered in 2010, which highlighted the advanced capabilities of cyber weapons developed by governments.

Stuxnet, believed to have been created by the **United States** and **Israel**, was specifically designed to infiltrate and disrupt Iran's nuclear facilities. The worm's primary target was the **centrifuges** used in uranium enrichment, and it caused significant physical damage to the equipment while remaining undetected for some time. This attack represented a new frontier in cyber warfare, demonstrating how digital tools could be used to achieve geopolitical objectives without traditional military intervention.

The use of cyber weapons by nation-states has blurred the lines between conventional warfare and cyber conflict, raising complex **legal** and **ethical** challenges. As cyber capabilities continue to evolve, there are growing concerns about the potential for **escalation** and the unpredictable consequences of cyber-attacks, especially when employed in the context of international conflict. The growing sophistication and frequency of state-sponsored cyber operations underscore the urgent need for new frameworks to address the evolving nature of cyber threats and their potential impact on global security.

The Era of Advanced Persistent Threats: Targeted Attacks and Espionage

In addition to state-sponsored cyber warfare, the rise of **Advanced Persistent Threats (APTs)** has significantly complicated the cybersecurity landscape. APTs are highly sophisticated, prolonged cyber-attacks typically carried out by nation-states or well-funded organizations with specific, long-term objectives. Unlike conventional cybercrime, which often seeks quick financial gains, APTs are characterized by their patient and methodical approach, aiming for deeper and more strategic impacts over an extended period.

APTs are known for their persistence and their ability to remain undetected for months, or even years. These attacks often target high-value individuals, organizations, or government entities, and involve a range of advanced tactics, such as **targeted phishing campaigns**, exploiting **zero-day vulnerabilities**, and **supply chain attacks**. These strategies are carefully crafted to breach specific targets and evade detection, allowing attackers to maintain access to sensitive information or infrastructure for as long as possible.

The actors behind APTs vary widely, from nation-states seeking to gather intelligence, conduct espionage, or disrupt their adversaries, to criminal organizations involved in **industrial espionage** or data theft. The resources and capabilities behind APT groups make them highly dangerous and difficult to defend against, as their objectives often go beyond immediate financial gain and aim at extracting valuable intellectual property, trade secrets, or sensitive governmental data. The emergence and sophistication of APTs highlight the growing complexity of the cyber threat landscape and the need for advanced security measures to defend against these stealthy, prolonged attacks.

The Future of Cyber Threats: Challenges and Opportunities

As technology continues to evolve, so too will the landscape of **cyber risks**. The rapid expansion of the **Internet of Things (IoT)**, the rise of **artificial intelligence (AI)**, and the increasing interconnectedness of digital systems present new and complex challenges for cybersecurity professionals. As these technologies advance, malicious actors will likely seek to exploit them for harmful purposes, underscoring the need for innovative defensive strategies to stay ahead of emerging threats.

At the same time, there are significant opportunities to address these risks through collaboration, education, and technological innovation. **Public-private partnerships** can play a crucial role in enhancing information sharing and improving coordination between government agencies, private enterprises, and cybersecurity experts. By working together, these entities can strengthen the collective defense against cyber threats.

Moreover, investment in **research and development** holds the potential to drive the creation of cutting-edge cybersecurity technologies that can more effectively detect, mitigate, and neutralize new forms of attack. As cyber risks evolve, it will be critical for stakeholders to remain proactive, agile, and collaborative in their efforts to protect digital infrastructure and ensure the security of interconnected systems.

Importance of Cybersecurity Measures

As our society rapidly embraces digitalization, with technology woven into nearly every aspect of daily life, **cybersecurity** has become a matter of paramount importance. Safeguarding against **cyber-attacks** is essential, as insufficient protection can lead to devastating consequences, such as **financial fraud**, **identity theft**, **espionage**, and even **cyber warfare**. Strong cybersecurity measures are vital not only for protecting individuals, businesses, and governments but also for maintaining trust in the digital ecosystem.

Cybersecurity is a broad field, encompassing a variety of **technologies**, **techniques**, and **processes** specifically designed to defend against harmful cyber activities. These activities include unauthorized access to sensitive data, disruption of critical services, and the exploitation of vulnerabilities in computer systems and networks. Given the highly interconnected nature of the digital landscape, **cyber threats** can arise from a wide range of sources, including **hackers**, **criminal**

organizations, **nation-states**, and even **insiders** within an organization. To address the ever-present and evolving risk of cyber-attacks, both individuals and organizations must stay vigilant and adopt proactive cybersecurity strategies.

Preventive measures are the cornerstone of effective cybersecurity. These measures involve proactive steps to identify and mitigate potential threats before they cause harm. For example, organizations deploy **firewalls**, **intrusion detection systems**, and **antivirus software** to monitor and block suspicious network traffic and malicious software. On a personal level, individuals can strengthen their security by using strong, unique passwords, enabling **two-factor authentication**, and regularly updating software to incorporate the latest security patches. By adopting these preventive measures, organizations can significantly reduce their vulnerability to cyberattacks. However, it is essential to recognize that, in the ever-evolving threat landscape, relying solely on prevention is not enough.

In addition to prevention, **detection** and **response** capabilities are critical components of a comprehensive cybersecurity plan. Despite our best efforts to prevent breaches, determined attackers may still find ways to circumvent defenses. To address this, organizations must invest in advanced technologies and well-established procedures that allow for early detection of security incidents and prompt responses to mitigate their impact. For instance, organizations can build **advanced threat detection systems**, establish dedicated **incident response teams**, and conduct regular **security assessments** to identify and address vulnerabilities.

Moreover, **human factors** play a significant role in cybersecurity, as human error is often a major contributor to security breaches. Actions like clicking on **phishing links** or accidentally sharing personal information can lead to serious compromises. To combat this, it is crucial to foster a **security-conscious culture** within organizations. This can be achieved by implementing ongoing **training** and **awareness programs** that educate employees on common cyber threats and best practices for safeguarding sensitive data. Additionally, fostering collaboration and **information sharing** among employees is vital for building a resilient cybersecurity system.

Cyber threats are not confined to specific industries or geographical regions; they can impact businesses of all sizes and sectors. Sharing threat intelligence and applying best practices across organizations can dramatically enhance collective defense. Public-private collaborations, industry alliances, and **information-sharing platforms** can help strengthen cybersecurity efforts and improve response capabilities to emerging threats. **Incident response** is another critical area of focus in cybersecurity. Despite all preventive measures, security breaches may still occur, and organizations must be prepared with robust incident response strategies. These strategies should include clear reporting procedures, dedicated response teams, and effective coordination with law enforcement and regulatory authorities. A well-executed incident response plan can minimize the damage from a breach and facilitate a swift return to normal operations.

Furthermore, the importance of cybersecurity extends beyond businesses and individual privacy. **National security** and **geopolitical stability** are also at risk in the digital age. As cyber-attacks are increasingly used for **espionage**, **sabotage**, and **coercion**, protecting **critical infrastructure** has become a top priority for governments worldwide. As a result, there has been an international push to create and adopt **cybersecurity policies**, **frameworks**, and collaborative efforts aimed at enhancing cyber defenses and promoting responsible conduct in cyberspace.

The growing adoption of technologies like the **Internet of Things (IoT)**, **cloud computing**, and **artificial intelligence (AI)** has added new layers of complexity to the cybersecurity landscape. Many IoT devices, such as **smart home appliances** and **industrial control systems**, often lack adequate security measures, leaving them vulnerable to exploitation. Similarly, the increased reliance on **cloud services** and **AI-powered systems** introduces new attack vectors that adversaries can exploit. To address these emerging risks, a comprehensive cybersecurity strategy is essential, one that integrates both **technical innovation** and **regulatory oversight**. This strategy should not only focus on developing advanced defensive technologies but also on implementing regulatory measures that promote secure design, development, and deployment practices across industries.

In conclusion, as digital technologies continue to evolve, so too will the **cyber risks** we face. By adopting a multifaceted approach that includes prevention, detection, response, human education, and collaboration, we can work to stay one step ahead of cyber threats. As a global community, it is essential that we invest in cybersecurity to safeguard both our digital infrastructure and the broader security and stability of our interconnected world.

Key concepts and terminologies

Cybersecurity has become an essential aspect of today's digital age, encompassing a wide range of concepts and terms designed to safeguard our digital assets from malicious actors. In this comprehensive exploration, we will examine the core principles and terminology that define the field of cybersecurity, providing a clearer understanding and deeper insight into this crucial area.

Analysis of Threats and Vulnerabilities

- **Threats**: Threats refer to any potential dangers or risks to information systems, including, but not limited to, viruses, malware, cyberattacks, and even natural disasters.
- **Vulnerabilities**: Vulnerabilities are weaknesses or flaws within a system that could be targeted by threats, potentially compromising the security of data or operations.

Analysis of Potential Attack Vectors

- **Attack Vector**: An attack vector is the specific route or technique an attacker uses to gain unauthorized access to a computer system, network, or application.
- **Common Attack Vectors**: Common attack vectors include phishing, malware, social engineering, brute-force attacks, and zero-day exploits.

Exploring Defense Mechanisms

- **Firewalls**: Firewalls are network security tools designed to monitor and control both incoming and outgoing traffic. By enforcing predefined security rules, they ensure that only authorized traffic is allowed to pass through the network. Acting as a barrier between internal and external networks, firewalls are essential for protecting against unauthorized access and potential security threats.
- **Intrusion Detection Systems (IDS)**: Intrusion Detection Systems are specialized software or hardware solutions that detect and respond to unauthorized access attempts or suspicious activity within a network or system.
- **Encryption**: Encryption is the process of converting data into a coded format that makes it unreadable without the appropriate decryption key, ensuring that sensitive information remains secure from unauthorized access.

Cybersecurity Frameworks

The NIST Cybersecurity Framework

- **NIST**: NIST stands for the National Institute of Standards and Technology, a U.S. government agency responsible for developing cybersecurity standards and guidelines.
- **Framework Core**: The Framework Core is a structured framework used to organize cybersecurity activities, consisting of functions, categories, and subcategories that guide organizations in managing cybersecurity risks.
- **Implementation Tiers**: Implementation Tiers represent the classification of an organization's cybersecurity risk management practices, based on their level of maturity and sophistication.

ISO/IEC 27001

- **ISO/IEC**: ISO/IEC stands for the International Organization for Standardization and the International Electrotechnical Commission, two organizations that collaborate to establish global standards for a wide range of technologies and systems, including cybersecurity.

- **Information Security Management System (ISMS)**: An ISMS is a systematic framework designed to help organizations manage and protect sensitive information, ensuring its confidentiality, integrity, and availability.
- **Risk Management**: Risk management involves identifying, assessing, and prioritizing potential risks, followed by the strategic allocation of resources to reduce, monitor, and control the impact and likelihood of negative events.

Cybersecurity Threats and Trends
Ransomware

- **Ransomware**: Ransomware is a type of malicious software that encrypts a victim's files and demands payment in exchange for the decryption key to restore access to the files.
- **Double Extortion**: Double extortion is a tactic used by ransomware attackers, where, in addition to encrypting data, they threaten to release or sell the stolen information unless the ransom is paid.

Advanced Persistent Threats (APTs)

- **APTs (Advanced Persistent Threats)**: APTs are highly sophisticated and prolonged cyberattacks executed by skilled and organized threat actors, typically with specific objectives and resources.
- **Attribution**: Attribution refers to the process of identifying the individuals or groups behind a cyberattack. This can be challenging due to advanced techniques used to conceal the attackers' identities and methods.

- **Internet of Things (IoT) security**

- **IoT (Internet of Things)**: The Internet of Things (IoT) refers to a network of devices that are connected to the internet and can collect, share, and exchange data with each other.
- **Security Challenges**: Security challenges in IoT include issues such as weak authentication, absence of encryption, and vulnerability to botnet attacks due to poorly secured device configurations.

Compliance and Regulation
The General Data Protection Regulation (GDPR)

- **GDPR (General Data Protection Regulation)**: The European Union implemented the General Data Protection Regulation (GDPR) to safeguard the personal data and privacy of its citizens.

- **Key Principles**: The fundamental principles of data processing under GDPR include lawfulness, fairness, and transparency. It also emphasizes the need for data minimization, accuracy, and accountability in handling personal data.

The Health Insurance Portability and Accountability Act (HIPAA)

- **HIPAA (Health Insurance Portability and Accountability Act)**: HIPAA is a U.S. law that establishes standards for the security and privacy of healthcare information, ensuring the confidentiality and integrity of medical data.
- **Protected Health Information (PHI)**: Protected Health Information (PHI) refers to any healthcare-related data that can identify an individual and is transmitted or stored by a covered entity or its business associates, in compliance with HIPAA regulations.

- **Emerging Technologies in Cybersecurity**
  - **Artificial Intelligence (AI)**
- **AI (Artificial Intelligence)**: Artificial Intelligence (AI) refers to the capability of machines to mimic human cognitive functions, such as learning, reasoning, and self-correction.
- **AI in Cybersecurity**: AI plays a vital role in cybersecurity by enabling automated threat detection, identifying anomalies, and responding to security incidents in real-time to enhance protection and efficiency.

Blockchain Technology

- **Blockchain**: Blockchain is a decentralized, distributed ledger technology that records transactions across multiple computers, ensuring transparency and security without the need for a central authority.
- **Security Benefits**: The security benefits of blockchain are significant, including immutable record-keeping, cryptographic hashing, and decentralized consensus mechanisms, all of which enhance data integrity and protect against tampering or manipulation.

The World without Cybersecurity

It's crucial to highlight that people are often the weakest link in cybersecurity due to their unpredictable behavior and the complex mix of motivations, vulnerabilities, and beliefs. Even the most robust systems can be compromised through social engineering tactics. No security measure, whether network defenses or firewalls, can fully eliminate the risks when an individual is tricked into falling for phishing scams or social engineering ploys—such as unknowingly sharing passwords with someone pretending to be from a legitimate customer service team.

The rise of automation also brings to light certain vulnerabilities, which could have severe consequences if exploited, particularly within communication and transportation networks. As self-driving vehicles become more prevalent, it is crucial to assess the risks associated with developing automated products without giving adequate attention to cybersecurity. This case study will explore the potential ramifications of such oversight.

Looking ahead, society will likely be governed by automated transportation systems, incorporating a variety of modes such as autonomous cars, trains, and buses. Additionally, drones may play a key role in crime prevention and the detection of infrastructure issues. One clear advantage of this technological shift is improved efficiency, with reduced traffic congestion being one of the most anticipated outcomes. The widespread adoption of electric vehicles (EVs) is also expected to lower pollution levels and reduce dependence on fossil fuels. Moreover, EV technology could drastically reduce transportation costs, potentially eliminating many associated expenses altogether.

However, in a worst-case scenario, a cyberattack could cripple the entire system, disrupting the coordination of transportation networks and halting city-wide operations. Such an event would severely impact workers' commutes, leading to a significant drop in productivity. People dependent on life-support systems or other essential services would face major hardships, and without access to these services, chaos could ensue. Basic needs might go unmet, leading to widespread fear and unrest.

The possibility of foreign entities gaining control of a city's infrastructure without resorting to physical force is particularly concerning. The ease with which such influence could be exerted is unsettling and presents a dystopian vision of the future. This scenario underscores the importance of prioritizing cybersecurity in the development of these systems.

The internet has played a major role in introducing new business models that have transformed global industries. While successful internet companies like search engines, social media platforms, and e-commerce giants have reshaped the business landscape, cybercrime remains the most profitable and rapidly growing sector. This highlights the significant threat posed by fraudulent activities, exploiting the lack of awareness among billions of people worldwide.

An Exploration of Threats

Cybercrime encompasses a wide range of illicit activities, such as denial-of-service attacks on websites, blackmail, unauthorized access to computer systems, and sabotage. The threats posed by cybercrime are varied and include the use of ransomware, malware, spyware, and even physical tampering with devices. The scope of these attacks is broad, and the situation is exacerbated by the attack surface—the vulnerabilities found in both hardware and software systems.

For example, if a cybersecurity vulnerability affects Apple devices and all members of an organization use products from the same brand, such as iPads, iPhones, or MacBooks, the potential attack surface may be limited to a specific group of users. However, the total number of employees in an organization can vary significantly, and if a vulnerability were to be exploited on a global scale, the potential pool of targets could reach millions. It's important to recognize that both software and hardware can serve as entry points for attackers. For instance, an iPhone could have several vulnerabilities that hackers might exploit. There are multiple ways to gain unauthorized access to computing devices, and some attackers may justify their actions by claiming they are working for the greater good, such as protecting public safety and security.

The potential damage caused by hacking becomes even clearer when considering interconnected systems like those in power grids or transportation networks. In these cases, the attacks are often more focused and targeted, meaning their impact can be devastating. Disrupting the power grid, for instance, could lead to life-threatening consequences and is difficult to detect because the system is embedded within the complex infrastructure of fiber-optic networks and switches that underpin the internet.

Cyberattacks are a persistent issue, occurring regularly even at this very moment. For instance, your home modem, which provides internet access, is constantly defending against incoming requests that attempt to probe open ports associated with your IP address. These ports serve as virtual gateways for applications to communicate with the network. According to cybersecurity firm Fortinet, its servers routinely face around 500,000 attacks daily, underscoring the scale of the problem.

The central concern is that almost any component of a technological system—whether it's hardware or software—is vulnerable to exploitation, and malicious actors are always searching for weaknesses to exploit for their own gain. To fully grasp the magnitude of these risks, the importance of cybersecurity, and the legal implications, it's crucial to conduct a comprehensive analysis of all possible attack vectors.

Examining the Risks Addressed by Cybersecurity Measures

It is often emphasized that the primary value of cybersecurity lies in its ability to block unauthorized access by hackers, thereby preventing data breaches and financial losses. However, this perspective overlooks the broader impact of cybersecurity on the functioning of modern families, organizations, and society at large, as well as its role in safeguarding individuals from potential physical harm. When examined from a wider lens, the role of cybersecurity can be approached from multiple angles, each with distinct objectives. While the following points may not cover every aspect, they provide a solid foundation for reflection and underscore the importance of acquiring knowledge on how to protect yourself and those you care about in the digital age.

The objective of cybersecurity: The CIA Triad

Cybersecurity experts often emphasize that the core mission of cybersecurity is to ensure the Confidentiality, Integrity, and Availability (CIA) of data—collectively known as the CIA Triad, with a lighthearted reference to the acronym's wordplay.

- **Confidentiality** refers to the protection of information from unauthorized access or disclosure, whether by individuals, organizations, or automated systems. It ensures that sensitive data remains private and secure.
- **Integrity** focuses on maintaining the accuracy and completeness of data. This involves ensuring that data is not tampered with by unauthorized users or corrupted by technical failures. "Completeness" means that data remains intact, with no portions missing or altered without permission. Integrity also includes **non-repudiation**, which means ensuring that data cannot be disputed or denied once created or transmitted, thus verifying its authenticity. A common threat to data integrity is the "man-in-the-middle" attack, where cybercriminals intercept and alter data during transmission, compromising its accuracy.
- **Availability** ensures that information and the systems used to store, process, and transmit it remain accessible and functional. This includes maintaining the uptime of communication systems and security protocols to meet a set standard—such as 99.99% uptime. While some may view availability as secondary to confidentiality and integrity, it is a crucial aspect of cybersecurity, and its protection can often be more challenging than safeguarding data confidentiality or integrity. Achieving high availability often involves coordination across various departments, not all of which may have cybersecurity expertise, particularly in larger organizations. Distributed Denial of Service (DDoS) attacks are a prime example of cyberattacks that target system availability by flooding a system with traffic, rendering it inaccessible. In contrast to the vast resources often used by cybercriminals in launching DDoS attacks, defenders typically have fewer resources to fend them off.

Cybersecurity also addresses various **risks** that affect individuals, businesses, and society, which can be categorized as follows:

- **Privacy Risks**: These involve the potential loss of control over personal or confidential information. Improper use or exposure of this data can have serious consequences for individuals, including identity theft or reputational harm.
- **Financial Risks**: Cyberattacks can result in both direct and indirect financial losses. Direct losses might include funds stolen from personal accounts, while indirect losses could stem from damage to a business's reputation or loss of customer trust, leading to reduced revenue.
- **Professional Risks**: Cybersecurity breaches can jeopardize careers, particularly for professionals in charge of managing security. If a breach occurs due to negligence, the consequences can include job loss or legal action. Executives and board members might face similar repercussions, such as termination or lawsuits. Additionally, breaches may expose sensitive professional communications or actions that could harm an individual's career or professional reputation.
- **Business Risks**: For companies, cybersecurity breaches can have severe implications, much like the personal professional risks mentioned. For example, the 2014 Sony Pictures hack exposed embarrassing internal emails and personal employee data, damaging the company's public image and financial standing.
- **Personal Risks**: Many people store sensitive or personal content on their devices—such as private images or potentially embarrassing information. If this data is accessed by unauthorized parties, it can cause significant harm to personal relationships or lead to blackmail. Additionally, cybercriminals might use stolen personal information for identity theft, creating ongoing personal challenges for the victim.
- **Physical Danger Risks**: Cyberattacks on critical infrastructure, like utilities, hospitals, or sewage treatment plants, can have serious real-world consequences, including potential threats to human health and safety. There have been alarming instances where weak cybersecurity measures have allowed attackers to compromise these vital systems, putting lives at risk.

In sum, cybersecurity plays a vital role in protecting not only digital information but also the physical, financial, and social well-being of individuals, organizations, and society. By understanding the various risks involved, individuals and businesses can better safeguard themselves against the ever-evolving threats in the digital world.

Frequently Asked Questions

- How would you describe cybersecurity?
- What is the evolution of cybersecurity over time?
- What are the fundamental principles and terms in cybersecurity?
- Why are cybersecurity measures essential?
- What does it entail to have a career in cybersecurity?

CHAPTER TWO
GETTING TO KNOW COMMON CYBER ATTACKS

Overview

Chapter Two discusses the most prevalent cyberattacks occurring globally and explains how to recognize the dangerous ones that can compromise your digital environment.

Damage-Dealing Attacks

Cyber attackers employ a range of strategies to execute their malicious goals and cause significant harm to their targets. This paragraph highlights the potential damage these attacks can inflict, emphasizing that the attackers' primary motive is often personal gain—whether financial, political, military, or physical—and the resulting harm they cause to their victims.

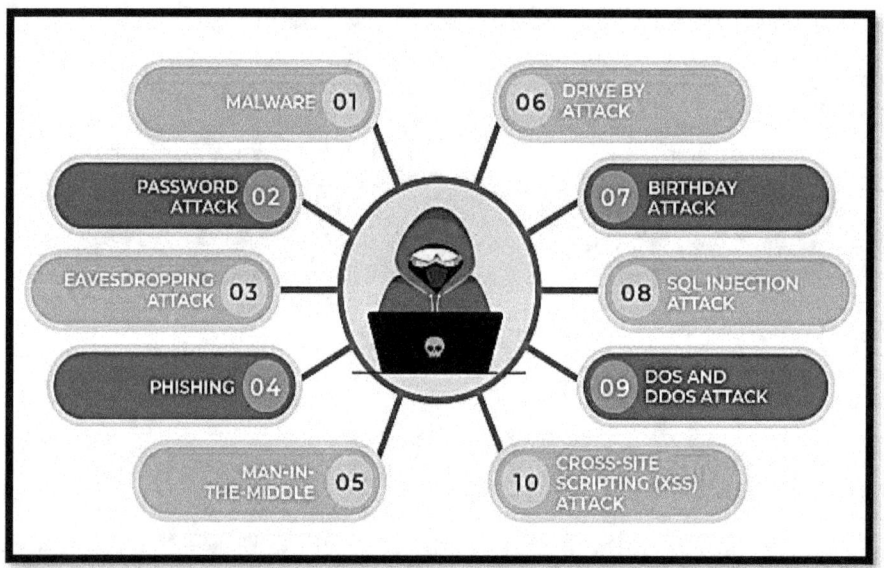

Different forms of attacks can result in significant harm, including:

- Denial-of-Service (DoS) attacks
- Distributed Denial-of-Service (DDoS) attacks
- Botnets and zombie networks
- Data destruction attacks

Denial-of-service (DoS) attacks

A Denial-of-Service (DoS) attack is an intentional attempt by an attacker to disrupt or disable a computer or network by overwhelming it with an excessive volume of requests or data. This overload prevents the target from properly processing legitimate requests. Often, the requests sent by the attacker appear innocuous, like a standard web page load request. However, in some cases, the attacker may exploit their knowledge of various protocols to craft more complex requests that escalate the attack's impact. DoS attacks primarily target a system's central processing units (CPUs), memory, network bandwidth, and infrastructure resources, such as routers, ultimately causing system slowdown or failure.

Distributed denial-of-service (DDoS) attacks

DDoS (Distributed Denial-of-Service) attacks are a type of cyberattack that can severely disrupt online services by overwhelming a target system with an excessive amount of traffic, rendering it unable to function properly. These attacks can be highly damaging, affecting organizations and industries across various sectors.

A DDoS attack occurs when multiple computers or connected devices, often from different locations, collectively flood a target with traffic, leading to service outages. The frequency of DDoS attacks has grown significantly in recent years. Nowadays, these attacks are more distributed, with attackers increasingly using Internet-connected devices like cameras and IoT gadgets, rather than relying solely on traditional personal computers.

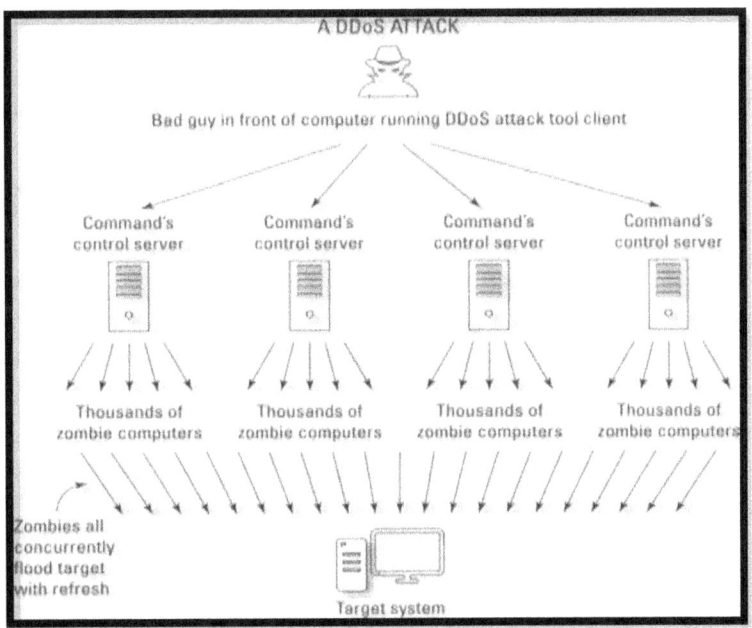

The primary objective of a DDoS (Distributed Denial-of-Service) attack is to disrupt the target's online presence, and the motivations behind these attacks can vary widely. In some cases, financial gain is the driving force. For instance, imagine a dishonest competitor launching a DDoS attack on an online retailer's website during the busy Black Friday period, potentially crippling the business. Alternatively, a malicious individual might target a popular toy store just weeks before the holiday season, with the aim of damaging their reputation and causing a drop in stock value through a well-timed DDoS assault. As these threats continue to grow, DDoS attacks have become an increasingly serious concern.

Criminal organizations even offer DDoS-for-hire services, advertising them on the dark web as a way to take down competitors' websites for a fee. However, financial motives aren't always the driving force. Some attackers are motivated by political agendas. For example, during election seasons, unethical politicians may target their opponents' websites to hinder their ability to communicate with voters or accept campaign donations. Additionally, some hacktivists use DDoS attacks as a form of protest, believing they are acting for "justice." In these cases, DDoS attacks might target government agencies or law enforcement websites in response to incidents such as police violence against unarmed individuals.

A 2017 survey by Kaspersky Lab and B2B International revealed that many organizations who had fallen victim to DDoS attacks expressed concern that their competitors might have been behind the assaults.

DDoS attacks have a significant impact on individuals and organizations in three key ways:

1. **Slowed Network Performance**: A DDoS attack on a local network can drastically reduce the internet speed for all users, often causing severe slowdowns or even complete connection failures due to session timeouts. This happens when requests take longer to process than the system allows, resulting in the termination of connections.
2. **Website Inaccessibility**: DDoS attacks can render websites unavailable, frustrating users and disrupting services. For example, on October 21, 2016, a massive DDoS attack disrupted access to major websites like Twitter, PayPal, CNN, and HBO Now by targeting a third-party company that provided technical services to these sites. This kind of attack can also pose risks for online banking, particularly when attempting to complete transactions at the last minute, as DDoS attacks can make banking sites inaccessible.
3. **Redirection and Misinformation**: A DDoS attack can make one website unavailable, leading users to seek out alternatives. This redirection can have serious consequences, particularly if it results in the spread of misinformation or limits access to diverse viewpoints on critical issues. In some cases, DDoS attacks can be used as a short-term tool to silence dissenting opinions or obstruct the free flow of information.

Botnets and zombies

Botnets are commonly used in DDoS attacks. A botnet is a network of computers that have been compromised and controlled by hackers, often without the knowledge or consent of the device owners. These infected devices, often referred to as "zombies," can be remotely manipulated to carry out various tasks, including launching large-scale attacks.

When cybercriminals infect a large number of machines with malware, they can command these devices to flood a target server or server farm with simultaneous requests, overwhelming the system. This coordinated surge of traffic can cripple the target's infrastructure, rendering it unable to process legitimate requests and causing service outages. Botnets are a powerful tool for attackers because they leverage the processing power of numerous devices, making the attack harder to defend against and more difficult to trace back to the source.

Data destruction attacks

Malicious actors sometimes have objectives that extend beyond temporarily disrupting a target with a flood of requests. In some cases, their aim is to cause lasting damage by corrupting or destroying critical data and information systems. For instance, a cybercriminal might use a data destruction attack to erase a victim's data, especially if the victim refuses to comply with a ransom demand, such as in a ransomware attack. As with DDoS attacks, the motivations behind these attacks—whether financial, political, or personal—can also drive hackers to target and destroy sensitive information.

One particularly destructive method used by cybercriminals is a **wiper attack**, which is a highly sophisticated form of data destruction. In a wiper attack, the attacker completely erases data from a victim's hard drive or SSD, making recovery nearly impossible. If the victim lacks proper backups, they face the permanent loss of all data and software stored on the targeted device. This kind of attack can be catastrophic, as it leaves the victim with no way to recover their lost files or restore their systems.

The internet, while a powerful tool for legitimate purposes, also poses significant risks, especially in the hands of malicious individuals. It has become easier than ever for fraudsters to impersonate others and deceive unsuspecting victims. In the past, criminals faced significant challenges in mimicking legitimate institutions, like banks or retailers, and convincing people to hand over money. However, the rise of the internet has provided fraudsters with a vast new arena to exploit. Today, it's remarkably simple to create a website that closely resembles the official site of a trusted bank, company, or government agency—often in just a matter of minutes.

The abundance of domain names that look nearly identical to legitimate ones offers cybercriminals a variety of opportunities to deceive people. By setting up fake websites that appear authentic, attackers can easily trick users into divulging sensitive information, laying the groundwork for online fraud and impersonation schemes.

Phishing

Phishing is a form of online deception where attackers impersonate a trusted entity in order to manipulate individuals into taking specific actions. For example, a cybercriminal might send an email that appears to be from a well-known bank, claiming there has been a data breach and urging recipients to click on a link to reset their passwords. The link leads to a counterfeit website that closely resembles the bank's legitimate page, but was crafted by the attacker. Once users enter their usernames and passwords on the fake site, the attacker collects this sensitive information, which can then be used for malicious purposes, such as unauthorized access to bank accounts.

Spear phishing

Spear phishing is a more targeted and sophisticated form of phishing, where attackers specifically craft their emails to deceive a particular individual, business, or organization. Unlike generic phishing attempts, spear phishing involves a high level of personalization. Cybercriminals often conduct in-depth research on their targets, gathering personal details from social media and other online sources, in order to create messages that seem highly legitimate and credible.

For example, an attacker might send a carefully designed email to an employee within a company, pretending to be a colleague or a superior, in order to gain access to sensitive systems like the company's email server. The email could read something like this:

"Hey, I just wanted to let you know that I'm about to board my flight in ten minutes. Could you kindly log in to the Exchange server and verify the details of my upcoming meeting? I'm having trouble accessing it on my end. If you have any issues, feel free to call me for security purposes, but if you can't reach me, please gather the information and email it to me. I'll be boarding shortly, so I would really appreciate your quick assistance."

This message appears harmless and might even seem urgent, making the recipient more likely to comply. It combines a legitimate-sounding request with personal context, increasing the chances that the victim will fall for the scam. In spear phishing, the attacker's deep knowledge of the target and their professional environment makes the scam much more persuasive and dangerous.

CEO fraud

CEO fraud, a type of social engineering attack similar to spear phishing, involves a cybercriminal impersonating a CEO or other high-ranking executive within an organization. However, unlike typical phishing attacks that focus on stealing login credentials, CEO fraud typically seeks to trick the victim into taking immediate actions, such as transferring funds or sharing sensitive information, without attempting to gather usernames, passwords, or other personal data.

A common tactic in CEO fraud is for the attacker to send an email to the company's CFO, requesting that a payment be made to a new, supposedly urgent vendor, or that sensitive documents, like W2 forms, be sent to an "accountant's" email address. The criminal may craft the email to appear urgent and authoritative, often using pressure tactics to prompt quick compliance. This can result in significant financial losses for the company, with funds being transferred to the fraudster's account or confidential information being exposed.

CEO fraud is particularly dangerous because it can be difficult for employees to verify the legitimacy of such requests, especially when they appear to come from a trusted leader in the organization. Victims of CEO fraud are often left facing severe consequences, including job loss, as their failure to detect the scam can make them seem negligent or unskilled.

The rise in CEO fraud during the COVID-19 pandemic can be attributed to the shift to remote work. With fewer in-person interactions and less opportunity to verify communications through traditional means, employees became more vulnerable to such scams. In this new work environment, it became even easier for attackers to exploit the lack of physical oversight and communication barriers, making CEO fraud a growing concern for businesses worldwide.

Smishing

Smishing is a form of phishing where attackers use text messages (SMS) rather than email to target victims. The goal of smishing is similar to other types of phishing: to steal sensitive information such as usernames and passwords or to trick the victim into downloading malware onto their device. These text messages often contain urgent or enticing messages, such as a fake security alert or prize notification, prompting the recipient to click on a malicious link or provide personal information. Because text messages are typically perceived as more personal or immediate than emails, smishing attacks can be especially effective in deceiving users into taking harmful actions.

Vishing

Vishing, or voice phishing, involves using phone calls to deceive and manipulate individuals. Despite advances in technology, criminals still rely on this longstanding method to exploit victims. While most of these fraudulent calls are now made through Voice over Internet Protocol (VoIP) systems, scammers continue to use traditional landline phones to target people, just as they have for many years.

Pharming

Pharming is a type of cyberattack that, while similar to phishing, takes advantage of vulnerabilities in internet routing technology. Like phishing, pharming involves impersonating a trusted entity to trick victims into taking specific actions. However, instead of luring users to a fake website through deceptive emails or messages, pharming attacks manipulate network infrastructure, such as routing tables, to redirect users who click on a link or type in a legitimate URL to a fraudulent copy of the original website.

Tampering with Other People's Belongings: A Serious Matter

Attackers often have motives beyond simply disrupting an organization's operations—they seek to profit from their actions. One common method they use to achieve this is through **tampering**, where they alter data during its transfer or storage within targeted systems. For example, imagine a customer instructs their bank to wire money to a specific account. A criminal could intercept the request and change the routing and account information, diverting the funds for themselves.

Another example involves unauthorized access to systems to manipulate information for personal gain. In one scenario, a criminal might alter the payment details of a recipient, so when the Accounts Payable department processes the payment, the money is sent to a fraudulent account instead of the intended one.

Tampering can also extend to other areas, such as financial markets. For instance, if a criminal modifies an analyst's report on a particular stock before it is made public, they could use the false information to manipulate stock prices, buying or selling based on the expected (but incorrect) market reactions to the report. This kind of manipulation can lead to significant financial gains for the attacker, while causing harm to others who rely on the accurate information.

Interception: Captured in Transit

Interception happens when attackers capture data as it is being transmitted from one point to another. In cybersecurity, this typically involves the transfer of data between computers or electronic devices. However, interception can also extend to interactions between humans and devices, such as when spoken words are recorded for a voice recognition system. To protect against unauthorized access, it is essential to implement strong data encryption during transmission. However, one challenge is that data received directly from humans, like voice recordings, often cannot be easily encrypted, making it more vulnerable to interception.

Man-in-the-middle attacks

Man-in-the-middle (MitM) attacks are a specific form of data interception, where an attacker secretly intercepts and manipulates communication between two parties. In a typical MitM attack, the attacker acts as an intermediary, or "middleman," between the sender and the recipient, making it appear as though the communication is taking place directly between the two legitimate parties. This process is known as **proxying**.

In this scenario, the attacker intercepts the data sent by the sender, forwards it to the intended destination, and then relays the response back to the sender. The attacker can either pass the response along unchanged or alter it before sending it back. The use of proxying makes it difficult for the sender or recipient to detect that the communication has been intercepted, as the conversation appears to proceed normally.

For example, a fraudster might create a fake bank website that mimics the legitimate one, and when an unsuspecting user enters their login details, the attacker captures the data. The fraudster can then pass the same information to the real bank, making it seem as though the user is interacting directly with the bank's website. If the user enters the wrong password, the attacker can modify the response, prompting the user to try again with the correct password. This method allows the attacker to collect sensitive information, such as login credentials, without the victim noticing any irregularities during the transaction.

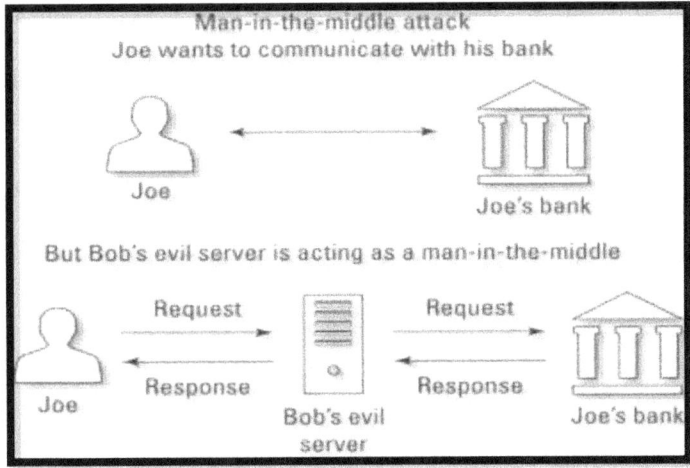

Data Theft

Cyberattacks frequently involve the unauthorized theft of sensitive data, which can have serious consequences for individuals, businesses, and government organizations. The motivations behind data theft are varied, ranging from financial gain to espionage or even sabotage. Regardless of the attacker's intent, data theft poses significant risks, including identity theft, financial loss, reputational damage, and security breaches. Whether targeting individuals, corporations, nonprofit organizations, or government entities, the impact of stolen data can be profound and far-reaching.

Personal data theft

Malicious actors often seek to steal personal information to uncover valuable assets that can be exploited for financial gain. In the digital age, the value of data has surged, making it an attractive target for cybercriminals. Depending on the type of data, the risks and consequences of a breach can vary greatly. When this information falls into the wrong hands, the impact can be severe. Some examples of valuable assets that criminals target include:

- **Personal Information**: This can be used for identity theft or sold on the black market. Cybercriminals may open fraudulent accounts, make unauthorized purchases, or commit other types of fraud in the victim's name, leading to financial losses and long-term damage to the victim's credit.
- **Photos and Health Data**: Sensitive images or health-related information are especially vulnerable, as they can be used for blackmail. If a hacker gains access to compromising photos or private medical details, they could threaten to release or publish this data unless a ransom is paid, causing both emotional distress and financial harm.
- **Ransomware Attacks**: In some cases, cybercriminals steal data from a user's device and then encrypt it, locking the victim out of their own files. This data can range from personal documents to critical business records, and the attacker demands payment in exchange for restoring access. Ransomware attacks can cripple both individuals and organizations, with potentially devastating consequences.
- **Passwords and Credentials**: Lists of stolen passwords are a highly valuable commodity for cybercriminals. These can be used to gain unauthorized access to other accounts, especially if victims reuse the same password across multiple platforms. Once an attacker breaches one account, they may be able to infiltrate more sensitive systems, amplifying the damage.
- **Confidential Work-Related Information**: Data relating to company strategies, financial plans, or upcoming mergers is particularly valuable. Cybercriminals who acquire insider knowledge could use it for illegal purposes, such as insider trading, profiting from the information before it becomes public.
- **Travel Plans**: Details about future trips or travel schedules can be exploited by criminals to target homes or properties when the owners are away. Often shared carelessly on social media or stored insecurely, this information can be used to plan burglaries or other criminal activities, compromising the victim's safety and security.

These examples highlight just a few of the ways data theft can lead to significant harm, underscoring the importance of safeguarding personal, financial, and sensitive information against malicious actors.

Business data theft

Data stolen from businesses can be exploited in a variety of ways, often with serious financial and reputational consequences. Here are some of the most common malicious uses of stolen business data:

- **Insider Trading**: Cybercriminals may steal confidential financial data to gain advance knowledge of a company's quarterly earnings or other sensitive business information. They can then use this insider knowledge to engage in illegal stock or options trading, potentially reaping significant financial gains before the information is made public.
- **Selling to Competitors**: Stolen business data, such as sales pipelines, upcoming product plans, or proprietary documents, can be sold to unscrupulous competitors or even employees. This gives the buyers an unfair advantage, enabling them to gain insights into a company's strategies and outperform it, often without management's knowledge.
- **Data Leaks to the Media**: Exposing sensitive business information to the public or media can cause significant embarrassment and harm to the company's reputation. It can also lead to a loss of customer trust and, in some cases, a drop in stock value if the leaked information damages the company's public image.
- **Privacy Violations**: If stolen data contains personal information covered by privacy regulations (such as GDPR or CCPA), the company responsible for the breach may face heavy fines and legal penalties. The fallout from these violations can also cause reputational damage and loss of consumer confidence.
- **Recruiting from Stolen Emails**: Cybercriminals may access employee communications to identify individuals who are dissatisfied with their current positions. This information can be sold to other firms looking to recruit skilled employees, giving competitors an edge by poaching talent with insider knowledge of company systems and operations.
- **Intellectual Property Theft**: Criminals may steal valuable intellectual property, such as source code or design plans, allowing them to bypass licensing fees or reduce their own research and development costs. In the case of stolen design documents, this could lead to major cost savings, potentially amounting to millions or even billions of dollars, by circumventing the need for original innovation and development.

The financial and strategic impact of such data theft can be devastating, often leading to both immediate losses and long-term consequences. As highlighted in the sidebar titled *"How a Cyber-Breach Cost One Company $1 Billion Without a Single Cent Being Stolen"*, the effects of a cyberattack can go far beyond direct financial theft, with organizations facing crippling costs even when no funds are taken.

Data exfiltration

Data exfiltration, while it may sound technical, essentially refers to the unauthorized transfer of data from one system to another. This can be carried out through various methods, such as using malware, automated tools, or even manual commands sent to a remote computer. When cybercriminals manage to breach a system and steal sensitive information, this act is known as data exfiltration.

The impact of data breaches involving exfiltration can be profound. They can significantly erode customer trust, undermine confidence in government agencies, compromise the privacy of personal information, and even pose risks to national security, depending on the nature of the data involved. Whether targeting individuals, businesses, or government entities, data exfiltration can have lasting repercussions, both for the victims and for society at large.

Unauthorized access

Compromised credentials refer to account login details—such as usernames and passwords—that have been accessed by someone other than the legitimate user. These credentials are typically stolen through a cybersecurity breach, and criminals often exploit them to gain unauthorized access to systems or networks. Once in, attackers can carry out further malicious activities, such as data theft or system manipulation.

The use of compromised credentials is a common attack method because many users tend to reuse the same username and password across multiple platforms, making it easier for cybercriminals to exploit them. Additionally, the misuse of one employee's login information by another—whether for malicious intent or otherwise—also falls under this type of attack. Such breaches can be particularly damaging, as they allow unauthorized individuals to bypass security measures, potentially leading to more significant breaches and operational disruptions.

Forced policy violations

A **forced policy violation attack** occurs when a user or device is coerced or manipulated into violating cybersecurity policies. This type of attack often involves the attacker exploiting vulnerabilities, such as social engineering or technical weaknesses, to force the victim into actions that breach established security protocols. The goal is typically to bypass security measures or gain unauthorized access to systems, data, or networks by manipulating the victim into compromising their own security practices.

Malware: Cyber Bombs That Infiltrate Your Devices

Malware, short for "malicious software," refers to any software designed to harm or exploit a computer, network, or device without the user's consent or knowledge. It comes in many forms, each with different methods of attack. Some common types of malware include:

- **Viruses**: Malicious programs that attach themselves to legitimate files or programs and spread to other systems.
- **Worms**: Self-replicating malware that spreads across networks without needing to attach to a host file.
- **Trojans**: Malicious software disguised as legitimate programs, often used to gain unauthorized access to systems.
- **Ransomware**: Malware that locks or encrypts a victim's data and demands a ransom for its release.
- **Scareware**: Software that tricks users into believing their system is infected, prompting them to pay for unnecessary or fake services.
- **Spyware**: Programs that secretly monitor a user's activities and collect sensitive information, such as passwords or financial details.
- **Cryptocurrency Miners**: Malware that hijacks a victim's computer resources to mine cryptocurrency without their permission.
- **Adware**: Software that displays unwanted advertisements, often used to generate revenue for the attacker or disrupt the user experience.

All of these types of malware are designed to exploit computer resources, steal information, or cause damage, making them significant threats to both individuals and organizations.

Viruses

Computer viruses are a type of malware that spread by inserting their code into a system when executed. This insertion often occurs through data files, such as malicious macros embedded in Word documents, or within the boot sectors of hard drives and solid-state drives, which contain essential code and data for booting a computer. Viruses can also hide within other applications.

Much like biological viruses, computer viruses can spread rapidly. However, to propagate, they need to infect a host system—whether that's another computer, device, or file. The impact of a computer virus on its host system can vary greatly. Some viruses cause significant performance issues, slowing down the system or damaging files, while others may operate quietly in the background, making them harder to detect but still harmful. Regardless of their visibility, viruses remain a serious threat to system security and stability.

Worms

Computer worms are self-replicating forms of malware that can spread autonomously without the need for a host file or program. Unlike viruses, which rely on user interaction or host systems to propagate, worms exploit security vulnerabilities in targeted systems or networks to spread. Once they've infiltrated a system, worms can replicate themselves and move across the network to infect other connected devices.

Although worms don't always modify system files or steal data, they can still cause significant disruption. One of the primary ways worms can harm a network is by consuming excessive bandwidth, which can slow down or even halt normal network operations. This degradation in speed can be frustrating for users who rely on smooth, fast internal and internet connections, making worms a considerable nuisance and potentially affecting business operations or productivity.

Trojans

Trojans are a type of malware that masquerades as legitimate software or hides within trusted applications and digital files. They get their name from the historical story of the Trojan Horse, where something harmful is concealed within something seemingly harmless. Unlike viruses or worms, which spread autonomously, Trojans rely on social engineering tactics to infect systems. Attackers often trick individuals into clicking malicious links, downloading deceptive apps, or opening infected email attachments.

Once inside a system, Trojans can carry out various harmful actions, such as stealing data, giving attackers remote access to the system, or installing other forms of malware. However, Trojans do not self-replicate or spread on their own—they rely on human error or manipulation to propagate. This makes user awareness and caution key to preventing Trojan infections.

Ransomware

Ransomware is a type of malicious software that forces victims to pay a ransom to prevent damage or loss of their data. Typically, ransomware encrypts the user's files, making them inaccessible, and then demands payment for the decryption key. In some cases, criminals may also steal sensitive data and use it to blackmail the victim, threatening to release it publicly unless a ransom is paid.

There are also more destructive forms of ransomware that not only encrypt data but also permanently delete it from the victim's machine, leaving no recovery options unless the ransom is paid. This makes the threat especially harmful, as victims are left with no means of restoring their files on their own.

Ransomware is often spread through various means, including Trojans, viruses, and worms, which criminals use to infect systems and propagate the malicious software. Over time, cybercriminals have become more sophisticated, launching targeted ransomware campaigns tailored to specific organizations or individuals. By understanding their targets' valuable data and their ability to pay, attackers can maximize the effectiveness of their ransom demands, making ransomware an increasingly dangerous and profitable form of cybercrime.

Scareware

Scareware is a type of malware that uses fear tactics to manipulate users into taking specific actions, typically by convincing them they need to buy unnecessary or fake security software. A common example of scareware involves a fake alert or pop-up notification that claims the user's device is infected with a virus or malware. The message often urges the user to purchase a particular security program to fix the issue, even though no infection exists.

These deceptive tactics prey on users' fear of security threats and can lead them to install malicious software or give away sensitive information, such as credit card details, to the attackers behind the scareware. By exploiting this fear, cybercriminals profit from tricking victims into unnecessary purchases or giving up personal information.

Spyware

Spyware is a type of malicious software that covertly collects data from a device without the user's knowledge or consent. It can capture a wide range of information, including keystrokes, screenshots, audio, video, and browsing activity. The primary purpose of spyware is to gather sensitive or personal data, which can then be used for malicious purposes, such as identity theft or selling information to third parties.

It's important to distinguish between spyware and other invasive software. Some technologies used by legitimate businesses—like tracking tools—may seem invasive but aren't necessarily classified as malware. For instance, **tracking cookies** and **web beacons** are commonly used by websites and apps to track user behavior, but they are typically disclosed to users and are often part of standard privacy agreements.

However, these technologies could become spyware if users aren't properly informed or given a choice about their use. There is also an ongoing debate among experts regarding software that monitors users' activities, such as tracking a smartphone's location even when the app is not in use. Apps like Uber, which track a user's location for convenience, may not be considered spyware if users are informed about it and consent to the tracking. However, some argue that this type of behavior—tracking location without clear user awareness—blurs the line between legitimate functionality and spyware.

Thus, the key issue lies in whether users are informed about the data being collected and have control over it. When transparency is lacking, even legitimate tracking tools can be perceived as spyware.

Cryptocurrency miners

Cryptocurrency miners, also known as crypto miners, are a type of malware that secretly takes control of infected devices, using their processing power (CPU cycles) to mine cryptocurrencies without the device owner's knowledge or consent. These malicious programs solve complex mathematical problems to create new units of a cryptocurrency, such as Bitcoin, and the attackers who deploy the miners profit from the process.

The use of crypto miners surged in 2017 as the value of cryptocurrencies skyrocketed. Although cryptocurrency prices later dropped, crypto miners remain prevalent because attackers find them a cost-effective way to profit from others' computing resources. Once cybercriminals develop or acquire crypto mining software, they can deploy it across multiple systems to generate steady, albeit small, rewards.

As cryptocurrency values began to rise again in 2019, new variants of crypto miners were developed, including some targeting Android devices specifically. Crypto miners are particularly attractive to lower-level cybercriminals because they require fewer resources to execute. Unlike other types of malware that may involve multiple stages or complex command-and-control systems, crypto miners can be quickly deployed and provide attackers with immediate, albeit incremental, financial gains. This makes them a low-cost, high-reward tool for cybercriminals looking to take advantage of infected devices.

Adware

Adware is a type of software that generates revenue by displaying advertisements on a user's device. While some adware is legitimate and installed as part of free software that users knowingly accept (such as in ad-supported apps or programs), there is a key distinction between this and adware that is considered **malware**. Malicious adware is typically installed without the user's consent, often bundled with other programs or disguised as a harmless app, and can interfere with the user's experience by flooding their device with intrusive ads.

The key difference lies in consent: **legitimate adware** is voluntarily installed by users who are aware that ads will be shown in exchange for free access to software, whereas **malicious adware** is secretly installed, often without the user's knowledge, and can lead to performance issues, privacy concerns, or further security risks.

Blended malware

Blended malware is a type of malicious software that combines elements from multiple types of malware, such as **Trojans**, **worms**, and **viruses**, to execute more complex and effective attacks. By merging features from different malware categories, blended malware can exploit a wider range of vulnerabilities and cause more damage. For example, it might use a Trojan to gain unauthorized access to a system, a worm to spread across networks, and a virus to replicate itself and infect additional devices.

This hybrid approach makes blended malware particularly dangerous, as it leverages the strengths of various attack methods to bypass security defenses, evade detection, and carry out its objectives more efficiently. Typically, blended malware is crafted by skilled cybercriminals who are looking to maximize the impact of their attacks, making it a sophisticated and challenging threat to defend against.

Zero-day malware

Zero-day malware refers to newly discovered malicious software that exploits vulnerabilities in software or hardware that have not yet been publicly disclosed or patched by the vendors. Because these vulnerabilities are unknown to both the public and security providers, zero-day attacks can be extremely powerful and difficult to defend against, making them highly dangerous.

Creating zero-day malware requires significant expertise, resources, and development effort. Due to the sophistication involved, zero-day exploits are often developed by well-funded groups, such as **nation-state cyber operations**, rather than individual hackers. These attacks are particularly valuable, and commercial vendors who specialize in selling these vulnerabilities may charge exorbitant prices—sometimes exceeding **$1 million** for a single exploit. As a result, zero-day malware represents one of the most advanced and expensive forms of cyberweaponry.

Fake malware on computers

Surprisingly, some attackers don't bother with complex hacking techniques. Instead, they use a simple yet effective tactic: sending messages to potential victims, falsely claiming that their computers are infected with malware. To restore security, the victims are instructed to pay a fee or purchase specific security software, which is often bogus.

These messages are typically delivered through pop-up windows that appear on the victim's screen or through more straightforward methods, such as phishing emails. The goal is to create a sense of urgency or fear, pressuring the target into taking immediate action—often paying for software or services that do nothing to resolve the non-existent issue. This type of scam, sometimes referred to as "tech support fraud" or "scareware," preys on users' concerns about their security to trick them into making unnecessary payments.

Malicious software targeting mobile devices

Malicious software is increasingly common on mobile devices, often surpassing its presence on laptops and desktops. While hacking mobile devices can be more technically challenging due to factors like app sandboxing and tighter security controls, many cybercriminals take a different approach. Rather than directly compromising mobile devices, they frequently trick users into believing their device has been infected or compromised.

One method involves **mobile ransomware**, which displays fake ransom demands on the device, even though no data has been encrypted. These types of attacks are designed to create fear and urgency, pressuring users into paying a ransom to supposedly restore their device's security or access. In many cases, no actual data loss occurs, but victims are still deceived into making unnecessary payments to the attackers. This form of **scareware** is becoming a growing concern as mobile usage continues to rise, with criminals exploiting people's reliance on their devices.

Phony security subscription renewal notifications

One common form of social engineering that takes advantage of people's concern for internet security is the use of fake "renewal notices" from fraudulent anti-malware companies. These emails typically claim that your security software subscription is about to expire and prompt you to renew or make a payment to continue your coverage. While these messages may look legitimate, it's important to be cautious. Do not click on any links or provide payment information in response to such emails.

To stay safe, always verify the authenticity of the email by checking directly with the security software provider using official contact details. This type of scam has become more prevalent, particularly during the COVID-19 pandemic, when many people shifted to remote work and managed their own security software subscriptions. With the increased reliance on digital tools, the risk of falling victim to such scams has never been higher. Staying vigilant and questioning unsolicited renewal requests can help you avoid these deceptive tactics.

Attacks on Web Services: A Dangerous Threat

Cybersecurity experts are continuously working to safeguard servers from the ever-changing vulnerabilities exploited by various types of cyberattacks. As new flaws are discovered regularly, their role demands constant vigilance. While there is a vast body of research on this topic, delving into all of it is outside the scope of this discussion. However, it's crucial to grasp the fundamental concepts behind server-based attacks, as they can have direct implications for you.

One such attack is known as a "poisoned" web service or webpage attack. This occurs when an unauthorized individual gains access to a web server and injects malicious code. As a result, when users visit the compromised site, the server may launch attacks against them. For instance, a hacker could breach the server hosting www.abc123.com, alter the homepage, and inject malware that infects visitors to the site.

It's important to note that a hacker can also poison web pages without fully compromising the system. Weak security measures on the site could create vulnerabilities. For example, users might post comments containing commands that, if properly crafted, are executed by the browser whenever the page is loaded. An attacker could insert a malicious script in such a comment, which would then capture the user's login credentials when the script is triggered from the original site. This type of attack, known as cross-site scripting (XSS), remains a persistent issue despite efforts to address it over the past decade.

Network Infrastructure Poisoning

Similar to web servers, network infrastructure is also a frequent target for cyberattacks, with new vulnerabilities being discovered regularly. However, it is essential to understand the risks associated with server-based attacks, especially when dealing with poisoned web servers, as they can have a direct impact on you.

One such attack involves malicious individuals exploiting weaknesses to inject corrupted Domain Name System (DNS) data into a DNS server. The DNS functions as the Internet's directory, translating human-readable domain names into computer-readable IP addresses. For instance, when you enter *https://JosephSteinberg.com* into your browser, the DNS directs your request to a numerical address (e.g., 104.18.45.53) that identifies the server hosting the website.

An attacker can manipulate the DNS tables, providing a false IP address to a user's computer. This allows the attacker to redirect the user's traffic to a machine of their choosing, rather than the intended destination. For example, the attacker could set up a fake banking site on the server and make it appear as though the user is accessing their legitimate bank. As a result, even if the user types the correct bank URL directly into their browser, they could still be tricked into visiting the fraudulent site. This type of attack, known as DNS poisoning or pharming, can lead to serious security breaches and identity theft.

Malvertising

Malvertising is a form of malicious advertising where cybercriminals use online ads to distribute malware or launch cyberattacks. Many websites display ads provided by third-party networks, which often contain links to external sites, making these ads a potential entry point for attackers. Even though some websites may be secure, they might fail to adequately protect users from hazardous ads created and managed by third-party vendors.

Malvertising enables criminals to discreetly place harmful content on reputable, high-traffic websites, allowing them to reach a wide audience, including security-conscious users who might not typically encounter such threats on less trustworthy sites. Additionally, websites often generate revenue by encouraging users to click on ads, which means site owners strategically position ads to maximize engagement. This creates an opportunity for malvertising to target large audiences without the need for direct hacking.

The mechanics of malvertising can vary. In some cases, users must click on an ad to trigger the malware infection. However, in other instances, merely displaying the ad can be enough to infect a user's device, with no interaction required from the user. This makes malvertising a particularly insidious and widespread threat.

Drive-by downloads

Drive-by downloads can be easily misunderstood as simply software that people unintentionally download without realizing the risks. In reality, these downloads occur when a user visits a compromised website, and malware is automatically installed on their device without their knowledge or consent. Drive-by downloads are particularly deceptive because users often don't recognize the potential dangers of installing certain software.

For example, a user might encounter a webpage claiming to detect a security vulnerability on their device, prompting them to click a button labeled "Download to install a security patch." In doing so, the user unknowingly authorizes the malicious download, believing they are improving their device's security. This type of trickery leads the user to think the download is beneficial, when, in fact, it is a malicious payload designed to infect their system.

Password theft

Criminals use various techniques to acquire passwords, and some of the most common methods include:

1. **Theft of Password Databases**: Cybercriminals often target online businesses to steal password databases. If a hacker successfully obtains such a database, users whose credentials are stored there are at risk of having their passwords compromised. Even if the passwords are encrypted, attackers can still launch hash attacks, which attempt to break the encryption. This means that passwords—especially commonly used ones—may still be vulnerable. Stealing passwords in this way remains one of the most widespread methods of compromise.
2. **Social Engineering Attacks**: In social engineering attacks, criminals manipulate individuals into performing actions they wouldn't normally take, often tricking them into revealing passwords. A common example is when an attacker impersonates a member of a company's tech support team, convincing the target to reset their password for "security testing" following a breach. The target, unaware of the deception, complies, unknowingly giving the attacker access. (For more details, see the section on phishing.)

3. **Credential Attacks**: These attacks aim to gain unauthorized access by using a valid username and password combination. There are several types of credential attacks:
    - **Brute Force**: Attackers use automated tools to try every possible password until they find the correct one.
    - **Dictionary Attacks**: Criminals use automated tools to attempt every word in a dictionary, hoping to guess the correct password.
    - **Calculated Attacks**: Attackers use personal information—like the target's mother's maiden name or other easily discovered details from social media profiles—to make educated guesses about the password.
    - **Blended Attacks**: Some attacks combine multiple methods for greater effectiveness. For example, attackers may use a combination of brute force and knowledge of common password patterns, or they may reference personal data to improve the accuracy of their guesses.
4. **Malware**: If criminals manage to infiltrate a user's device with malware, they can capture passwords directly from the system. Malware can record keystrokes, monitor web activity, and steal login information without the user's knowledge.
5. **Network Sniffing**: When users enter passwords on websites that lack sufficient encryption, especially over unprotected public Wi-Fi networks, there's a risk that an attacker on the same network could intercept and capture the passwords while they are transmitted. Similarly, other attackers along the route between the user and the website could also monitor the data in transit.
6. **Credential Stuffing**: This method involves attackers trying to gain access to accounts on one site by using stolen username and password combinations obtained from previous breaches of other websites. Since many people reuse passwords across different sites, attackers often succeed in compromising multiple accounts with a single set of stolen credentials.

These techniques highlight the wide range of ways criminals can obtain passwords and stress the importance of using strong, unique passwords and taking extra security measures such as multi-factor authentication (MFA).

Highlighting Maintenance Challenges

Maintaining computer systems is a critical task, as software vendors frequently release updates that can impact the performance of other programs running on a device. However, some patches are particularly important because they address software bugs that could create security vulnerabilities. Balancing the need for security with routine maintenance is an ongoing challenge, and security often ends up taking a backseat. As a result, many computers fail to receive regular updates.

Even users who have set up automatic updates on their devices may not always have the latest versions of software. This is because updates are typically checked at intervals rather than in real time, and not all software supports automatic updating. Furthermore, it's important to note that installing updates for one program can occasionally introduce vulnerabilities in other software running on the same system, creating potential new risks.

Advanced Attacks

When large-scale cyber breaches are reported, commentators often highlight the involvement of sophisticated attacks. While there is no universally accepted definition of an "advanced" cyberattack, it is clear that some attacks are more complex and require a higher level of technical expertise to execute. From a subjective standpoint, an attack could be considered sophisticated if it demands significant investment in research and development to be successful. However, what constitutes a "substantial" investment varies depending on the perspective. There have been instances where R&D costs have soared, and the complexity of an attack has been so impressive that there is broad agreement on its sophisticated nature.

There is ongoing debate among experts about whether zero-day attacks should be classified as sophisticated. Advanced attacks can take various forms, including opportunistic, targeted, or a combination of both.

- **Opportunistic Attacks**: These attacks aim to target a wide range of potential victims in the hopes of discovering vulnerabilities that can be exploited. The attacker does not have specific targets in mind; instead, any system within reach that shows weaknesses becomes a potential victim. These attacks are akin to firing a shotgun in a crowded area, hoping that at least one pellet will hit a vulnerable target.
- **Targeted Attacks**: In contrast, targeted attacks focus on a specific individual, organization, or system. The attacker uses a range of tactics to breach the target's defenses, and once inside, they may launch additional attacks to navigate deeper into the system. These attacks are much more deliberate and focused compared to opportunistic ones.

Opportunistic attacks

Opportunistic attacks are typically driven by the pursuit of financial gain. Attackers are often indifferent to whose systems they compromise, as their primary objective is monetary profit. In many instances, they may not even attempt to conceal the breach, especially if they stand to profit from it—such as by selling stolen login credentials or credit card information. While not all opportunistic attacks are highly sophisticated, some certainly are. It's important to distinguish between opportunistic attacks and targeted ones, as there is a notable difference between the two.

Targeted attacks

In the context of targeted attacks, breaching systems outside the intended scope does not count as a success, regardless of the scale. For example, if a Russian operative is assigned to hack into the email systems of both the Democratic and Republican parties to steal all stored emails, the success of the mission depends solely on whether the operative accomplishes that specific goal. Even if the hacker manages to steal $1 million from an online bank using the same tactics, the mission would still be considered a failure if the original target— the parties' email systems— was not compromised. In a targeted attack, the attacker's objective is highly specific, such as sabotaging a former employer's website over a personal dispute. Attacking unrelated websites is seen as pointless in this case.

Targeted attacks typically involve advanced techniques to bypass strong security measures, often exploiting vulnerabilities that are unknown to the public or the companies tasked with patching them. These attacks are generally carried out by individuals or groups with far greater technical expertise than those behind opportunistic, less sophisticated attacks. The motivations behind targeted attacks often go beyond financial gain, such as stealing sensitive data or causing significant harm. After all, if the goal is to make a profit, why risk attacking a highly secure site? A more strategic approach would be to focus on less protected, yet relevant targets.

These advanced threats in targeted attacks are commonly referred to as **Advanced Persistent Threats (APTs)**, characterized by the following:

- **Advanced**: Involves sophisticated hacking techniques, often supported by considerable financial investment in research and development.
- **Persistent**: Continuously adapts and tries multiple methods to infiltrate the target system, remaining persistent even when faced with strong defenses.
- **Threat**: Represents a serious risk of significant damage, whether through data theft, system disruption, or other harmful outcomes.

Blended (opportunistic and targeted) attacks

Another type of advanced assault is the opportunistic or semi-targeted attack. In these cases, attackers are less focused on specific targets and more concerned with gathering as much valuable data as possible. For instance, when fraudsters aim to steal credit card information, they don't care whether they breach Best Buy, Walmart, or Barnes & Noble. Their main objective is to capture as many active credit card numbers as possible, regardless of the retailer. For these attackers, targeting sites without access to credit card data is a waste of time and resources. The goal is clear: maximize the haul of valuable information, so focusing on sites without that data doesn't serve their purpose.

Various Technical Attack Techniques

While it's not necessary for most people to dive deep into the technical details of how cyberattacks target system vulnerabilities, understanding the basic concepts behind common hacker techniques can be both interesting and enlightening. Below are some of the key methods hackers use to infiltrate and exploit technical systems.

Rootkits

Rootkits are software tools designed to allow attackers to perform unauthorized actions with elevated privileges on a compromised system. The term "root" refers to the administrator account on UNIX-based systems. These tools often include features that help the attacker maintain ongoing access to the device, often without the knowledge of the legitimate users.

Brute-force attacks

Brute-force attacks involve an attacker systematically trying numerous potential combinations until they find the correct one. In the case of account access, the attacker will repeatedly attempt every possible password until the right one is found. Alternatively, they might try various decryption keys until they manage to unlock an encrypted message or communication.

Injection attacks

Injection attacks happen when a system expects user input, but instead, it receives malicious content, such as code. This harmful input can be executed by the system itself or passed along to other systems for execution. While proper coding practices can reduce the risk of injection attacks, many systems still remain vulnerable, making injection attacks a persistent and commonly used technique among hackers.

Cross-site scripting

Cross-site scripting (XSS) is a specific type of injection attack where an attacker inserts malicious code into a legitimate website. When users visit the site, this code is delivered to their devices and executed through their web browser or app. This typically happens because the site allows users to submit content that is then displayed to others. Online platforms like forums, social media sites, and comment sections on news stories are particularly vulnerable to XSS attacks. For example, an attacker might inject harmful code into a comment, which is then executed in another user's browser when the comment is viewed. To prevent these types of attacks, it's crucial for websites to implement strong safeguards, especially on platforms that allow user-generated content.

SQL injection

SQL injection attacks target relational databases by exploiting vulnerabilities in SQL (Structured Query Language) interfaces, which are commonly used to manage and access data in systems. An SQL injection occurs when an attacker deliberately sends data containing malicious SQL commands instead of expected user input. For instance, if a system asks for a user ID to retrieve information, an attacker may input SQL code alongside the user ID. If the attacker knows the SQL query the system is likely to use, they can manipulate it by injecting commands that could display all the database entries. If the system lacks proper protection against such attacks, it may unintentionally execute the attacker's code. While the primary goal of an SQL injection attack might not be to expose data directly, the system's response to the malicious input can unintentionally reveal critical details about its structure, security measures, and vulnerabilities, offering the attacker valuable information for further exploitation.

Session hijacking

Session hijacking occurs when an unauthorized individual gains control of an active communication session between two parties. For example, if an attacker intercepts the connection between a user and their bank during an online banking session, they can take over the session, effectively replacing the legitimate user. Once successful, the attacker assumes the identity and privileges of the authorized user, allowing them to perform any actions the user would normally be able to do. This type of attack often arises from flaws in how an application manages user sessions. It becomes especially problematic when systems rely too heavily on technological methods to validate a session's legitimacy, rather than using stronger, more secure measures to confirm the user's identity.

Malformed URL attacks

Malformed URL attacks involve altering URLs to mislead users into believing they are visiting a legitimate website, while in reality, the URL contains special characters designed to carry out malicious actions. Attackers can spread these deceptive URLs through channels like email, text messages, social media, or blog comments. Another variation of URL-based attacks involves deliberately crafting a URL with specific components aimed at causing disruption or exploiting vulnerabilities in the targeted system.

Buffer overflow attacks

Buffer overflow attacks happen when an attacker intentionally overloads a system's memory buffer with excessive data, causing it to overwrite adjacent memory areas and potentially compromise the system's security. By carefully crafting the overflow input, the attacker can manipulate the memory, potentially overwriting critical areas where the system stores instructions or control data. This can lead to unintended behavior, including executing malicious code or gaining unauthorized access.

Frequently Asked Questions

- What are the various types of cyber-attacks?
- How can cybercriminals gain access to your devices?
- How can you protect your systems and prevent cyber-attacks?
- What are the different methods used in technical attacks?
- What distinguishes opportunistic attacks from targeted attacks?

CHAPTER THREE
CYBERATTACKERS AND THEIR COLORED HATS

Overview

In this chapter, you will explore the different types of cyberattackers, represented by various "hat" colors, and how they can profit from their cyberattacks against businesses and individuals.

Cyberattackers categories

Cyberattackers are typically classified based on their goals and motivations:

- **Black hat hackers** are individuals who engage in malicious activities with the intent to steal, alter, or destroy data. They are typically associated with illegal and harmful actions, contributing to the negative image of hackers in general.
- **White hat hackers** are ethical hackers who use their skills to test, fix, and enhance the security of systems and networks. These experts, often specializing in penetration testing, are hired by businesses and governments to identify and address security vulnerabilities. White hat hackers only operate with the explicit permission of system owners, ensuring their actions are lawful and legitimate.
- **Grey hat hackers** fall somewhere between black and white hats. While they do not typically engage in malicious activities, they may sometimes act unethically or break anti-hacking laws. Grey hat hackers often explore vulnerabilities without authorization but tend to report their findings responsibly, without causing harm. However, some may seek financial gain, for instance, by charging system owners for helping fix discovered vulnerabilities. While some grey hat hackers might be mistaken for black hat hackers, they don't always have harmful intentions.
- **Green hat hackers** are newcomers to the hacking world who aspire to become experts. Their position on the spectrum from white to black hat hackers can evolve as they gain more experience and refine their skills.
- **Blue hat hackers** are hired to thoroughly test software for security flaws before it is released to the public. They act as an external layer of protection, ensuring software is free from vulnerabilities before it reaches the market.

Among these, black and grey hat hackers pose the greatest threat to cybersecurity, potentially compromising not only your personal data but also the safety of those around you.

Exploring the Monetization Strategies of Cybercriminals

Some cyberattackers are driven by financial motives, though not all engage in malicious activities for monetary gain. There are several ways these attackers can profit from their actions, including:

- **Direct financial fraud**: This involves outright theft of money, such as stealing credit card details or engaging in unauthorized financial transactions.
- **Indirect financial fraud**: This includes activities like identity theft or selling stolen data (e.g., personal information, login credentials) on the black market to facilitate further financial exploitation.
- **Ransomware**: Cybercriminals use ransomware to encrypt a victim's data, demanding payment (usually in cryptocurrency) to restore access to the files or systems.
- **Cryptomining**: Attackers may use infected devices to mine cryptocurrency without the owner's knowledge, essentially hijacking system resources for profit.

These methods represent just a few of the ways cybercriminals exploit digital environments for financial gain.

Direct financial fraud

Hackers are constantly finding new ways to directly steal money using various techniques. For example, they may install malware on victims' computers to intercept online banking sessions and manipulate the bank's server to transfer funds into their own accounts. While financial institutions often have strong security measures in place, many cybercriminals are shifting their focus to systems with weaker defenses.

One such strategy involves targeting apps or systems that store prepaid card balances, such as those used at coffee shops or for other small-scale purchases. Hackers can steal funds from these accounts, or if the accounts are set up with auto-refill features, they can repeatedly siphon off money with each automatic reload.

In addition, fraudsters are also eyeing frequent traveler accounts. By gaining access, they may transfer loyalty points to other accounts, make unauthorized purchases, or redeem points for plane tickets and hotel bookings that they can then sell for cash.

Credit card information is another common target. Hackers may either use stolen credit card numbers themselves or sell them to others involved in fraudulent activities.

The reality of cybercrime is complex: it's not simply a matter of good versus evil. The methods are varied and often involve exploiting systems in subtle and indirect ways. The line between legitimate and illicit activity in cyberspace can be blurry, making it crucial to stay vigilant against these evolving threats.

Indirect financial fraud

Cybercriminals with more advanced skills often avoid direct financial theft because these types of scams typically involve smaller amounts of money and are easier for victims to reverse—such as by disputing fraudulent transactions or canceling unauthorized purchases. Moreover, such crimes carry a higher risk of detection and capture. Instead, more sophisticated hackers tend to focus on collecting data that can be exploited for fraudulent purposes in the future.

Several types of these data-driven offenses include:

- **Illicit trading of securities**: Hackers may manipulate stock markets or trade sensitive information to profit illegally from securities, using insider knowledge or unauthorized access to financial data.
- **Unauthorized access to payment information**: This includes stealing credit card, debit card, or other payment details to conduct fraudulent transactions or sell the stolen information.
- **Theft of goods**: Cybercriminals may steal physical goods or digital products, often by accessing secure systems or bypassing security measures.
- **Unauthorized data acquisition**: Hackers may unlawfully access personal, financial, or business-related data, which can then be sold or used for further exploitation, such as identity theft or corporate espionage.

These types of crimes often involve more complex schemes and can have long-term impacts, making them harder to trace and stop compared to straightforward financial theft.

Profiting off illegal trading of securities

Illegal trading of securities, including stocks, bonds, and options, presents an enticing opportunity for cybercriminals to make significant profits. These criminals use various sophisticated tactics to manipulate the financial markets:

- **Pump and Dump**: In this scheme, hackers gain unauthorized access to a company's data, often through infiltration or theft. They then short-sell the company's stock, betting that its value will decrease. After releasing the stolen information (often causing panic or uncertainty), they drive the stock price down. Once the price drops, the hackers buy back the stock at a lower price to cover their short positions, pocketing the difference.

- **Misleading Press Releases and Social Media Posts**: Cybercriminals may exploit their access to a company's official communication channels, such as press releases or social media accounts, to spread false or misleading information. By either posting fake news or manipulating social media accounts, they create artificial market fluctuations. These individuals may either buy or sell the company's stock before the news hits, profiting from the resulting price changes.
- **Insider Information**: Criminals often target a company's internal communications to obtain insider information, such as press release drafts. For example, they may learn about a company's upcoming earnings report that is expected to surpass Wall Street's expectations. Armed with this knowledge, they might buy call options (which allow them to purchase stock at a set price) in anticipation of the stock price rising. Conversely, if they know a company is about to release negative news, they might purchase put options or short-sell the stock, profiting when the price falls.

These tactics of indirect financial fraud are not only common but also grounded in reality, with concrete evidence of their use by cybercriminals. Compared to direct theft, these scams are often seen as less risky for the perpetrators. Regulators face significant challenges in detecting such activities in real-time, and even when discovered, reversing the fraudulent transactions can be nearly impossible. For sophisticated hackers, this creates a low-risk, high-reward environment, where the potential for financial gain is substantial, and the chances of getting caught are relatively low.

Stealing credit cards, debit cards, and other payment-related information

In news reports, it's common to see criminals targeting credit and debit card information for theft. They can exploit these stolen numbers to make unauthorized transactions. Thieves often employ tactics like acquiring electronic gift cards, software serial numbers, and other valuable items that can be quickly resold for cash. Some may even use the stolen card details to purchase physical goods or services, having them shipped to vacant addresses for easy collection. Many criminals don't directly use the stolen credit cards themselves. Instead, they sell the card information on the dark web, where it's typically bought by other criminals who can quickly exploit the cards before the fraud is detected and the accounts are frozen.

Stealing goods

In addition to the types of theft previously mentioned, some criminals focus on high-value, easily transportable items such as jewelry. They often gather information about high-value shipments with the intent to steal the items when they are delivered, rather than relying on fraudulent transactions.

Stealing data

Some individuals steal data with the intent to commit various financial crimes, while others do so to sell it or make it public. For example, data stolen from a business can be extremely valuable to a dishonest competitor seeking to gain an unfair advantage.

Ransomware

Ransomware is a type of malicious software that blocks users from accessing their data, demanding payment from victims to restore access. This form of cyberattack has already generated billions of dollars for criminals, while also putting lives at risk, particularly when it disrupts critical systems, such as hospital networks. In some cases, ransomware attacks have been linked to tragic outcomes, including preventable deaths, when medical professionals are unable to access patient records or essential equipment due to system lockouts.

As hackers continue to improve their tools and refine their techniques, the threat posed by ransomware grows. Some cybercriminals design ransomware specifically to maximize financial gain, infecting computers to infiltrate entire networks and gain access to high-value systems and sensitive data. Rather than simply encrypting the first data it encounters, the ransomware is programmed to target the most valuable information, knowing that the higher the value of the data to its owner, the more likely they are to pay a ransom.

Ransomware has also become more sophisticated, often bypassing antivirus software and evading detection. In many cases, attackers specifically target organizations they believe can afford to pay large ransoms. Criminals tend to focus on high-profile targets—such as hospitals, where the consequences of system downtime are especially severe. For example, a hospital's inability to access patient records can be life-threatening, making it more likely that they will pay a ransom to restore their operations quickly.

Moreover, attackers are often strategic, preferring to target regions or individuals with a higher capacity to pay. For instance, they know that an American business or government entity may be more likely to pay a higher ransom than a victim in a country with less economic power, such as China.

Cryptominers

A crypto miner is a type of malware that secretly hijacks a computer's resources to perform complex mathematical calculations required for generating new cryptocurrency. The cryptocurrency produced by these calculations is then sent to the cybercriminal running the crypto miner. Often, these malware programs use networks of compromised computers—sometimes known as botnets—to carry out the mining operations.

Crypto miners have become a popular tool for hackers who may not have the skills to carry out more sophisticated attacks, like ransomware. For criminals, crypto miners offer a relatively simple and low-risk way to profit from their hacks, as they generate income without directly affecting the victims. While the value of cryptocurrencies can fluctuate wildly, some reports suggest that certain large-scale mining operations can generate over $30,000 per month for their operators.

Dealing with Non-Malicious Threats: Not All Dangers Come From Attackers

While some individuals seek to exploit others, there are also those who, although well-intentioned, can unknowingly create risks that may be even more dangerous than those posed by malicious actors.

Human error

Human error represents a major cybersecurity risk for individuals, businesses, and government organizations alike. Many of the high-profile data breaches reported in the media over the past decade can be traced, at least in part, to mistakes made by people. Cybercriminals are keenly aware that exploiting human error is often a crucial factor in the success of their attacks.

The vulnerability of cybersecurity lies in humans

People often become the weakest link in the cybersecurity chain, leading to major breaches due to their mistakes. The reasons for this are rooted in the rapid pace of technological advancement and the limitations of the human mind. Technology has made extraordinary leaps in recent years, far outpacing the expectations once set by science fiction. Today, there is an abundance of electronic devices, and security technology has advanced to the point where intrusion detection systems now bear little resemblance to those from just a decade ago. These systems are constantly improving, with each new release offering better protection than the last.

In contrast, the human brain has evolved over tens of thousands of years and remains relatively unchanged within a single lifetime or even across generations. While technology progresses at a rapid rate, the human mind struggles to keep pace. As a result, people are regularly expected to manage and understand an increasingly complex array of devices, systems, and software, which increases the likelihood of mistakes. Human limitations, combined with the growing demand for intellectual capacity to handle advanced technologies, significantly heighten the risk of error.

Think about the difference in how many passwords your grandparents needed to remember when they were your age. Now compare that to how many passwords you are required to keep track of today. How secure were passwords in your grandparents' time? How vulnerable were they to hacking? Today, passwords are more susceptible to remote attacks, and the burden of remembering complex passwords is greater than ever.

This challenge is further complicated by modern work environments, especially with the rise of remote work and the need to supervise children's education at home. The lack of direct interaction with colleagues or the constant juggling of responsibilities can lead to distractions and mistakes, which may compromise security. These situations create more opportunities for errors, whether it's forgetting a password, clicking on a malicious link, or failing to recognize a phishing attempt.

It's essential to acknowledge that human error can have a profound impact on cybersecurity. As technology becomes more sophisticated, so too does the potential for mistakes. To mitigate this risk, it's critical to take proactive steps to safeguard against human error, such as implementing stronger security protocols, using multi-factor authentication, and providing regular training to keep individuals aware of the threats they face.

Social engineering

In information security, **social engineering** refers to the manipulation of individuals' psychology to convince them to take actions they would typically avoid—actions that often lead to negative consequences for them and their organizations. Essentially, social engineering exploits human trust to bypass security measures.

Here are a few common examples of social engineering attacks:

- A hacker impersonating a member of the IT department over the phone, tricking someone into resetting their email password.
- Deceptive emails designed to trick users into revealing sensitive information.
- Emails that impersonate a CEO or other high-ranking official, convincing an employee to take harmful actions.

While the perpetrators of social engineering attacks often have malicious intentions, those who unknowingly create the vulnerabilities—such as the individuals who fall for these tactics—typically do so without any intention to harm anyone. For example, the user who resets their password in response to a call from someone pretending to be from the IT department believes they are helping fix an issue, not realizing they are giving hackers access to the system. Similarly, the targets of phishing emails or CEO fraud are not intentionally aiding cybercriminals, but rather, they are deceived into acting against their own interests.

Human error can compromise cybersecurity in many ways, including unintentionally deleting data, misconfiguring systems, unknowingly downloading malware, or accidentally disabling security features. These innocent mistakes can be easily exploited by criminals to further their malicious goals. It's important to recognize that human error is an undeniable part of cybersecurity risks. Everyone makes mistakes, including you and me—it's just a part of being human.

To minimize the risk of falling victim to such attacks, it is essential to double-check critical actions and be vigilant in verifying any suspicious activities. If you receive an unexpected email, phone call, or request, especially one that seems to come from a high-ranking person like a CEO or IT staff, it's crucial to confirm its legitimacy before taking action. Even if you've dealt with similar issues in the past, it's better to err on the side of caution and verify before responding. It's always better to be safe than sorry.

External disasters

Cybersecurity focuses on protecting the confidentiality, integrity, and availability of your data. External disasters can severely threaten data availability, and may also indirectly affect its confidentiality and integrity. These disasters can be divided into two types: natural disasters and human-made disasters.

Natural disasters

Many people live in regions susceptible to various natural disasters. Nature's unpredictable force can damage computers and the valuable data they store. Hurricanes, tornadoes, floods, and fires can all cause widespread destruction. As part of their certification, cybersecurity professionals are trained in continuity planning and disaster recovery. Statistically, most individuals will experience at least one natural disaster in their lifetime, making it crucial to plan for safeguarding systems and data against such risks. Businesses with well-established continuity plans fared better than those without when the COVID-19 pandemic forced a shift to remote work. Relying on backup storage at two different locations—especially if both are basements in flood-prone areas—may not be the most effective solution.

Pandemics

A specific category of natural disasters includes pandemics and other health crises. The events of 2020 clearly demonstrated how the emergence of a highly contagious disease can force the sudden shutdown of workplaces and schools, triggering a swift move to online platforms. However, this shift also introduces a range of cybersecurity issues.

Issues caused by human activity in the environment

External challenges we face are not solely caused by nature. It's important to recognize that human actions can also trigger disasters, such as floods and fires. Unfortunately, the consequences of these man-made events often exceed those of natural catastrophes.

Additionally, disruptions like power outages, voltage surges, protests, riots, strikes, terrorist attacks, internet failures, and telecom service interruptions can all impact the availability of data and systems. Following the tragic events of 9/11, businesses came to understand the importance of storing backups away from their primary systems. Those who had backed up their data from systems in the World Trade Center to nearby systems in the World Financial Center learned this lesson the hard way, as the World Financial Center became inaccessible for an extended period after the destruction of the World Trade Center.

Cyberwarriors and cyberspies

Modern nations often command powerful teams of cyberwarriors who specialize in identifying vulnerabilities in software and systems. These teams typically use their findings for offensive purposes, such as hacking or espionage against adversaries, or even for law enforcement objectives. However, this approach carries significant risks for individuals and businesses alike. While government agencies tend to keep vulnerabilities secret, rather than sharing them with the relevant vendors, this strategy can expose organizations, governments, and individuals to attacks from adversaries who may discover and exploit the same weaknesses.

Additionally, governments may use their cyberwarfare teams to combat criminal activity or, in some cases, to monitor their own populations and maintain political control. After the events of 9/11, the U.S. government initiated several large-scale data collection programs that affected law-abiding citizens. This presents a potential risk to U.S. individuals, especially if the databases created in these operations were accessed by foreign entities, leading to various cybersecurity challenges.

The dangers of governments creating large repositories of data and exploiting cyber vulnerabilities are not theoretical. In recent years, several powerful cyberweapons believed to have originated from U.S. intelligence agencies have surfaced on the internet. These tools were reportedly stolen by individuals or groups with motives contrary to those of the agency that developed them. It remains unclear whether these weapons have been used against U.S. interests by the perpetrators of the theft.

The ineffective Fair Credit Reporting Act

The Fair Credit Reporting Act (FCRA) is a set of regulations that many Americans recognize. First enacted nearly fifty years ago, it has since undergone multiple updates. The FCRA governs how credit reports are collected, managed, and shared, with a focus on ensuring fairness, accuracy, and privacy for individuals' credit information. Its primary aim is to protect consumers from inaccuracies and misuse of their credit data.

FAIR CREDIT REPORTING ACT

The Fair Credit Reporting Act (FCRA) requires credit reporting agencies to remove certain negative information from individuals' credit reports after a specified period. For example, if you miss a credit card payment during your college years, it is illegal for that late payment to appear on your credit report years later when you're applying for a mortgage. Even individuals who file for bankruptcy to get a fresh start can have their bankruptcy records expunged under the law, ensuring that they are not permanently penalized. The intent of the law is to give people the opportunity to rebuild their financial lives.

However, today, some technology companies are undermining the protections established by the FCRA. For instance, it is alarmingly easy for a bank loan officer to access court records of bankruptcies with a simple Google search, allowing them to pull up relevant details about a potential borrower's financial history. Similarly, it is just as easy to find foreclosure records tied to a person's name, even if those events occurred many years ago. These records are accessible online, and there are no legal restrictions preventing them from being used inappropriately. In the U.S., Google and other search engines are not regulated to block links to these databases, meaning that outdated or irrelevant financial information can still surface, potentially harming an individual's ability to secure loans or credit based on old financial troubles.

Expunged records are no longer expunged

The court system has various regulations designed to help young people keep minor offenses off their permanent criminal records. Laws allow courts to seal certain files and remove specific types of information, providing individuals with a chance for a fresh start. These legal protections are widely recognized as crucial for helping people move on from past mistakes, and many successful individuals credit these safeguards with enabling their achievements.

However, the effectiveness of these protections is questioned when a simple Google search can reveal allegedly erased information. Google provides access to local police blotters and court records, once published in newspapers but now stored in online archives. As a result, even individuals who were charged with minor offenses but had all charges dropped may still face lasting consequences, such as damage to their career prospects or personal lives. This happens despite the fact that they were never convicted, prosecuted, or even formally indicted. The availability of such information online undermines the intent of the legal protections meant to allow people a clean slate.

Social Security numbers

In the past, it was common practice for colleges to use Social Security numbers (SSNs) as student identifiers. During that time, the world was very different, and schools often posted grades using SSNs instead of names for privacy reasons. However, with the advent of online archives, many of these pre-web-era materials, including student records from the 1970s, 1980s, and early 1990s, are now accessible, raising questions about whether it's appropriate to expose students' SSNs to the public.

Additionally, there are instances where the last four digits of a person's phone number are used for user authentication, and this information is easily found through a quick search on search engines like Google or Bing. Given the widespread awareness of the security risks posed by past practices, it's puzzling why the government continues to rely on Social Security numbers as a form of secure identification, treating them with an expectation of privacy that no longer holds true.

Moreover, online archives of community newsletters from churches, synagogues, and other local organizations often contain detailed personal information, such as birth announcements with the baby's name, parents' names, birthdate, hospital, and even the names of grandparents. With this information so readily accessible, one might question whether a single security question for a user could be easily bypassed by someone with access to such public data.

These examples highlight the privacy risks created by technological advancements and the potential cybersecurity threats they pose. They also underscore how these vulnerabilities could lead to legal challenges, eroding existing protective measures and putting individuals' personal information at greater risk.

Social media platforms

Social networking platforms pose significant cybersecurity risks for businesses and their employees. Hackers increasingly target social media sites, often using automated tools, to gather personal information that can be exploited for malicious purposes. With this data, attackers can launch various types of cyberattacks, including those involving ransomware. For example, they may craft highly convincing spear-phishing emails, which trick employees into clicking on links to ransomware-infected websites or opening infected attachments.

In recent years, virtual kidnapping schemes have also become more prevalent. Criminals use social media to gather detailed information about potential victims, such as their routines, family members, and key moments in their lives. They then exploit this information to time their attacks and choose their targets carefully. Once a target is identified, the criminals often call relatives of the victim, claiming that the person has been kidnapped and demanding a ransom for their release, despite the victim being completely unharmed and unaware of the threat.

These examples illustrate how social media, while connecting people, has become a tool for cybercriminals to exploit, posing significant threats to both individuals and organizations.

Google's highly advanced computers

Computer systems often use security questions as a verification method, where users are asked questions that only they should be able to answer. However, the widespread availability of personal information online, easily accessible through search engines like Google, undermines the effectiveness of this authentication process. In recent years, the amount of personal data available with a simple search has grown exponentially, making it easier for criminals to find the answers to security questions used on many websites.

While some websites may have safeguards in place to detect and block delayed or incorrect answers to security questions, many others do not. This lack of consistency means that individuals with the know-how to effectively use search engines can bypass certain security measures with relative ease. By simply looking up answers to questions like "What is your mother's maiden name?" or "What was the name of your first pet?" thieves can quickly compromise accounts and gain unauthorized access.

As the availability of personal information continues to grow, traditional security questions are becoming increasingly ineffective as a means of authentication. This highlights the need for stronger, more secure verification methods to protect sensitive information from being exploited.

Tracking the location of mobile devices

Google, along with other app providers, collects a vast array of data through services like Android phones, Google Maps, and Waze, which track users' locations and behaviors. This data collection impacts a significant portion of the population in the Western world. However, it's important to note that other companies with access to location data—such as those with apps installed on multiple devices—are capable of similar tracking activities. By monitoring a person's movements and the length of time they stay in various locations, these companies can build detailed databases that pose several risks.

One major concern is that this data could be used to undermine security mechanisms like knowledge-based authentication, where answers to questions (e.g., "Where were you born?" or

"What is your favorite vacation spot?") may be easily derived from location data. Additionally, this information could facilitate social engineering attacks, where attackers manipulate personal data to trick individuals into revealing sensitive information.

The security of these databases is also a serious issue. Even if the company collecting the data does not have malicious intent, unauthorized parties could potentially access or steal critical information, leading to significant security breaches. Beyond cybersecurity risks, this extensive tracking raises privacy concerns, as companies may collect sensitive details about people's routines, such as visits to healthcare facilities or sleep patterns. This data could be used to make inferences about individuals' health or personal lives, which could then be exploited for targeted advertising, manipulation, or even more intrusive purposes.

The combination of widespread data collection, weak security measures, and potential privacy violations underscores the need for stronger regulations and protections to safeguard personal information in the digital age.

Protecting against These Attackers

It's important to recognize that achieving total cybersecurity is simply not possible. A common misconception is that using manual typewriters offers perfect security, but this is far from true. Even with a typewriter, someone could deduce the content of a message by carefully listening to the keystrokes. The reality is that rather than striving for impossible perfect security, we should focus on achieving **adequate** cybersecurity.

Adequate cybersecurity means understanding the current risks, acknowledging which threats have been effectively managed, and addressing those that remain. No single security measure is foolproof—what works well against one type of threat or attacker may be ineffective against others. For example, the security requirements for a personal computer may differ drastically from those needed to protect a sophisticated online banking server. Similarly, the security standards for a smartphone used by the President of the United States to communicate with advisors are orders of magnitude higher than those for an average sixth grader's device.

The key takeaway is that cybersecurity is about risk management—it's about making informed decisions to safeguard against the most likely and impactful threats, rather than chasing an unattainable ideal of total security.

Frequently Asked Questions

- What are the various types of cyber attackers?
- What are the best strategies to protect against these cyber threats?
- In what ways do cybercriminals generate profit?

CHAPTER FOUR
PROTECTION AGAINST CYBER ATTACKS

Overview

Chapter four outlines effective strategies for safeguarding yourself and your online business from cyber-attacks, detailing the protective measures you should implement.

Understanding Your Current Cybersecurity Posture

Recognizing what needs protection is crucial for strengthening your cyber defenses. With a clear understanding of this, you can evaluate key procedures to ensure proper security and pinpoint any potential areas that require improvement.

It's essential to assess the type of data you hold, the potential threats to its security, and its level of sensitivity. Consider the consequences if this data were to be exposed publicly on the internet. Once you evaluate the time and financial resources you're willing to invest, you can better determine how much you should allocate to securing it.

Threat to Computers

Your home computers may face several major cybersecurity risks, including:

- **Breach of Security:** Unauthorized individuals may gain access to your computer, potentially using it for malicious activities. They could view your data, communicate with other devices, launch attacks on other systems, steal cryptocurrency, or access information across your network.
- **Malware:** Malware is a form of malicious software that can infiltrate your home computer, much like an attacker. It allows cybercriminals to steal information, interact with other devices, mine cryptocurrency, and more. Malware can also monitor network traffic and spread across connected devices within your home network.
- **Sharing Devices:** Allowing others—such as family members or roommates—to use your computer increases the risk of exposure. Different levels of cybersecurity awareness may lead to unintentional malware infections, breaches, or damage to your system.
- **External Networks and Storage Connections:** Connecting your computer to other networks, such as through a Virtual Private Network (VPN), introduces the risk of network-based malware or hacking attempts from external sources. Similarly, using cloud storage or remote services could expose your system to similar vulnerabilities.
- **Physical Security Risks:** The physical location of your computer can affect its security. If it's easily accessible or in a shared space, there is a greater risk of theft, tampering, or unauthorized access to your data.

Your mobile devices

Mobile devices present significant information security risks due to several factors:

- **Constant Connectivity:** Mobile devices are always connected to the internet, which exposes them to public, often insecure networks where hackers and cybercriminals are active, increasing the risk of attacks.
- **Sensitive Data Storage:** Mobile devices typically store large amounts of personal and sensitive data, such as financial details, passwords, and private communications, making them prime targets for theft or exploitation.
- **Communication Channels:** Mobile devices are used to communicate with a wide variety of people and systems, some of which may not be entirely trustworthy. This increases the likelihood of interacting with malicious actors or untrusted sources.
- **Inbound Threats:** Mobile devices are susceptible to receiving unsolicited messages, calls, or notifications from unknown sources, some of which may carry malware or attempt phishing attacks.
- **Limited Security Tools:** Due to resource constraints, mobile devices may not always have robust security software installed, or they may rely on pre-installed apps that can't be upgraded or customized to meet specific security needs.

- **Risk of Loss or Theft:** Mobile devices are portable and therefore prone to being lost or stolen, exposing sensitive data to unauthorized individuals.
- **Vulnerability to Damage:** Mobile devices are also at risk of accidental damage, which can lead to data loss or make them more vulnerable to attacks if compromised.
- **Untrusted Wi-Fi Networks:** Mobile devices frequently connect to Wi-Fi networks that may be insecure, increasing the risk of data interception or malware attacks.
- **Improper Disposal:** Mobile devices are often replaced without properly decommissioning them, leading to the risk of leftover data being accessed or recovered by others when the devices are discarded or traded in.
- **Upgrades Without Decommissioning:** When upgrading to newer devices, old phones may be traded in or sold without securely wiping or disabling data, leaving sensitive information vulnerable to recovery.

Your Internet of Things (IoT) devices

In recent years, the landscape of connected computing has undergone a significant transformation. Not long ago, the Internet was primarily accessed through traditional devices like desktops, laptops, and servers, which handled a wide array of computing tasks. Today, however, the world has changed, with computers now representing only a small fraction of all connected devices. A wide range of everyday electronics—such as smartphones, security cameras, refrigerators, cars, coffee makers, and even gym equipment—are now embedded with sophisticated computing systems that remain continuously connected to the Internet. This network of interconnected devices, known as the Internet of Things (IoT), has expanded rapidly in recent years. However, the security measures in place for these devices often fall short. Many IoT devices lack the necessary security technologies to protect them from potential cyberattacks. Even when security features are enabled, they are often poorly configured or insufficiently robust. Hackers can exploit these vulnerabilities to spy on users, steal personal information, launch attacks on other systems or devices, carry out denial-of-service attacks on networks, or cause other types of harm.

Your networking tool

Networking equipment is a common target for hackers, as vulnerabilities in these devices can lead to unauthorized traffic rerouting, data breaches, cyberattacks, and even disruptions to internet access.

Your work environment

Understanding the risks associated with sensitive data in the workplace is essential, especially when considering the behavior of coworkers. One significant risk arises from connecting electronic devices to multiple networks, such as when moving them between the office and home. In these situations, malware and other security threats can transfer from your employer's or coworkers' devices to your own, potentially spreading to other devices on your home network. The COVID-19 pandemic has further complicated this issue by blurring the lines between work and home environments, creating significant cybersecurity challenges.

Risk Identification

To effectively protect something, you must first fully understand what you're trying to safeguard. Without this understanding, securing an environment becomes a difficult, if not impossible, task. To ensure your security, it's crucial to assess your assets—both digital and physical—and determine what you want to protect. These assets may not always be located in one place; some, like data, could be stored in various cloud services such as Google Drive, Apple iCloud, or Microsoft OneDrive, which might not be physically accessible to you. It's essential to have a clear understanding of the risks associated with each of your assets in order to implement effective security measures.

Understanding Endpoints

Endpoints are devices that connect to networks and facilitate communication. For example, a laptop is an endpoint when it connects to your home network, while a smartphone becomes an endpoint when connected via Wi-Fi or a cellular network (e.g., 4G or 5G). The term "endpoint" refers to the point at which a communication channel ends. Internet traffic typically passes through several nodes before reaching its final destination, but once it reaches an endpoint, the data transfer stops. Given the potential risks associated with these devices, securing all endpoints is crucial. Laptops, smartphones, tablets, and other electronic devices should all have robust security software installed. Similarly, IoT devices need to be protected based on their specific vulnerabilities.

In enterprise settings, endpoint management is often centralized. Security systems communicate with client applications on the devices to enforce policies, detect unusual activity, prevent data breaches, and thwart cyberattacks. This centralized approach helps ensure consistency and improves the overall security posture.

For individuals, creating an inventory of all connected devices is a straightforward process. Start by listing every device connected to your home network. One way to do this is by checking your router's settings under the "connected devices" section. Don't forget to include devices that may not always be connected or are only occasionally used. Be sure to also list external storage devices like hard drives, flash drives, and memory cards, as well as any third-party storage or computing services you use. Document this list carefully—either typed or printed—to avoid missing any devices and ensure proper tracking.

Ensuring Safety from Potential Hazards

Once you've identified the assets that need protection, it's essential to implement and enforce appropriate measures to secure them and minimize the impact of any potential security breaches. For home users, protection primarily involves creating barriers to prevent unauthorized access to both your digital and physical assets, establishing processes to safeguard sensitive data (even if informal), and regularly backing up system configurations and restore points.

Most individuals should focus on a few key elements of protection:

- **Perimeter Defense:** Establishing strong boundaries around your network to prevent unauthorized access from external sources.
- **Firewall/Router:** Using firewalls and secure router settings to monitor and control incoming and outgoing network traffic.
- **Security Software:** Installing and maintaining up-to-date antivirus, anti-malware, and other security software on all devices to detect and block threats.
- **Devices:** Ensuring that all devices, including computers, smartphones, tablets, and IoT devices, are properly secured with strong passwords and encryption.
- **Backup Procedures:** Regularly backing up important data and creating system restore points to recover in case of data loss or a cyberattack.

It's also crucial to develop a thorough understanding of cybersecurity practices, including how to detect potential threats, respond effectively, recover devices after incidents, and improve overall defense strategies to stay ahead of evolving risks.

Perimeter defense

Securing your cyber-perimeter is similar to building a moat around a castle, with the aim of preventing unauthorized access and closely monitoring any potential intruders. One effective way to create this digital moat is by avoiding the direct connection of any computer to your Internet modem. Instead, you should connect a firewall/router to the modem and then link your computers to the firewall/router.

The modem can function as both a router and a firewall in many cases, so it's perfectly fine if you're connecting to the firewall/router part of the device rather than the modem itself. Typically, the connection between the firewall and the modem is made using a physical network cable. In some setups, the modem and firewall/router may be combined into a single device, which simplifies the process while still providing the necessary protection.

Firewall/router

Modern routers, commonly used in residential settings, offer firewall capabilities that help block most inbound traffic unless it originates from an action initiated by a device already protected by the firewall. This means that while a router's firewall can prevent unauthorized access from outside sources, it won't block responses from a web server when your computer requests a webpage. Routers use various technologies to provide this level of protection, with **Network Address Translation (NAT)** playing a key role. NAT allows devices on a private network to use private IP addresses, which are not recognized by the public Internet. To the outside world, all devices behind the NAT firewall appear to have the same public IP address. The firewall manages the NAT function, acting as an intermediary between your devices and the Internet.

To enhance the security of your home router/firewall, consider these essential steps:

1. Regularly Update Your Router

- Keeping your router's firmware up-to-date is crucial for protecting your network from vulnerabilities. Before setting up your router, ensure it has the latest updates installed. Enable the auto-update feature, if available, to ensure ongoing protection against newly discovered threats.

2. Replace Outdated Routers

- If your router is no longer supported by the manufacturer or is too old to receive regular updates, it's time to replace it. An outdated router may become vulnerable to newer cyber threats. Upgrading your router can also improve overall network performance as newer models support faster, more secure protocols.

3. Change the Default Administrative Password

- Many routers come with default administrative passwords that are widely known and easily guessable. Change this password to a strong, unique one and store it securely. It's a good idea to write down both the default and new passwords and keep them in a safe location, like a safe deposit box, rather than on any connected devices.

4. Choose a Unique SSID (Wi-Fi Network Name)

- Set a unique name for your Wi-Fi network instead of using the default SSID provided by your router. Avoid using personal information such as your last name or address. Opt for something neutral or creative to keep potential attackers guessing.

5. Enable Strong Wi-Fi Encryption

- Ensure your Wi-Fi network uses **WPA2** encryption at a minimum. If possible, upgrade to **WPA3** for stronger protection. Additionally, choose a robust password for your Wi-Fi network, and ensure that all devices connecting to it know this password to prevent unauthorized access.

6. Disable Older Wi-Fi Protocols

- If your devices support newer Wi-Fi standards like **Wi-Fi 5** (802.11ac) or **Wi-Fi 6** (802.11ax), disable older protocols like **802.11b**, **802.11g**, and **802.11n** on your router. These older standards have known security vulnerabilities and lower performance. Upgrading to the latest standards enhances both security and speed.

7. Enable MAC Address Filtering

- MAC (Media Access Control) address filtering allows you to restrict network access to devices with specific MAC addresses. While not foolproof, it adds another layer of security by making it harder for unauthorized users to connect to your network. Ensure all devices on your network are secure before enabling this feature.

8. Position Your Router Strategically

- To reduce the risk of outsiders accessing your network, place your router centrally in your home. This helps ensure the Wi-Fi signal stays within your home and doesn't extend too far beyond your property line. For mesh networks, follow placement instructions carefully to optimize both coverage and security.

9. Disable Remote Router Access

- Unless absolutely necessary, disable remote access to your router's administrative settings. Managing your router should be done only from inside your secured network using trusted devices. This minimizes the risk of unauthorized access from outside your home network.

10. Monitor Connected Devices

- Keep a list of all devices connected to your network, including both active and permitted devices. Regularly review this list to ensure only authorized devices are connected, and promptly disconnect any that should not have access.

11. Use a Guest Network for Visitors

- Set up a **guest network** for visitors to keep their devices separate from your main network. This adds a layer of protection for your personal devices and data. Make sure to apply encryption and a strong password to the guest network as well.

12. Consider Advanced Security Adjustments

- If you're comfortable with more technical networking adjustments, consider disabling **DHCP** and changing the default IP address range used by your router for internal networks. This can help disrupt certain automated hacking tools and add another layer of protection. However, this step is not recommended for everyone, as it can cause complications if done incorrectly.

Conclusion:

By following these practices, you can significantly enhance the security of your home network and safeguard your personal information and devices from cyber threats. In today's interconnected world, securing your router and network settings is crucial, as cyberattacks are becoming increasingly common and sophisticated. Taking proactive steps to protect your network is essential for maintaining your privacy and security online.

Security software

To effectively safeguard your personal information, using security software is essential. Here are some best practices to follow when setting up and using security software:

1. Install Security Software on All Devices

- Ensure that antivirus and personal device firewall software are installed on every computer, smartphone, and tablet you use. This includes devices connected to your home network and those you use for work or personal activities. These tools are essential for detecting and blocking malware and other cyber threats.

2. Use Anti-Spam Software for Email Protection

- Make sure to install and enable anti-spam software on all devices where you access email. This will help block malicious or phishing emails, which are common vectors for cyberattacks and identity theft.

3. Enable Remote Wipe on Mobile Devices

- Enable the **remote wipe** feature on all of your mobile devices. This feature allows you to erase your data remotely in case your device is lost or stolen, ensuring that sensitive information remains secure even if the device falls into the wrong hands.

4. Set Strong Passwords for Device Access

- Use strong, unique passwords for logging into your computers, smartphones, and other devices. Avoid simple or easily guessable passwords (e.g., "123456" or "password"). Instead, use a combination of upper and lower case letters, numbers, and special characters. Consider using a password manager to securely store and manage complex passwords.

5. Enable Auto-Updates and Keep Devices Updated

- Ensure that auto-updates are enabled for your security software, operating systems, and all installed applications. Regular updates help protect your devices from newly discovered vulnerabilities and security flaws. Keeping your devices up to date ensures that you're always protected against the latest threats.

By following these best practices, you can significantly improve the security of your devices and reduce the risk of cyberattacks or data breaches that could compromise your personal information.

The physical computer(s) and any other endpoints

- To ensure the security of your computers and other devices, it's essential to control physical access and store them in a secure location. If someone gains access to your device, it could be stolen, tampered with, or damaged without your knowledge.
- If possible, avoid sharing your computer with other family members. To ensure safe and efficient sharing, create separate user accounts for each person. Additionally, be cautious about granting administrative privileges to other users, as this could expose your device to unnecessary risks.
- Simply deleting data is not enough when disposing of, recycling, donating, or selling an old device. To fully protect your privacy, use a multi-pass data erasure tool for both hard drives and solid-state drives. It's also a good idea to remove the storage media from the device entirely before disposal and consider physically destroying it for added security.
- Additionally, some devices that require security, such as smart home hubs or wireless camera systems, may not be considered "endpoints" as they connect to other devices. These systems may use proprietary communication methods to interact with smart gadgets or cameras. It's important to ensure these devices are also properly secured.

Backup solutions

Make it a habit to back up your files regularly. If you're unsure how often you should be backing up, it's a sign that you may not be doing it often enough.

Detecting

It's essential to implement measures that allow you to identify cybersecurity incidents as soon as they happen. While home users may not have access to specialized detection tools, the detection phase of security should not be overlooked. Modern personal computer security software offers a range of detection features, making it crucial to ensure that all devices you manage are equipped with security software that actively monitors for potential threats.

Responding

Reacting to a cybersecurity incident involves taking appropriate action in response to detected threats. Security software often automatically responds or alerts users when it identifies potential security issues, enabling them to take the necessary steps to mitigate the risk.

Recovering

Cybersecurity recovery focuses on returning a compromised computer, network, or device to full functionality, including restoring all critical operations. It's important to have a well-documented recovery plan in place ahead of time to streamline and clarify the recovery process. Although most home users don't create one, having a plan offers several benefits. Typically, these plans are straightforward and concise, often fitting on a single page.

Assessing Your Existing Security Protocols

Once you have a clear understanding of what you need to protect and the steps required to do so, it becomes easier to assess the gaps between your current setup and your ideal level of security. As you review the following points, keep in mind that not all of them will apply in every situation:

- Is all software on your computer, including the operating system, legally obtained?
- Were the software and operating system sourced from trusted, reputable vendors?
- Are all your software applications, including the operating system, still supported by their developers or vendors?
- Are all software programs, as well as the operating system, up to date?
- Have you set up your software, including the operating system, to automatically receive updates?

- Is security software installed and actively running on your device?
- Is the auto-update feature for your security software enabled?
- Is your security software updated to the latest version?
- Does your security software include anti-malware protection, and is it fully activated?
- Are automatic virus scans scheduled to run after each software update?
- Does your security software include a firewall, and is it fully enabled?
- Does your security software provide anti-spam protection, and is it fully enabled? If you use additional anti-spam software, is it active and functional?
- Does your security software include remote lock or wipe capabilities, and are these features fully operational? If you use other remote wipe software, is it active?
- Are all features of your security software enabled, or are any functions intentionally disabled?
- Do you have backup software in place to ensure your device is included in a comprehensive backup strategy?
- Is encryption enabled for all sensitive data stored on your device?
- Are user permissions properly configured to restrict access to sensitive software, ensuring only authorized individuals can use it?
- Are the appropriate permissions in place to prevent unauthorized software from making changes to your computer, especially for software that should not run with administrator privileges?

Software and Cybersecurity Considerations

When evaluating software on your device, consider the following questions for each device, especially those only accessible by trusted users and not exposed to external threats. For devices used in more publicly accessible roles, like a web server, additional security measures will need to be addressed.

Hardware

When evaluating the security of your hardware devices, consider the following questions to ensure they are adequately protected:

- **Where did the hardware come from?** Was it sourced from a reliable and trusted vendor? (For example, purchasing an IP-based camera from an unfamiliar online retailer in China may raise concerns about its reliability and potential security risks.)
- **How confident are you in the source of your hardware?** If you're confident, what specific factors or evidence support that confidence?
- **Is your hardware from a brand or manufacturer that is restricted by the U.S. Government due to security concerns, potential foreign surveillance, or cyber threats?**
- **Is your hardware adequately protected against theft, damage, and environmental hazards, such as moisture or electrical surges, while stored in its designated location?**

- **What measures are in place to safeguard your hardware during transit or movement?**
- **Does your hardware include a backup power source?** This is particularly important to prevent sudden shutdowns in the event of a power failure.
- **Is your hardware running the latest firmware?** Make sure to download firmware updates only from trusted sources, such as the manufacturer's website or the device's official configuration tool.
- **Is there a BIOS password set on your device?** This prevents unauthorized access by requiring the correct password to enter the system.
- **Have you disabled unnecessary wireless protocols?** For example, turning off Bluetooth on your laptop when not in use can improve both security and battery life.

These considerations help ensure that your hardware devices are secure, resilient, and protected from potential vulnerabilities or attacks.

Insurance

Cybersecurity insurance is often overlooked, particularly by small businesses and individuals, yet it can be an effective way to mitigate certain cyber risks. Depending on your specific situation, it may be worth considering a policy that protects against potential threats. For small business owners, who may be especially concerned about the financial impact of a breach, strong security measures are essential. However, since no security system can be completely foolproof, investing in cybersecurity insurance to cover unexpected, catastrophic events could be a wise choice. In recent years, such policies have become more accessible to consumers and small organizations, expanding beyond just large corporations.

Learning

Proper education plays a key role in reducing the risk of cybersecurity threats to individuals in your household (or any other group). Here are some important points to discuss and consider:

- **Do all family members understand their rights and responsibilities** when it comes to using technology at home, connecting devices to the home network, and allowing guests to connect to that network?
- **Have you educated your family members about common cybersecurity risks**, such as phishing emails? Are you confident that they can recognize these threats?
- **Are all family members familiar with cybersecurity best practices**, such as avoiding clicking on suspicious links in emails?
- **Have you made sure everyone understands the importance of creating strong, secure passwords** and how to protect them for their devices and online accounts?
- **Are family members who use social media aware of the risks associated with oversharing?** Have you discussed what information is safe to share online and what should be kept private?

- **Is it clear to everyone that careful consideration is important before taking action online?** Encourage a mindset of thinking before clicking, opening, or sharing anything.

Ensuring that all members of your household are well-informed can go a long way in protecting against cybersecurity threats.

Privacy

Technology poses numerous threats to personal privacy in today's world. Surveillance cameras can track your every movement, while tech companies monitor your online activities through sophisticated tracking methods. Furthermore, mobile devices constantly record your location. While it's true that technology has made it harder to maintain privacy compared to a few years ago, it's important to note that privacy is not completely lost. There are still many effective strategies and tools available to help safeguard your privacy in our increasingly connected world.

Consider the consequences before you decide to share

In today's data-driven society, people often share more personal information than necessary, particularly when prompted by institutions like medical facilities. A common example occurs during doctor's visits in the United States, where patients are typically handed forms to fill out. These forms may ask for extensive personal details—some necessary for medical evaluation and treatment, but others potentially irrelevant or unnecessary.

For example, many medical forms still request a patient's Social Security number. This practice dates back to a time when insurance companies commonly used Social Security numbers as identification, but this approach is now outdated and has been largely phased out due to security risks. While some medical facilities might still ask for Social Security numbers for purposes like credit reporting, this is increasingly seen as a potentially hazardous practice. In many cases, patients can opt to leave this field blank, reducing the risk of exposing sensitive information.

It's important to recognize that the assumption that those collecting your data will handle it responsibly is not always reliable. The more entities that have access to your personal information—and the more detailed that information is—the higher the risk of a privacy breach. These breaches can occur for various reasons, such as cyberattacks, mishandling of data, or even accidental exposure. The consequences can be severe, including identity theft, financial loss, and other significant impacts.

To protect privacy, individuals must be cautious about the information they share, whether with medical providers, government agencies, corporations, or even other individuals. Before disclosing personal details, it's wise to critically evaluate whether the information is truly necessary for the situation. For example, if a Social Security number isn't required for a specific form or transaction, leaving that field blank can be a smart choice.

The principle of minimizing data exposure applies beyond healthcare settings and extends to all aspects of life. For instance, when using online services, signing up for newsletters, or creating accounts, it's important to assess whether the data requested is truly needed. Often, companies collect more information than necessary to provide their services, creating additional risks if that data is compromised.

Reducing the amount of personal information shared and stored across multiple locations can significantly lower the risk of privacy breaches. This proactive approach helps protect individuals from potential misuse of their data and fosters a more secure digital environment. As data breaches become more frequent and their consequences more damaging, taking control of one's personal information is not just advisable but essential for safeguarding privacy and security.

Consider your words before sharing them online

It's crucial to carefully consider the potential consequences before posting anything on social media. Sharing personal details can lead to a variety of undesirable outcomes, including compromising your privacy and security. For instance, information about your family, job, or interests might be exploited by thieves to commit identity theft or gain access to your accounts.

One key example is the use of your mother's maiden name as a security question answer. Whether it's intentional or due to a service provider's oversight, this information can be easily discovered by thieves. To minimize this risk, avoid listing your mother as "Mother" on Facebook or connecting with several relatives who share the same last name as your mother's maiden name. Thieves can easily browse your Facebook friends list and identify the most common last name, which could potentially be your security question answer.

Additionally, sharing information about your children, your routines, or where you're located can expose you to serious risks such as kidnapping, burglary, or other dangerous situations. It's essential to be cautious when disclosing such details, as it can provide opportunistic criminals with the information they need to target you or your family.

Another area where caution is critical is in sharing medical information. Posting about medical visits, treatments, or even sharing location data from medical institutions can inadvertently reveal sensitive details about your health. For instance, if you share a photo or location at a specific clinic, it might suggest that you're receiving treatment for a particular condition, potentially violating your privacy.

Moreover, sharing personal activities or images can sometimes unintentionally disclose private details about your lifestyle. Photos or posts that hint at alcohol consumption, drug use, gun ownership, or affiliations with controversial organizations could expose you to unintended scrutiny or risks. Even innocently sharing where you are at a given time can jeopardize the confidentiality of your activities or personal life.

The issue of oversharing goes beyond social media. With the rise of digital platforms, many people unknowingly share too much personal information through emails, text messages, or file attachments. This kind of accidental oversharing can lead to privacy breaches, as it may include sensitive data, the wrong files, or even incorrect details that can be used against you.

In today's connected world, it's more important than ever to be mindful of what you share and to think critically about the potential impact on your privacy and safety. Taking steps to limit oversharing, both on social media and across digital platforms, can help protect you from various risks, including identity theft, unwanted attention, or worse.

Tips for maintaining your privacy

In addition to being mindful of what you share online, there are several practical steps you can take to minimize the risks of oversharing and protect your privacy:

- **Use privacy settings on your social media platforms**: It's important to configure your social media privacy settings to restrict access to your posts. Ensure that your personal information is visible only to those you trust and that public posts are intentionally shared. However, privacy settings shouldn't be your sole line of defense. Many platforms have security vulnerabilities, so don't rely entirely on them to protect your data.
- **Be cautious about storing sensitive information in the cloud**: Cloud storage can be convenient, but unless proper encryption is used, it's risky. Don't solely rely on the encryption offered by cloud providers. Encrypt your data before uploading it, even if the provider offers encryption. There are apps that can automate this process for major cloud services, ensuring your data remains secure even if the provider's systems are compromised.
- **Avoid storing sensitive information in cloud applications meant for sharing**: Refrain from using cloud-based services like Google Docs or collaborative platforms to store highly sensitive data, such as passwords, personal identification documents, or confidential medical records. While these platforms are useful for collaboration, they aren't designed with maximum security in mind.
- **Use browser privacy settings or consider Tor for enhanced anonymity**: To protect your browsing privacy, use your browser's Private or Incognito mode, though this offers only basic privacy. For stronger privacy, consider using the Tor Browser, which routes your traffic through a network of relays to anonymize your activity. Tor includes strong privacy settings and a range of privacy-enhancing tools by default.
- **Be mindful of tracking while browsing**: When you search for specific information, especially health-related topics, your browser activity can be tracked and used by third parties for advertising or data collection. You may notice targeted ads based on your recent searches, which is a sign that your browsing data is being exploited. To minimize this, consider using privacy-focused browsers or tools like Tor that reduce tracking.

- **Protect your phone number**: Your personal cellphone number is a key piece of sensitive information. To protect it, consider using a forwarding number from a service like Google Voice. This keeps your actual phone number private, helping to reduce risks like SIM swapping and unwanted spam.
- **Store highly sensitive content offline**: For maximum security, it's advisable to store sensitive documents, photos, and other files offline. You can keep these items in a fireproof safe, a bank safety deposit box, or on a computer that isn't connected to the internet. This reduces the likelihood of cybercriminals accessing your information through online breaches.
- **Encrypt your private information**: Whether it's documents, images, or videos, encryption adds an extra layer of security to your data. If you're handling sensitive information, always encrypt it before storing or transmitting it. This helps protect your data from unauthorized access, even if your storage system is breached.
- **Use end-to-end encryption for online communication**: Regular SMS text messages are not secure and can be intercepted. When sharing sensitive information in writing, use messaging apps that offer end-to-end encryption. This ensures that only the sender and recipient can read the messages, as they are encrypted on the sender's device and decrypted on the recipient's. Popular apps like WhatsApp provide this level of encryption, making it much harder for hackers to access your messages.
- **Practice proper cyber hygiene**: Finally, maintaining good cyber hygiene is essential for safeguarding your privacy and security. This includes using strong, unique passwords, enabling two-factor authentication, keeping software updated, and being cautious of phishing attempts. Regularly reviewing your privacy settings across all platforms and being selective about what you share online can significantly reduce your exposure to privacy risks.

By following these steps, you can take greater control over your personal information and reduce the likelihood of privacy breaches in an increasingly connected world.

Ensuring Secure Online Banking

In today's digital age, many consumers feel it's impractical to avoid internet banking, despite the security risks involved. While phone and in-person banking also present their own dangers, online banking remains essential for most people. Having used internet banking since its adoption by major financial institutions in the mid-1990s, I'm familiar with the associated risks, but there are steps you can take to safely enjoy the benefits of online banking.

Here are some recommendations to help enhance your online banking security:

1. Create a Strong, Unique Password

Make sure your online banking password is robust and difficult to guess, yet memorable. Avoid storing it in an electronic database or password manager, as they can be vulnerable to hacking. If necessary, you can store a physical copy in a safe deposit box for added security, though this is generally not required.

2. Use a Unique PIN for ATM and Phone Authentication

Choose a random PIN for your ATM card and phone-based identification, one that's completely unrelated to anything personal (e.g., birthdays, phone numbers). Never reuse a PIN that you've used for other purposes, and avoid using the same PIN for multiple accounts. It's important to keep your PIN private—never write it down or store it electronically, and don't share it with anyone, even bank employees.

3. Request an ATM-Only Card

Consider requesting an ATM card that is strictly for withdrawing money and cannot be used as a debit card for purchases. This reduces the chances of someone using your card to make unauthorized purchases. Since these cards lack purchasing capabilities, they're less useful to thieves, as they require the correct PIN to access funds.

4. Understand Fraud Protection

If your debit card is used fraudulently, you may be able to recover your losses. In the case of credit card fraud, however, you typically won't be held liable for fraudulent transactions unless a thorough investigation proves otherwise. Always notify your bank promptly if you suspect fraudulent activity.

5. Access Online Banking from Trusted Devices

Only log in to your online banking account from devices that you trust and have up-to-date security software installed. Keeping your devices secure with the latest antivirus programs and operating system updates is essential.

6. Use Secure Networks

When accessing online banking, always use secure, trusted networks. Public Wi-Fi, especially in places like cafes or airports, can be risky. Whenever possible, use your cellular data connection rather than public networks. Avoid logging into online banking from locations where providers may be targeting devices with malware.

7. Access Banking via Official Apps or Browsers

Always log in to online banking through the official app or the website's official URL. Be sure to download the bank's app from trusted app stores (Apple App Store, Google Play). Avoid using third-party apps or websites to access your bank account.

8. Set Up Alerts

Sign up for text or email alerts from your bank. Notifications can keep you informed of important account activities such as new payee additions, withdrawals, and suspicious logins. Timely alerts can help you quickly identify potential fraud.

9. Enable Multi-Factor Authentication (MFA)

If your bank offers multi-factor authentication (MFA), enable it. This adds an extra layer of security, requiring you to verify your identity with something you know (password) and something you have (e.g., a one-time password sent to your phone). Be sure to protect your phone, as it can act as a second factor for authentication. If your phone is stolen, it may temporarily allow access to your account, so consider enabling remote wiping for added security.

10. Do Not Store Passwords in Your Browser

Avoid saving your online banking password in your web browser. Many browsers offer to store passwords, but this can make your account vulnerable if someone gains access to your device. It's safer to manually enter your password each time you log in.

11. Always Enter Bank URL Manually

When accessing your bank's website, always type the URL directly into your browser rather than clicking on links in emails or other sites. Phishing scams often use fake links to redirect you to fraudulent websites designed to steal your login credentials.

12. Use a Separate Computer or Browser for Banking

If possible, use a dedicated device or a separate web browser for your online banking. If you must use the same device for banking and other activities, such as shopping or social media, regularly update your browser and ensure it's properly configured for maximum security.

13. Set Up Browser to Remember Incorrect Passwords

Consider setting your browser to remember incorrect passwords for banking websites. This can make it more difficult for someone to log in if they gain access to your device, as the browser will remember the incorrect credentials, alerting you to unauthorized access attempts.

14. Secure Your Devices

Ensure that your online banking devices are physically secure. For example, never leave your phone or laptop unattended in public places. Set strong passwords for all your devices, and enable features like remote wipes or tracking in case your devices are lost or stolen.

15. Monitor Your Accounts for Suspicious Activity

Regularly check your bank statements and account activity for any signs of unauthorized transactions. The earlier you spot suspicious activity, the quicker you can report it and minimize any potential damage.

By following these best practices, you can significantly reduce the risks associated with online banking while enjoying the convenience it offers. Security requires ongoing vigilance, but with the right precautions in place, you can protect your financial information from fraudsters and hackers.

Using Smart Devices with Safety in Mind

Smart devices and the Internet of Things (IoT) introduce several cybersecurity challenges. Here are some key strategies to improve your security when using these devices:

- **Ensure Device Fail-Safes:** Make sure your IoT devices have built-in safeguards in case of failure. For instance, smart locks should not prevent you from evacuating during an emergency, such as a fire, nor should they allow intruders access in the event of a power or network outage.
- **Segregate Networks:** If possible, place your IoT devices on a separate network from your computers. This isolation helps protect sensitive data and should be reinforced with a robust firewall for the IoT network.
- **Keep Devices Updated:** Regularly update your IoT devices. Cybercriminals often exploit outdated firmware to gain control and launch attacks. Enabling automatic updates, if available, is a simple yet effective way to ensure devices stay secure.
- **Track Connected Devices:** Maintain an up-to-date inventory of all devices connected to your network. It's also essential to have a record of all devices that are authorized to connect, even if they aren't currently active.

- **Disconnect When Not in Use:** Whenever possible, turn off IoT devices when they're not in use. Disconnecting them makes it much harder for hackers to access the device remotely.
- **Use Strong Passwords:** Always change the default passwords on your IoT devices. Secure each device with a unique password to prevent unauthorized access.
- **Review Device Settings:** Check the security settings on your devices. Many come with factory settings that may not be optimal for safeguarding against threats.
- **Secure Your Smartphone:** Since your smartphone likely controls or interacts with IoT devices, ensure it is both physically secure and protected with strong passwords or biometric authentication.
- **Disable Unnecessary Features:** Turn off features you don't need. This reduces the potential attack surface, making it harder for hackers to exploit vulnerabilities or access your devices.
- **Beware of UPnP Vulnerabilities:** While Universal Plug and Play (UPnP) simplifies device configuration, it also introduces risks. Flaws in UPnP implementations can allow hackers to easily discover and compromise devices. Additionally, UPnP can bypass firewall protections, enabling malware to exploit your router.

By taking these steps, you can significantly reduce the security risks associated with smart devices and IoT technology.

Frequently Asked Questions

- What steps do you take to protect against potential risks?
- How do you evaluate your current security measures?
- What are the best practices for safeguarding your privacy?
- How do you guarantee the safety of your online banking activities?
- How do you define and manage endpoints?

CHAPTER FIVE
INTRODUCTION TO ENCRYPTION

Overview

Chapter five delves into the crucial topic of encryption within the field of cybersecurity. In this section, you will explore the concept of encryption and its vital role in protecting data and securing communications in the digital world.

About Encryption

In today's rapidly evolving digital landscape, where information moves swiftly across extensive networks, protecting sensitive data is more important than ever. Cybersecurity has become a top priority for individuals, businesses, and governments. One of the most powerful and essential tools in data security is encryption, which offers a range of methods to effectively protect valuable information from unauthorized access.

Encryption plays a crucial role in protecting sensitive data in our increasingly connected world. It ensures that only authorized individuals can access encoded information, transforming readable data (plaintext) into an unreadable format (ciphertext) using cryptographic algorithms. Only those with the correct decryption key can revert the ciphertext to its original state, providing a high level of security to prevent unauthorized access or interception.

Encryption has a long history, with early civilizations using simple methods to hide messages. Over time, encryption techniques have evolved, and the development of modern cryptography in the

20th century brought about highly sophisticated methods of data protection. Today, encryption is a cornerstone of cybersecurity, securing communication channels and protecting stored data.

One of the key functions of encryption is ensuring the privacy and integrity of sensitive information. By encrypting data before transmission or storage, businesses can safeguard it from unauthorized access or tampering. This is especially crucial in sectors like banking, healthcare, and government, where the consequences of data loss or compromise can be severe. Encryption also plays a critical role in authentication and identity verification, with digital signatures verifying the authenticity and integrity of electronic documents and communications. This helps combat fraud and ensures that transactions and messages are legitimate.

Additionally, encryption helps protect the integrity of data by preventing unauthorized alterations, particularly in critical infrastructure systems and electronic voting systems. It also enables secure communication over public networks like the internet. Protocols such as SSL/TLS (Secure Sockets Layer/Transport Layer Security) ensure that sensitive data remains private during transmission, a key concern for activities like online banking, e-commerce, and remote work.

In addition to its security benefits, encryption is essential for compliance with industry regulations. Many sectors are required to adhere to stringent data protection laws, such as HIPAA (Health Insurance Portability and Accountability Act) in healthcare and GDPR (General Data Protection Regulation) in the European Union. Encryption helps organizations meet these regulatory requirements by ensuring that sensitive data is protected and privacy rights are upheld.

While encryption is indispensable in cybersecurity, it is not without challenges and limitations. One major issue is balancing security with usability. Although encryption offers robust protection, it can add complexity that may be inconvenient for end-users. Managing encryption keys securely is one such challenge; losing access to these keys can result in the permanent loss of encrypted data. Additionally, encryption can sometimes impact system performance, slowing down network speeds or system operations, which can be frustrating for users and organizations.

Despite these challenges, it is important to note that encryption is not a complete solution to all cybersecurity threats. While it significantly reduces the risk of unauthorized access, it cannot prevent all types of attacks. Sophisticated adversaries can bypass encryption using methods such as social engineering, where individuals are manipulated into revealing sensitive information or granting access to secure systems. Malware can also infiltrate a system and extract data before encryption occurs, making the encryption itself ineffective.

Moreover, the rise of emerging technologies, particularly quantum computing, presents potential risks to the long-term security of current encryption methods. Quantum computers, which are still in development, could eventually break many of the encryption algorithms that are widely used today. This potential vulnerability emphasizes the need for continued research and the development of new encryption techniques that are resistant to quantum-based attacks.

Despite these evolving challenges, encryption remains a vital component of cybersecurity. As technology advances, so too does encryption, with researchers and cybersecurity professionals working continuously to develop stronger, more resilient cryptographic techniques. Staying informed about the latest advancements in encryption technology and understanding its limitations is essential for organizations looking to protect their data and maintain the trust of their stakeholders.

In today's digital environment, where cyberattacks and data breaches are increasingly common, implementing effective encryption strategies is not just an advantage—it is a necessity. By adopting the latest encryption standards and being proactive about addressing potential vulnerabilities, organizations can safeguard sensitive data and continue to ensure the security and privacy of their users.

Encryption Basics

In today's interconnected digital landscape, where data is vital for both individuals and organizations, safeguarding sensitive information from unauthorized access is essential. Encryption is a cornerstone of cybersecurity, defending against malicious actors while ensuring the confidentiality, integrity, and authenticity of data. This guide provides a thorough exploration of encryption, covering its fundamental principles, techniques, and practical applications in securing digital assets.

What exactly is encryption?

The core concept of encryption involves converting readable data (known as plaintext) into an unreadable format called ciphertext using a cryptographic algorithm and key. This transformation ensures that the original data remains private and inaccessible to unauthorized parties, as it can only be decoded with the correct decryption key. Encryption is an effective technique for protecting a wide range of sensitive information, including personal communications, financial transactions, government data, and intellectual property.

Exploring the Fundamentals of Encryption

Encryption relies on two key components: **algorithms** and **keys**.

1. **Algorithms**: Encryption algorithms are mathematical procedures designed to transform data into a form that is unreadable to anyone without proper authorization. These algorithms can vary in complexity. In **symmetric encryption**, the same key is used for both encryption and decryption, meaning both the sender and recipient must share the same key. In **asymmetric encryption**, two different keys are used: one for encryption (the public key) and another for decryption (the private key).

2. **Keys**: Encryption keys are strings of data that control the encryption and decryption processes. In symmetric encryption, a single key is shared between the sender and recipient to both encrypt and decrypt the information. In asymmetric encryption, there are two keys: a **public key**, which is widely distributed and used to encrypt data, and a **private key**, which is kept secret and used to decrypt it. The effectiveness of encryption largely depends on the strength of the keys—specifically their length and randomness. Strong, unpredictable keys enhance security, making it more difficult for unauthorized parties to decrypt the data.

Various Encryption Methods

Encryption techniques are generally divided into two main categories: **symmetric encryption** and **asymmetric encryption**.

1. **Symmetric Encryption**: Also known as secret-key encryption, symmetric encryption uses the same key for both the encryption and decryption processes. Its simplicity makes it highly efficient, especially for encrypting large amounts of data. However, the key must be securely shared between the sender and recipient. Common symmetric encryption algorithms include **Advanced Encryption Standard (AES)**, **Data Encryption Standard (DES)**, and **Triple DES**.
2. **Asymmetric Encryption**: Also called public-key encryption, asymmetric encryption relies on two distinct keys: a **public key**, which is shared openly and used for encryption, and a **private key**, which is kept secret and used for decryption. This approach allows secure communication without the need for exchanging secret keys beforehand. Popular asymmetric encryption algorithms include **RSA (Rivest-Shamir-Adleman)** and **Elliptic Curve Cryptography (ECC)**.

Uses of Encryption

Encryption plays a critical role in various aspects of cybersecurity and beyond. Here are some of the key areas where encryption is essential:

- **Communication Security**: Encryption is vital for protecting communication channels, ensuring that sensitive data sent over networks remains private and inaccessible to unauthorized parties. This is particularly important for emails, instant messages, and voice calls, where data could easily be intercepted without encryption. Protocols like **HTTPS (Hypertext Transfer Protocol Secure)** use encryption to safeguard data transmitted between web browsers and servers. By encrypting this data, HTTPS prevents eavesdropping and tampering, making it a standard for securing websites, especially those handling sensitive transactions or personal information.
- **Data Storage**: Encryption is equally important for protecting data stored on various devices, such as computers, smartphones, and servers. Encrypting data at rest ensures

that information remains secure even if a device is lost or stolen. Disk encryption solutions that encrypt entire volumes make data unreadable without the proper decryption key. This added layer of security ensures that sensitive data, such as financial or healthcare records, remains protected, even if an attacker gains physical access to the storage device.
- **Authentication**: Encryption plays a foundational role in authentication processes, such as in **digital signatures** and **certificate-based authentication**. Digital signatures use encryption to verify the authenticity of digital documents and communications, ensuring that they are unaltered and originate from a legitimate source. This is vital for maintaining the integrity of electronic communications and verifying the identity of the sender. **Certificate-based authentication** further strengthens security by using encryption to establish trust between parties, such as in secure email communications or when accessing encrypted websites.
- **Ensuring Secure Transactions**: In online transactions, encryption is crucial for protecting sensitive information, such as payment card details, personal data, and transaction records. Whether it's an e-commerce purchase, online banking, or an electronic funds transfer, encryption ensures that transaction data remains confidential and protected from interception or fraud. By encrypting data before transmission, encryption helps maintain the integrity of these transactions, fostering trust and security in online financial systems.
- **VPN (Virtual Private Network)**: **VPNs** rely heavily on encryption to create secure, encrypted tunnels between users and remote servers. This is particularly important when accessing the internet from potentially insecure networks, like public Wi-Fi hotspots. Encryption within a VPN protects data traffic from unauthorized access and interception, ensuring privacy and anonymity. By encrypting all transmitted data, VPNs help users protect their online activities from hackers, ISPs, and other third parties, making them a popular choice for individuals and organizations looking to secure sensitive communications and online privacy.

In summary, encryption is essential in protecting data during transmission, storage, authentication, and transactions. It is a key tool for ensuring the security and privacy of information in today's digital world.

Challenges and Considerations

While encryption is a robust tool for protecting sensitive information, it also presents several challenges and considerations that organizations must address:

1. **Key Management**: The security of encrypted data is directly tied to how encryption keys are created, distributed, and stored. Poor key management practices can undermine encryption, making it vulnerable to attacks. Effective key management is essential to

ensure that encryption keys remain secure throughout their lifecycle, and failure to do so can lead to unauthorized access to encrypted data.
2. **Performance Overhead**: The encryption and decryption processes introduce computational overhead, which can impact system performance, especially in resource-limited environments like mobile devices or embedded systems. Finding a balance between strong encryption and maintaining acceptable performance levels is critical to avoid significant slowdowns or bottlenecks.
3. **Cryptographic Vulnerabilities**: Cryptographic algorithms and their implementations are not immune to flaws. Vulnerabilities in the encryption methods themselves, or errors in their implementation, can be exploited by attackers to bypass encryption and retrieve plaintext data. To mitigate this risk, regular assessments, audits, and updates to cryptographic techniques are necessary to address potential weaknesses and ensure continued security.
4. **Compliance with Regulations**: Organizations handling sensitive data, such as those in healthcare, banking, or government sectors, must adhere to encryption regulations. Laws like the **General Data Protection Regulation (GDPR)** and **Health Insurance Portability and Accountability Act (HIPAA)** require businesses to use encryption to protect personal and health-related data. Ensuring compliance with these regulations is not only a legal requirement but also a critical aspect of maintaining customer trust and data privacy.
5. **Emerging Technologies**: The rise of **quantum computing** poses a potential threat to conventional encryption algorithms, as these powerful machines could potentially break many of the cryptographic schemes in use today. Research into **quantum-resistant algorithms** and **post-quantum cryptography** is ongoing, as the cybersecurity community works to develop encryption methods that can withstand the computational capabilities of quantum computers in the future.

In summary, while encryption remains a fundamental security measure, addressing these challenges—such as key management, performance trade-offs, cryptographic vulnerabilities, regulatory compliance, and the impact of emerging technologies—is essential for maintaining robust data protection in an evolving digital landscape.

An Overview of Encryption Algorithms

Encryption is the process of encoding information in such a way that only authorized parties can access it. Using cryptographic algorithms and keys, plaintext data is transformed into ciphertext, making it unreadable to unauthorized individuals who might intercept it. Decryption is the reverse process, where ciphertext is converted back into its original, readable form, accessible only to those with the correct decryption key.

Various Encryption Algorithms

Encryption algorithms are generally classified into two main categories: **symmetric encryption** and **asymmetric encryption**.

1. Symmetric Encryption:

Symmetric encryption, also known as secret-key encryption, uses the same key for both the encryption and decryption processes. It is essential to protect the shared key, as both the sender and the recipient rely on it to secure the data. Some widely used symmetric encryption algorithms include:

- **Advanced Encryption Standard (AES)**: AES is one of the most commonly used symmetric encryption algorithms, offering strong security and high efficiency. It is employed in various applications, including securing data during transmission and protecting stored information.
- **Data Encryption Standard (DES)**: DES was one of the earliest encryption standards but has largely been replaced by AES due to its vulnerability to brute-force attacks. Despite its age, it laid the groundwork for modern encryption techniques.
- **Triple DES (3DES)**: Triple DES applies the DES algorithm three times to each data block, offering enhanced security compared to standard DES. However, it is slower than AES and is gradually being phased out in favor of more secure and efficient methods.

2. Asymmetric Encryption:

Asymmetric encryption, also known as public-key encryption, uses a pair of keys: a **public key** for encryption and a **private key** for decryption. The public key is shared openly, while the private key is kept secret. Although asymmetric encryption provides stronger security, it tends to be more computationally intensive. Common asymmetric encryption algorithms include:

- **Rivest-Shamir-Adleman (RSA)**: RSA is one of the oldest and most widely used asymmetric encryption algorithms. Its security is based on the difficulty of factoring large prime numbers, making it highly secure when large key sizes are used.
- **Elliptic Curve Cryptography (ECC)**: ECC has gained popularity due to its efficiency and the ability to provide strong security with smaller key sizes compared to RSA. This makes ECC ideal for use in resource-constrained environments, such as mobile devices and IoT (Internet of Things) devices, where computational power and storage are limited.

In summary, **symmetric encryption** is faster and more efficient but requires secure key management, while **asymmetric encryption** offers stronger security for key exchange and data protection, though at the cost of higher computational resources. Each has its strengths and applications depending on the specific use case.

Advantages and Disadvantages

Each encryption algorithm has its own advantages and limitations, influencing its suitability for various use cases:

- **Symmetric Encryption**: Symmetric encryption techniques are fast and efficient, making them well-suited for encrypting large volumes of data. However, the challenge lies in securely distributing the secret key, which is crucial for ensuring safe communication between parties.
- **Asymmetric Encryption**: Asymmetric encryption addresses the key distribution challenge by using a pair of public and private keys. This method enhances security and allows for secure communication without the need for a pre-shared key. On the downside, asymmetric encryption requires more computational power and may not be the best choice for encrypting large datasets.

Applications in Cybersecurity

Encryption algorithms play a crucial role in various cybersecurity applications, safeguarding the confidentiality, integrity, and authenticity of data. Here's how they are applied across different areas:

1. **Communication Security**: Encryption protects the privacy and integrity of data transmitted between parties. It is employed in secure communication protocols such as SSL/TLS to safeguard sensitive information, including financial transactions, personal messages, and login credentials, ensuring secure connections over the internet.
2. **Data Storage**: Encryption is essential for securing data stored on devices like computers, smartphones, and servers. Full disk encryption protects the entire storage drive, ensuring data is secure even if the device is lost or stolen. Additionally, file-level encryption allows users to encrypt individual files or folders, offering enhanced security for sensitive data.
3. **Digital Signatures**: Asymmetric encryption is key to digital signatures, which verify the authenticity and integrity of digital documents and messages. In this process, the sender's private key is used to encrypt a hash of the message. The recipient can then decrypt the hash using the sender's public key, confirming the message's integrity and the sender's identity.
4. **Password Protection**: Encryption methods are used to securely store and transmit passwords and other sensitive authentication data. Hashing passwords with one-way hash algorithms ensures that the original password cannot be easily retrieved, providing strong protection against unauthorized access.

Public Key Infrastructure (PKI)

Public Key Infrastructure (PKI) is essential for maintaining cybersecurity, as it provides the foundation for secure communication and authentication in digital environments. Let's explore the key aspects of PKI, including its components, functions, and its vital role in protecting sensitive information in the digital world.

At its core, PKI is a comprehensive system that integrates rules, processes, technologies, and personnel for managing digital certificates and public-key encryption. Its primary objective is to facilitate secure communication over unsecured networks, such as the internet. PKI enables entities to authenticate identities, encrypt data, and ensure the integrity of information, making it an indispensable tool for safeguarding sensitive digital assets.

By using asymmetric encryption, PKI allows users to exchange confidential information securely, ensuring that both the sender and recipient can trust the authenticity of the communication. In doing so, PKI supports critical activities like secure email exchanges, online banking, and access to protected systems, helping to prevent fraud, data breaches, and unauthorized access.

PKI Components

The components of Public Key Infrastructure (PKI) work together to create a secure and trusted framework for digital communication. These components include:

- **Certificate Authority (CA)**: The Certificate Authority is a trusted entity responsible for issuing digital certificates that validate the identity of individuals, organizations, or systems within a digital ecosystem. The CA's main role is to associate a public key with the identity of its holder, thus enabling secure communication. By issuing digital certificates, the CA ensures that the public key truly belongs to the identified party, preventing issues like impersonation or man-in-the-middle attacks. The trustworthiness of the CA is essential, as the entire PKI system relies on the integrity of the certificates it issues.
- **Registration Authority (RA)**: The Registration Authority acts as an intermediary between the user or entity and the Certificate Authority. Its primary responsibility is to authenticate the identities of those applying for digital certificates. Before a certificate request is sent to the CA, the RA verifies the identity of the applicant, ensuring they are who they claim to be. This step is crucial for maintaining the integrity of the PKI system, as it helps prevent unauthorized or fraudulent certificate requests. The RA is integral to the system, ensuring only legitimate entities receive certificates from the CA.
- **Public Key Cryptography**: Central to PKI is asymmetric encryption, which uses a pair of public and private keys. Public key cryptography enables secure communication by allowing anyone to encrypt data using the recipient's public key, while only the holder of the corresponding private key can decrypt it. This ensures that even if the public key is

widely distributed, only the intended recipient can access the encrypted data. The use of asymmetric cryptography within PKI ensures secure data exchange and identity verification without requiring a shared secret key.
- **Digital Certificates**: Digital certificates are fundamental to PKI, acting as electronic documents that confirm the identity of a certificate holder and include their public key. These certificates are issued and digitally signed by the Certificate Authority, ensuring their authenticity. The digital signature guarantees that the public key belongs to the entity it is supposed to represent. Digital certificates enable secure communication, authenticate identities, and establish trust for transactions. They are widely used in various applications, including secure email, online banking, and encrypted web browsing.
- **Revoking Certificates**: Certificate revocation is a critical aspect of PKI, ensuring that certificates can be invalidated if they are compromised, expired, or no longer trustworthy. Revocation mechanisms, such as Certificate Revocation Lists (CRLs) and the Online Certificate Status Protocol (OCSP), allow certificates to be promptly identified as invalid. CRLs are periodically updated lists containing revoked certificate serial numbers, while OCSP provides real-time certificate status verification. These mechanisms ensure that compromised certificates are not used for secure communications.

In summary, the components of PKI—Certificate Authority, Registration Authority, public key cryptography, digital certificates, and certificate revocation systems—work in tandem to create a secure and trustworthy environment for digital interactions. Together, they protect sensitive information, enable secure transactions, and help build confidence in the digital world. PKI is indispensable for safeguarding data, verifying identities, and maintaining the integrity of secure communications.

PKI functions

Here's how PKI (Public Key Infrastructure) enhances cybersecurity across various aspects:

1. **Verification**: PKI enables secure authentication by allowing parties to verify each other's identities using digital certificates. This ensures that only authorized users can access sensitive information or services, safeguarding security and preventing unauthorized access.
2. **Encryption**: PKI enables secure communication by utilizing public and private key pairs. This process ensures data confidentiality and integrity during transmission, making it virtually impossible for unauthorized parties to intercept or alter the data while in transit.
3. **Digital Signatures**: By using private keys to create digital signatures, PKI ensures the authenticity and integrity of messages, providing strong non-repudiation. The recipient can use the sender's public key to validate the signature, ensuring trust and accountability in the communication process.

4. **Secure Transactions**: PKI plays a vital role in securing online transactions, such as e-commerce and online banking. By combining encryption and authentication methods, PKI helps prevent fraud and unauthorized access, making digital transactions safer for all parties involved.
5. **Access Control Security**: PKI enables organizations to implement robust access control mechanisms by verifying the identity of users and devices before granting access to critical data or systems. This ensures that only authorized individuals or devices can enter the system, protecting against internal threats and unauthorized access.

In summary, PKI provides essential security features like identity verification, encryption, digital signatures, secure transactions, and access control, which are crucial for maintaining a safe and trusted digital environment.

The Significance of PKI in Cybersecurity

Here's how PKI (Public Key Infrastructure) supports cybersecurity and digital trust in various contexts:

1. **Building Confidence**: PKI fosters trust in digital transactions by verifying the identities of all parties involved and ensuring data integrity and authenticity. This foundational trust is essential for secure online interactions and helps maintain confidence in digital communication and transactions.
2. **Maintaining Confidentiality**: Through public key cryptography, PKI protects sensitive data during transmission over insecure networks. By encrypting communications, PKI ensures that confidential information remains private, safeguarding it from unauthorized access and malicious actors.
3. **Ensuring Regulatory Compliance**: PKI plays a key role in meeting regulatory requirements, especially in sectors like healthcare, banking, and government, where strict data privacy and security standards are mandatory. By implementing PKI, organizations can comply with regulations, ensuring data protection and avoiding potential legal and financial penalties.
4. **Addressing Potential Risks**: PKI helps mitigate a wide range of cybersecurity risks, such as data breaches, identity theft, and man-in-the-middle attacks. With its strong authentication and encryption capabilities, PKI enhances organizational security and reduces vulnerabilities to cyber threats.
5. **Embracing Digital Transformation**: In today's digital era, PKI is crucial for enabling secure communication and transactions across multiple platforms and devices. It supports digital transformation by ensuring the security of technologies like IoT, cloud computing, and mobile applications, providing a secure foundation for the digital ecosystem.

In summary, PKI is integral to building trust, maintaining confidentiality, ensuring compliance, reducing risks, and supporting digital transformation efforts in an increasingly interconnected world.

Challenges and Considerations

While PKI implementation offers numerous benefits, it also presents several challenges and considerations that organizations must address to ensure successful deployment. Here are some key challenges to keep in mind:

1. **Complexity of Management**: Implementing and managing a PKI infrastructure can be complex and resource-intensive. It requires dedicated personnel and robust systems to handle tasks like certificate issuance, renewal, and revocation efficiently. Without proper management, PKI systems may become difficult to maintain and prone to errors.
2. **Managing Keys**: Effective key management is crucial for maintaining the security and integrity of PKI systems. Organizations must ensure that private keys are securely stored and protected from unauthorized access or theft. Improper key management can lead to security breaches, making it essential to adopt stringent practices for key storage and handling.
3. **Scalability**: As businesses grow and expand their digital operations, scalability becomes a critical factor. PKI systems must be capable of scaling to meet the increasing demands for certificate issuance, renewal, and overall administration. Without scalability, the PKI infrastructure could become overwhelmed, leading to delays or security gaps.
4. **Interoperability**: Ensuring seamless integration between different PKI components, applications, and systems is essential for smooth operation. Interoperability can be a challenge, especially when different standards (like X.509) are in use across various systems. While standards can improve compatibility, they may require careful configuration and ongoing management to ensure all components work together efficiently.
5. **Compliance Requirements**: Adhering to regulatory requirements such as GDPR, HIPAA, or PCI DSS can complicate PKI implementation. Organizations must ensure their PKI systems meet the relevant legal and regulatory standards for data protection and privacy. Non-compliance can result in penalties or reputational damage, making it essential to align PKI processes with applicable regulations.

In summary, while PKI provides significant security advantages, organizations must carefully address the complexities of management, key handling, scalability, interoperability, and regulatory compliance to ensure the successful implementation and ongoing effectiveness of their PKI infrastructure.

Anticipated Developments in PKI

Several emerging trends are shaping the future of PKI (Public Key Infrastructure) and cybersecurity. These developments are driving innovation and adaptation in how digital identities and data are protected:

1. **Exploring Quantum-Safe Cryptography**: As quantum computing advances, there are growing concerns about the ability of current encryption techniques to withstand quantum attacks. To address this, PKI is expected to evolve toward quantum-safe cryptography, which uses algorithms resistant to quantum computing threats, ensuring the long-term security of encrypted communications and digital certificates.
2. **Streamlining Processes**: Automation and orchestration technologies are increasingly being integrated into PKI management. These tools help streamline processes such as certificate issuance, renewal, and revocation, reducing human error and enhancing operational efficiency. By automating repetitive tasks, organizations can better manage their PKI systems while ensuring consistency and accuracy.
3. **Decentralized Identity**: Decentralized identity systems, powered by technologies like blockchain, are transforming the way digital identities are managed. These systems allow individuals to have more control over their personal information, reducing the reliance on centralized authorities. This shift could significantly impact PKI by enabling more secure, user-controlled identity management and reducing the risks associated with centralized data storage.
4. **Security with Zero Trust**: The Zero Trust security model, which assumes no trust by default and continuously verifies identities and access permissions, is reshaping PKI architectures. This approach requires stronger, more granular authentication mechanisms, and integrates with PKI to enforce strict access control policies, ensuring that only verified and authorized users can access sensitive resources.
5. **Cloud-Based PKI Solutions**: Cloud-based PKI is gaining traction as organizations move more of their infrastructure to the cloud. These solutions offer greater scalability, flexibility, and cost-effectiveness compared to traditional on-premises PKI implementations. As more businesses adopt cloud technologies, the demand for cloud-based PKI solutions is expected to grow, enabling faster certificate management and more efficient security operations.

In summary, these trends—quantum-safe cryptography, automation in PKI management, decentralized identity systems, Zero Trust security, and cloud-based PKI—are paving the way for more secure, efficient, and adaptable PKI solutions in the future. As cybersecurity continues to evolve, these developments will help organizations stay ahead of emerging threats while ensuring the protection of sensitive data and identities.

Encrypting Data at Rest and in Transit

Data at rest refers to data that is stored on physical or digital media—such as hard drives, databases, or cloud storage—rather than actively being transmitted across networks or systems. Protecting data at rest involves implementing encryption techniques that render the data unreadable to unauthorized individuals, even if they gain access to the storage media. Without the proper encryption key, the data remains secure and inaccessible, safeguarding it from potential threats like theft or unauthorized access.

Methods for Securing Data in Storage

1. **Full Disk Encryption (FDE)**: FDE provides robust security by encrypting the entire storage device, protecting all data stored on it. This approach is particularly useful for portable devices like laptops and smartphones, where the risk of physical theft is higher. With FDE, even if a device is lost or stolen, the data remains encrypted and inaccessible without the decryption key.
2. **File-Level Encryption**: Unlike FDE, which encrypts the entire disk, file-level encryption allows for selective encryption of individual files or folders. This gives users more control over which data is encrypted, making it ideal for situations where only certain files contain sensitive information that requires additional protection.
3. **Database Encryption**: Databases often contain valuable and sensitive information, making them prime targets for cyberattacks. Encrypting the data within databases helps secure sensitive records from unauthorized access, adding an extra layer of protection to critical business data and personal information.

Encrypting Data in Transit

Data in transit refers to data being transferred between systems, such as when sending an email or browsing the internet. Encrypting data in transit ensures that the information is protected while it is moving across networks, making it extremely difficult for unauthorized parties to intercept or decipher the data. This encryption helps safeguard sensitive information from potential threats like eavesdropping or man-in-the-middle attacks during transmission.

Methods for Securing Data during Transmission

- **Transport Layer Security (TLS)**: TLS, the successor to SSL, is the most widely used protocol for encrypting data in transit over the internet. It is highly regarded for its ability to secure communication between clients and servers by using a combination of symmetric and asymmetric encryption methods to establish a secure connection.
- **Secure Shell (SSH)**: SSH is a network protocol that ensures secure communication over unsecured networks through encryption. Commonly used for remote login, command

execution, and secure file transfer (via SFTP), SSH provides a reliable and secure method for accessing and managing systems remotely.
- **Virtual Private Networks (VPNs)**: VPNs create a secure, encrypted tunnel between a user's device and a remote server, ensuring that online activities remain private and protected from unauthorized access. VPNs are often used to enhance security when connecting to public Wi-Fi networks, safeguard user privacy, or bypass geo-restrictions by masking the user's IP address.

Challenges and Considerations

Encryption is a powerful tool for protecting data, but it also presents several challenges and considerations that organizations must address to ensure its effectiveness. Here are some key obstacles to keep in mind:

1. **Key Management**: Proper key management is critical to maintaining the security of encrypted data. This involves securely generating, storing, rotating, and revoking encryption keys. Any weakness in key management can undermine the encryption's effectiveness, making it essential to follow best practices to ensure the integrity of both keys and encrypted data.
2. **Performance Impact**: Encryption and decryption processes can introduce overhead, which may impact system performance, particularly in high-throughput environments. Striking the right balance between robust encryption and optimal system performance is important, as poor performance can hinder operational efficiency and user experience.
3. **Compliance and Regulation**: Organizations, especially those in regulated industries, must comply with data protection laws such as GDPR, HIPAA, and PCI DSS. These regulations often require the implementation of specific encryption measures to protect sensitive data. Compliance demands careful planning to ensure that encryption practices meet regulatory standards while aligning with broader organizational goals.
4. **User Experience**: While encryption is essential for security, it should not compromise the usability or accessibility of data for legitimate users. Striking a balance between strong encryption and ease of use is key to ensuring that security measures do not create unnecessary barriers to productivity or frustrate end-users.

In summary, while encryption is a vital tool for data protection, organizations must carefully address key management, performance, regulatory compliance, and user experience to implement effective and efficient encryption strategies.

Using Secure Communication Protocols

Communication protocols are essential for establishing secure channels of communication in digital environments. These protocols ensure that data exchanged between parties remains private, tamper-proof, and authenticated. By using cryptographic methods, they protect information, validate identities, and prevent unauthorized access or interception by malicious actors.

The key objectives of secure communication protocols are:

1. **Privacy**: Ensuring that the information exchanged between parties remains confidential and is not accessible to unauthorized individuals or entities. Privacy protection prevents sensitive data from being exposed during transmission.
2. **Integrity**: Protecting the integrity of data ensures that it remains unaltered during transmission. This guarantees that the data has not been tampered with or modified by unauthorized parties, preserving its authenticity and reliability.
3. **Authentication**: Authentication verifies the identities of the parties involved in the communication. It helps establish trust by ensuring that each party is who they claim to be, preventing impersonation, and mitigating the risk of spoofing attacks.
4. **Non-repudiation**: Non-repudiation provides accountability, ensuring that the sender cannot deny having sent the message and the recipient cannot deny receiving it. This guarantees that both parties can be held responsible for their actions, reinforcing trust and legal assurance in digital communications.

In summary, secure communication protocols leverage cryptographic techniques to achieve privacy, integrity, authentication, and non-repudiation, forming the foundation for safe and reliable digital interactions.

Secure Communication Protocols Types

Communication protocols are essential for securing various applications and environments, employing a wide range of technologies and standards to ensure data privacy, integrity, and authentication. Here are some of the most commonly used protocols in securing digital communications:

1. **Transport Layer Security (TLS) / Secure Sockets Layer (SSL)**: TLS and its predecessor SSL are cryptographic protocols designed to secure network communication. These protocols are widely used in web browsing, email, instant messaging, and other applications requiring secure data transmission. TLS/SSL ensures that data exchanged between clients and servers is encrypted, maintaining both confidentiality and integrity during transit.
2. **Internet Protocol Security (IPsec)**: IPsec is a suite of protocols that secures IP communications by authenticating and encrypting each IP packet in a session. Operating at the network layer of the OSI model, IPsec is commonly used in Virtual Private Networks (VPNs) to create secure, encrypted connections between remote sites or devices, ensuring that data sent across public networks remains protected.
3. **Secure Shell (SSH)**: SSH is a cryptographic network protocol that provides secure remote access to computers or servers over an unsecured network. It offers strong encryption

and authentication capabilities, making it ideal for secure command-line operations, file transfers, and tunneling applications. SSH is widely used for managing systems remotely while ensuring data integrity and confidentiality.
4. **Pretty Good Privacy (PGP) / OpenPGP**: PGP is a data encryption standard that provides robust security for email communication, file encryption, and digital signatures. OpenPGP is an open-source implementation of PGP that offers high levels of privacy and authenticity by using public-key cryptography. PGP and OpenPGP are commonly used to secure sensitive communications and ensure the authenticity of digital documents.
5. **Wireless Security Protocols (WPA2, WPA3)**: WPA2 (Wi-Fi Protected Access 2) and its successor WPA3 are security protocols designed to protect wireless networks. They use encryption techniques, such as Advanced Encryption Standard (AES), to safeguard data transmitted over Wi-Fi networks from eavesdropping and unauthorized access. WPA3 provides enhanced security features compared to WPA2, further improving the protection of wireless communications.

In summary, these communication protocols are critical for securing digital communications, each addressing specific security needs like encryption, authentication, and data integrity. They help ensure that sensitive data remains protected during transmission, whether over the internet, private networks, or wireless connections.

The Importance of Secure Communication Protocols in Cybersecurity

Communication protocols that prioritize security play a vital role in enhancing cybersecurity for both individuals and organizations. These protocols address a wide range of cyber threats and vulnerabilities, ensuring the protection of sensitive data during transmission. Here's an overview of their key roles and importance:

1. Protection of Sensitive Information

Secure communication protocols are crucial in today's digital world, where the confidentiality of sensitive information is paramount. They use strong encryption methods to protect data during transmission, ensuring that it remains secure and inaccessible to unauthorized parties. This level of protection is especially important for safeguarding personal credentials, financial transactions, and proprietary business data. By encrypting data in transit, these protocols help mitigate the risk of data breaches and cyberattacks, ensuring that sensitive information doesn't fall into the wrong hands.

2. Prevention of Man-in-the-Middle (MitM) Attacks

One of the key functions of secure communication protocols is to defend against Man-in-the-Middle (MitM) attacks. In a MitM attack, a malicious actor intercepts communication between two parties, potentially stealing or manipulating sensitive information. To counter this threat, secure protocols utilize cryptographic techniques like digital certificates and key exchanges to authenticate the identities of the communicating parties and detect any unauthorized interception or tampering. By ensuring the authenticity of both parties and the integrity of the data being exchanged, these protocols help protect against MitM attacks, thus securing sensitive data in transit.

3. Enabling Secure Remote Access

With the rise of remote work, secure communication protocols have become essential for enabling secure access to corporate networks and resources. As employees access systems from remote locations, protocols like SSL VPNs (Secure Sockets Layer Virtual Private Networks) and SSH (Secure Shell) ensure that data remains encrypted and secure. These protocols enforce stringent authentication measures to protect corporate information while enabling remote employees to access sensitive data without risking security breaches. This is critical in maintaining data confidentiality and integrity in a distributed work environment.

4. Securing Online Transactions

Protocols like **TLS/SSL** (Transport Layer Security / Secure Sockets Layer) are widely used to protect online transactions, such as e-commerce purchases, online banking, and electronic payments. By encrypting sensitive financial data (like credit card numbers and personal information) during transmission, these protocols ensure that data is secure from interception or tampering. TLS/SSL protection helps prevent fraud, identity theft, and unauthorized access to payment details, which is crucial for maintaining consumer trust in online financial transactions.

5. Enabling Safe Collaboration and Information Sharing

Secure communication protocols also facilitate safe collaboration and information exchange between individuals and organizations, even when they are geographically dispersed. Whether it's sending encrypted emails, sharing confidential documents, or holding secure video conferences over VPNs, these protocols ensure that sensitive information is protected from unauthorized access or interception. This is especially important in scenarios involving critical collaboration—such as legal discussions, business partnerships, or government communications—where confidentiality and integrity are paramount. By implementing these secure protocols, organizations can maintain the privacy of their communications, no matter where the parties are located.

Conclusion:

In summary, secure communication protocols are integral to protecting sensitive data, preventing attacks, and ensuring safe remote access, secure financial transactions, and confidential collaborations. By leveraging strong encryption, authentication, and integrity checks, these protocols play a pivotal role in safeguarding digital interactions, minimizing vulnerabilities, and fostering trust in online systems. Whether for everyday communication, business transactions, or remote work, these protocols are essential for securing the modern digital landscape.

Challenges and Considerations

Secure communication protocols face a range of challenges that must be addressed to maintain strong cybersecurity defenses. Here are some key considerations:

1. **Evolving Cyber Threats:** Cyberattacks are becoming increasingly sophisticated, with adversaries exploiting vulnerabilities in communication protocols and systems. To counteract these threats, continuous monitoring, threat intelligence, and proactive security measures are essential to stay ahead of attackers.
2. **Compatibility and Interoperability:** Ensuring that secure communication protocols work seamlessly across different systems and technologies can be challenging, particularly in environments that involve a variety of standards. Organizations need to carefully evaluate and implement protocols that integrate smoothly with their existing infrastructure and applications.
3. **Impact of Encryption on Performance:** The encryption and decryption processes used in secure communications can introduce latency and overhead, potentially affecting system performance, especially in high-traffic network environments. Balancing high network performance with strong security measures is critical.
4. **Key Management:** Effective key management is fundamental to the security of cryptographic systems. This includes generating, distributing, and revoking cryptographic keys. It is also important to maintain trust in certificate authorities (CAs) that issue digital certificates, to prevent attacks targeting certificates and ensure the authenticity of cryptographic entities.
5. **Regulatory Compliance:** Organizations handling sensitive data must comply with relevant data protection regulations such as GDPR, HIPAA, and PCI DSS. Communication protocols must align with these standards to ensure the confidentiality, integrity, and security of personal and sensitive information.

Frequently Asked Questions

Here are clear and concise responses to each of the questions:

1. **What do you understand by encryption?** Encryption is the process of converting readable data, known as plaintext, into an unreadable format, called ciphertext, using a cryptographic algorithm and an encryption key. This process ensures that only authorized parties who have the corresponding decryption key can access the original data. The purpose of encryption is to protect the confidentiality and integrity of data, especially during storage or transmission over insecure networks.
2. **How do you understand encryption algorithms?** Encryption algorithms are mathematical formulas or procedures used to transform plaintext into ciphertext during encryption and vice versa during decryption. They use a key (or multiple keys) to secure the data. The strength and security of an encryption algorithm depend on its design and the length of the key used. Common types of encryption algorithms include symmetric-key algorithms (where the same key is used for both encryption and decryption) and asymmetric-key algorithms (where different keys are used for encryption and decryption, such as in public-key cryptography).
3. **What are the uses of encryption?** Encryption is used for a variety of purposes, including:
    - **Data confidentiality:** Protects sensitive data, such as personal information, financial transactions, and confidential communications, from unauthorized access.
    - **Data integrity:** Ensures that data has not been altered or tampered with during transmission or storage.
    - **Authentication:** Verifies the identity of parties involved in a communication (e.g., through digital signatures).
    - **Secure communications:** Encrypts messages exchanged over the internet to safeguard privacy and security, such as in email, online banking, and messaging apps.
    - **Protecting data at rest and in transit:** Ensures that data is secure when stored on devices or transmitted over networks, preventing unauthorized access.
4. **What are the types/methods of encryption?** There are several types of encryption, broadly categorized as:
    - **Symmetric-key encryption (Private-key encryption):** The same key is used for both encryption and decryption. Common examples include the Advanced Encryption Standard (AES) and Data Encryption Standard (DES).
    - **Asymmetric-key encryption (Public-key encryption):** Different keys are used for encryption and decryption. One key is public and can be shared, while the other is private and kept secret. RSA (Rivest-Shamir-Adleman) and ECC (Elliptic Curve Cryptography) are examples.

- o **Hash functions:** Although not technically encryption, hashing is a process used to verify data integrity. It transforms data into a fixed-size hash value. Examples include SHA-256 (Secure Hash Algorithm) and MD5.
- o **Hybrid encryption:** Combines both symmetric and asymmetric encryption methods to take advantage of the speed of symmetric encryption and the security of asymmetric encryption. This is commonly used in protocols like SSL/TLS.

5. **What is the importance of secure communication protocols in cybersecurity?** Secure communication protocols are crucial in cybersecurity because they ensure the confidentiality, integrity, and authenticity of data exchanged over networks. These protocols protect against various cyber threats, such as eavesdropping, data tampering, and man-in-the-middle attacks. By encrypting data during transmission and verifying the identity of the communicating parties, secure communication protocols help maintain privacy, secure online transactions, and prevent unauthorized access to sensitive information. Examples of secure communication protocols include HTTPS (for secure web browsing), SSL/TLS (for secure email and data transmission), and IPsec (for secure VPN communications).

CHAPTER SIX
INCIDENT RESPONSE BASICS

Overview

Chapter six covers the incident response framework in cybersecurity, detailing strategies for addressing and mitigating breaches caused by cybercriminals. This chapter provides valuable insights on how to effectively prevent and manage security incidents.

Introduction to Incident Response

In the fast-evolving landscape of cybersecurity, where threats constantly shift and technology advances rapidly, having a robust incident response strategy is essential. This process involves effectively managing and mitigating security breaches, cyber-attacks, and other disruptive events that threaten the confidentiality, integrity, or availability of data and information systems. It requires the implementation of structured systems and procedures to address these challenges swiftly and efficiently. In today's interconnected world, where businesses heavily rely on digital infrastructure, the impact of security incidents can be devastating. A cyber-attack can lead to significant financial losses, reputational damage, regulatory penalties, and potential legal consequences. Additionally, the rising frequency of sophisticated threats—such as ransomware, advanced persistent threats (APTs), and zero-day vulnerabilities—underscores the need for proactive measures to detect, contain, and eliminate security risks.

Incident Response Lifecycle

The incident response process typically follows a well-structured lifecycle, consisting of several key phases:

1. **Preparation**: This phase focuses on planning and setting up the necessary rules, processes, and resources to ensure a swift and effective response to security incidents. Activities in this stage include developing an incident response plan, defining roles and responsibilities, conducting risk assessments, and implementing preventive controls and safeguards to reduce the likelihood of incidents.
2. **Detection and Analysis**: During this phase, security teams continuously monitor network traffic, system logs, and other data sources to identify potential security threats. Any suspicious activity or anomalies are thoroughly investigated to assess the scope, nature, and impact of the threat on the organization's systems and assets.
3. **Containment**: Once a security incident is confirmed, the immediate priority is to contain the threat and prevent further damage. This may involve isolating compromised systems,

disabling affected accounts, or blocking malicious network traffic. The goal is to limit the spread of the attack and minimize its impact on the organization.

4. **Resolution**: In this phase, the security team works to address the root cause of the incident and restore affected systems to a secure state. This may involve patching vulnerabilities, removing malware, or reconfiguring compromised devices. Ensuring a thorough clean-up is critical to prevent future incidents.
5. **Recovery**: The recovery phase focuses on returning the organization to normal operations and recovering lost or corrupted data. This may involve restoring backups, rebuilding infrastructure, and implementing additional security measures to prevent similar incidents. The goal is to minimize downtime and reduce the incident's long-term impact on the business.
6. **Lessons Learned**: After the incident has been resolved, it is essential to conduct a post-incident review to extract valuable insights and identify areas for improvement. This may include updating incident response plans, enhancing security controls, and providing additional employee training and awareness. The lessons learned from the incident can help strengthen the organization's defenses and better prepare for future threats.

Challenges and Considerations

While incident response frameworks provide a structured approach to managing security incidents, organizations often face several challenges when implementing them:

1. **Complexity of Attacks**: Cyber-attacks are becoming increasingly sophisticated, making them harder to detect and mitigate. Attackers use advanced techniques, such as polymorphic malware, encryption, and evasion tactics, to bypass traditional security defenses and evade detection.
2. **Resource Constraints**: Many organizations struggle with limited resources, including budget, skilled personnel, and technology, which can hinder their ability to effectively detect and respond to security incidents. This may impact their capacity to deploy advanced security measures, conduct proactive threat hunting, or maintain an adequately trained cybersecurity workforce.
3. **Legal and Regulatory Compliance**: Navigating the complex landscape of legal and regulatory requirements adds another layer of difficulty to incident response. Organizations must comply with various laws, industry standards, and regulations regarding data breach reporting, evidence preservation, and privacy protection, all while managing security incidents in a way that meets these obligations.
4. **Collaboration**: Successful incident response often requires coordination between multiple teams and stakeholders, including IT, security, legal, communications, and executive leadership. Clear communication and seamless collaboration are essential for ensuring a rapid and effective response to security threats.
5. **Evolving Threat Landscape**: The cybersecurity threat landscape is constantly shifting, with attackers continuously evolving their tactics, techniques, and procedures (TTPs). To

effectively address emerging threats, organizations must remain agile and continually adapt their incident response plans and strategies to keep pace with new and evolving attack methods.

Effective Strategies for Incident Response

Organizations can significantly enhance their incident response capabilities by adopting the following best practices:

1. **Develop an Incident Response Plan**: Establish a thorough incident response plan that clearly defines roles, responsibilities, processes, and communication protocols to ensure a swift and coordinated response to security incidents. The plan should be regularly reviewed, updated, and tested to keep pace with changes in the threat landscape and the organization's evolving needs.
2. **Form a Rapid Response Team**: Assemble a dedicated incident response team composed of skilled professionals from various disciplines, such as IT, security, legal, and communications. Equip the team with the necessary authority, resources, and training to respond quickly and effectively to security incidents.
3. **Implement Robust Security Controls**: Deploy a comprehensive set of security measures designed to detect and address security threats as they emerge. This includes tools such as network firewalls, intrusion detection systems (IDS), endpoint protection, security information and event management (SIEM) systems, and threat intelligence feeds to enhance real-time detection and response.
4. **Provide Regular Training and Drills**: Conduct ongoing training programs to raise awareness of security risks and ensure that employees understand best practices for incident response. Regularly run simulated cyber-attacks and tabletop exercises to test the organization's preparedness and identify areas for improvement in the response process.
5. **Establish Incident Reporting and Escalation Procedures**: Set up clear protocols for reporting security incidents, including defined channels for communication, escalation procedures, and criteria for incident severity. Encourage a culture of transparency where employees feel comfortable reporting suspicious activities or concerns without fear of reprisal.
6. **Leverage Threat Intelligence**: Stay informed about the latest threats, vulnerabilities, and attack trends by utilizing credible threat intelligence sources, such as industry information-sharing groups, government agencies, and commercial security firms. Use this intelligence to enhance threat detection, prioritize response efforts, and take proactive measures to defend against emerging threats.

Incident Handling Process

The incident handling process is a structured approach designed to detect, respond to, and recover from cybersecurity incidents. It involves a coordinated set of actions to identify the nature and scope of an incident, contain its spread, minimize its impact, and restore normal operations. Below are the key elements of the incident handling process and how to implement them effectively:

1. Preparation

Preparation is the foundation of an effective incident handling strategy. This phase involves setting up policies, procedures, and resources to ensure a quick and efficient response to incidents. Key activities include:

- **Developing an Incident Response Plan**: Organizations must create a comprehensive plan outlining team member roles, responsibilities, escalation procedures, communication protocols, and available technical resources. The plan should be regularly updated to reflect the changing threat landscape and organizational needs.
- **Assembling a Response Team**: Form a specialized incident response team consisting of experts from various areas such as IT, cybersecurity, legal, and communications. Regular training ensures the team is well-prepared to handle incidents efficiently and effectively.
- **Conducting Risk Assessments**: Regularly assess cybersecurity risks to identify vulnerabilities, potential threats, and areas of high exposure. This allows organizations to prioritize mitigation efforts based on the potential impact of different types of incidents.
- **Implementing Monitoring and Detection Systems**: Deploy advanced security technologies like intrusion detection systems (IDS), security information and event management (SIEM) systems, and endpoint detection and response (EDR) solutions to continuously monitor for suspicious activity and detect potential breaches early.

2. Detection and Analysis

Once an incident is suspected or detected, the focus shifts to identifying indicators of compromise (IOCs), analyzing the incident's scope and impact, and planning the appropriate response. Key activities in this phase include:

- **Incident Triage**: After detection, assess the severity, impact, and response priority of the incident. Gather information on the type of attack, affected systems, and the potential risks to the organization.
- **Forensic Analysis**: Collect and preserve evidence (e.g., log files, network traffic, memory dumps) to better understand the incident and identify the attackers. Forensic analysis is critical for tracking the source of the attack and supporting any necessary legal or disciplinary actions.

- **Root Cause Analysis**: Once the immediate threat is mitigated, investigate the root cause of the incident. This helps identify vulnerabilities that were exploited and informs future improvements to the organization's security posture and defenses.

3. Containment, Eradication, and Recovery

After identifying and analyzing the incident, the next priority is to contain its spread, eliminate the threat, and restore normal operations. Key activities include:

- **Containment**: The goal of containment is to isolate affected systems to prevent further spread of the incident. This may involve disconnecting compromised devices from the network, disabling user accounts, or applying emergency security controls to limit the attacker's access.
- **Eradication**: Once the incident is contained, the root cause must be addressed. This involves removing malware, unauthorized access, and any other remnants of the attack. It may also involve restoring systems from backups, applying security patches, and enhancing security measures to prevent recurrence.
- **Recovery**: The recovery phase focuses on restoring normal operations. This may involve recovering data from backups, rebuilding compromised systems, and ensuring that all security controls are functioning properly. Priority should be given to restoring critical systems to minimize downtime and resume business operations.

4. Post-Incident Activities

Once the incident is resolved and normal operations are restored, it's crucial to conduct a thorough review of the incident response process to identify lessons learned and areas for improvement. Key activities include:

- **Incident Debriefing**: A post-incident debriefing allows the organization to evaluate its response to the incident. This includes gathering feedback from responders, analyzing the strengths and weaknesses of the incident handling process, and identifying areas for improvement in future responses.
- **Documentation and Reporting**: A detailed incident report should be created, documenting the incident's cause, impact, and the actions taken during the response. This report should be shared with relevant stakeholders, such as internal teams, external partners, and regulatory bodies, in accordance with legal and compliance requirements.
- **Continuous Improvement**: The incident handling process should be reviewed and updated regularly based on insights gained from the incident and any changes in the threat environment. Ongoing activities such as tabletop exercises, penetration testing, and security audits can help assess the organization's preparedness and identify opportunities for strengthening incident response capabilities.

By following these structured phases, organizations can improve their ability to detect, respond to, and recover from cybersecurity incidents, reducing the impact of attacks and strengthening their overall security posture.

Roles within the Incident Response Team

In the fast-evolving landscape of cybersecurity, where new threats emerge constantly, organizations must be able to react swiftly to incidents in order to minimize damage and protect their assets. Incident Response (IR) teams are critical in this process, ensuring that security breaches are quickly identified, contained, and addressed. The success of an IR team largely depends on clearly defined roles and responsibilities within the group.

1. Incident Commander (IC)

The Incident Commander is responsible for overseeing the entire incident response process. This individual manages the response efforts, makes key decisions, and coordinates the activities of the team. An effective IC should possess strong leadership skills, decisiveness, and a thorough understanding of the organization's security posture. The main tasks of the Incident Commander include:

- Assessing the severity and potential impact of the incident.
- Coordinating resources and personnel efficiently.
- Establishing communication channels with stakeholders.
- Providing regular updates to executive leadership and relevant parties.
- Ensuring compliance with regulatory standards and internal policies.
The Incident Commander is essential in ensuring smooth communication and collaboration across all involved parties during an incident.

2. Incident Responder

Incident Responders are key players in investigating and mitigating security incidents as they unfold. With a deep technical background in areas like network security, forensics, malware analysis, and intrusion detection, these professionals work to limit the damage caused by threats. Their responsibilities include:

- Identifying and analyzing indicators of compromise (IOCs) to understand the nature and scope of the incident.
- Neutralizing the threat to prevent further damage.
- Conducting forensic analysis to collect evidence for later investigation and remediation.
- Implementing additional security measures to prevent similar incidents in the future.

- Collaborating with team members and external experts to exchange intelligence and best practices.
  Incident Responders must be able to perform effectively under pressure and quickly adapt to rapidly changing situations, as incidents can escalate quickly.

3. Forensic Analyst

Forensic Analysts are crucial after an incident occurs. Their primary responsibility is to conduct in-depth forensic investigations, reconstruct the event sequence, identify the root cause of the incident, and gather evidence for legal or regulatory purposes. Key tasks include:

- Collecting and preserving volatile data from affected systems.
- Performing disk and memory forensics to uncover traces of malicious activity.
- Analyzing logs, network traffic, and other digital evidence to track the attacker's actions.
- Compiling findings into detailed reports for internal stakeholders or law enforcement.
- Providing expert testimony in legal proceedings, if necessary.
  Forensic Analysts must be skilled in digital forensic techniques and well-versed in the legal aspects of data privacy and evidence handling.

4. Communications Coordinator

Clear, effective communication is vital during any incident response to keep all stakeholders informed and reassured. The Communications Coordinator manages internal and external communications, ensuring everyone involved stays up-to-date. Responsibilities include:

- Setting up communication protocols to relay information to stakeholders.
- Managing media relations and overseeing public communications, especially during high-profile incidents.
- Ensuring employees, customers, and regulatory bodies are consistently updated to maintain transparency and trust.
- Facilitating communication between the incident response team and executive management to ensure critical information is shared promptly.
- Monitoring social media and online platforms for misinformation or rumors about the incident.
  The Communications Coordinator must possess excellent communication skills, crisis management expertise, and the ability to convey complex technical issues clearly.

5. Legal Counsel

Legal expertise is essential during incident response, particularly when dealing with data breaches or compliance issues. The Legal Counsel guides the response team on legal obligations, potential liabilities, and regulatory compliance. Key duties include:

- Assessing the legal implications of the incident, such as potential fines, lawsuits, or reputational damage.
- Advising on legal requirements for breach notifications under data protection laws.
- Coordinating with external legal experts and law enforcement, if needed.
- Reviewing and drafting necessary documentation, such as breach notifications and settlement agreements.
- Ensuring the protection of sensitive information and maintaining attorney-client privilege.

Legal Counsel must have a strong understanding of relevant laws and regulations and practical experience in handling data privacy and cybersecurity legal issues.

By clearly defining these roles, organizations can ensure that their incident response teams operate efficiently and effectively when facing cyber threats.

Techniques for Detecting and Analyzing Incidents

Detecting unauthorized activity or security breaches within an organization's network or systems is a vital aspect of incident detection and response. Proactive detection plays a critical role in minimizing the impact of cyber-attacks by enabling quick identification, reaction, and containment of threats. Historically, incident detection relied heavily on signature-based methods, which involved identifying known patterns of malicious activity. However, as cyber threats evolve, these traditional methods are becoming less effective at identifying novel or sophisticated attacks.

Advanced Threat Detection Techniques

To address the growing complexity of cyber threats, organizations are increasingly turning to advanced detection techniques. These approaches leverage technologies such as machine learning, artificial intelligence (AI), and behavioral analytics to identify potential security incidents. Machine learning algorithms can analyze large volumes of data to detect anomalies and uncover previously unknown threats, while behavioral analytics focuses on monitoring normal user behavior and spotting deviations that might suggest malicious activity. By identifying unusual patterns early, these advanced techniques help organizations detect emerging threats more effectively.

Intrusion Detection and Prevention Systems (IDS/IPS)

Both Intrusion Detection Systems (IDS) and Intrusion Prevention Systems (IPS) are critical components of an organization's cybersecurity infrastructure. IDS monitors network traffic for signs of suspicious activity and generates alerts when potential threats, such as unauthorized access or unusual data transfers, are detected. In contrast, IPS actively blocks harmful traffic and prevents attacks in real-time, offering a more proactive defense. Together, IDS and IPS solutions enhance security by providing layered protection against various cyber threats, including malware, phishing, and denial-of-service (DoS) attacks.

Endpoint Detection and Response (EDR)

As remote work becomes more prevalent and the number of endpoints connected to corporate networks increases, endpoint security has become a growing concern. Endpoint Detection and Response (EDR) systems provide real-time monitoring and threat detection at the device level, helping organizations quickly identify and address security incidents. EDR tools collect and analyze data from endpoints to detect suspicious activities, such as unauthorized access, file modifications, and system anomalies. By integrating EDR with centralized threat intelligence and response mechanisms, organizations can enhance their ability to detect and mitigate sophisticated attacks targeting endpoints.

Security Information and Event Management (SIEM)

Security Information and Event Management (SIEM) systems are crucial for identifying and managing cybersecurity incidents. SIEM solutions aggregate and analyze data from multiple sources—such as network logs, system logs, and security devices—to provide a comprehensive overview of an organization's security status. By correlating and analyzing these data points, SIEM platforms help identify potential threats and detect patterns indicative of security incidents. Furthermore, SIEM solutions offer advanced features, such as threat intelligence integration, automated incident response, and forensic analysis, which strengthen an organization's ability to detect and respond to security threats efficiently.

Integrating Threat Intelligence

Incorporating threat intelligence into the incident detection and response process is essential for staying ahead of evolving cyber threats. Threat intelligence provides critical insights into emerging threats, attack tactics, and the activities of malicious actors. By integrating threat intelligence feeds from trusted sources—such as government agencies, cybersecurity firms, and industry groups—organizations can proactively detect and mitigate potential risks. Threat intelligence helps organizations map security events to known indicators of compromise (IOCs), allowing them to identify and address security incidents before they escalate. Leveraging threat intelligence enhances the effectiveness of incident detection and supports faster, more informed decision-making during incidents.

The Role of Forensic Analysis in Incident Response

Forensic analysis plays a key role in understanding the nature of security incidents and preventing future breaches. After a security event, forensic investigators analyze evidence to determine the root cause of the breach, gather evidence for legal and regulatory purposes, and identify areas for improvement in security measures. A thorough forensic investigation not only provides valuable insights into past incidents but also helps organizations strengthen their defenses by learning from previous attacks.

Effective Incident Response and Mitigation

Effective incident response is essential for limiting the damage caused by security breaches. By adhering to predefined response processes and policies, organizations can quickly contain and mitigate security incidents. Clearly defined roles and responsibilities within the incident response team ensure that everyone knows their tasks and can act swiftly and decisively. By combining advanced detection techniques, timely response, and forensic analysis, organizations can significantly reduce the impact of cyber threats and improve their overall cybersecurity posture.

Identifying Indicators of Compromise (IOCs)

Indicators of Compromise (IOCs) are observable artifacts or patterns that suggest a security incident has occurred or is currently in progress. These signs can manifest in various forms, such as unusual network traffic or abnormal system activity, and may point to a wide range of cyber threats, including malware infections, unauthorized access, or data exfiltration. IOCs can be classified into several categories, each focusing on different aspects of a system's behavior and security posture:

1. File-based IOCs

These indicators are related to specific files or software on a system. They include hashes of known malicious files, filenames, file paths, and digital signatures associated with suspicious or harmful software. Identifying these IOCs helps in detecting known malware or unauthorized files that may indicate a compromise.

2. Network-based IOCs

Network-based IOCs are observed in network traffic patterns. These include unusual data flows, communication with suspicious IP addresses, or connections using non-standard ports. Monitoring network traffic for these anomalies can help identify malicious activity, such as data exfiltration, command-and-control communications, or the spread of malware.

3. Host-based IOCs

Host-based IOCs focus on specific endpoints or devices within the network. These indicators may include unexpected system changes, unauthorized processes running in memory, or unusual modifications to system registries. Detecting these types of IOCs can reveal a compromised machine or unauthorized activity occurring on a particular host.

4. Behavioral IOCs

Behavioral IOCs involve detecting unusual patterns of behavior within the system or network. Examples include repeated failed login attempts, unauthorized privilege escalation, or abnormal access to sensitive data. These indicators often point to malicious actions such as credential stuffing, lateral movement, or attempts to gain unauthorized access to critical systems.

5. Artifact-based IOCs

These IOCs relate to physical or digital traces left by an attacker during the intrusion process. Artifacts may include log entries, error messages, or remnants of tools used during the attack (such as malware or hacking utilities). Analyzing these traces can help identify the tools and techniques used by the attacker, which can be critical for post-incident analysis and future prevention.

By carefully monitoring and analyzing these different categories of IOCs, cybersecurity professionals can gain a clearer understanding of ongoing or past security incidents. This allows them to take timely and effective action to mitigate risks, limit the impact of an attack, and strengthen the organization's defenses against future threats.

Identifying Signs of Compromise

Effectively identifying Indicators of Compromise (IOCs) requires a combination of advanced technology, expert human insight, and a proactive approach to threat intelligence. While automated tools and algorithms are essential for detecting patterns and potential threats, human analysts play an indispensable role in contextualizing data, identifying emerging threats, and detecting anomalies that might otherwise go unnoticed.

1. Integrating Threat Intelligence

Incorporating threat intelligence feeds into an organization's security infrastructure ensures that security teams stay up-to-date on the latest threat actors, tactics, and indicators of compromise (IOCs). By using threat intelligence platforms and services, organizations can enhance their understanding of potential threats and improve their ability to detect IOCs proactively. Threat intelligence helps security teams stay ahead of evolving attacks by providing real-time information on new attack methodologies, vulnerabilities, and emerging trends in the cybersecurity landscape.

2. Contextual Analysis

To effectively distinguish between legitimate threats and false positives, it's essential to understand the context in which IOCs occur. Security analysts must thoroughly assess the surrounding factors, including the systems involved, user activity, and potential attack vectors. By correlating various IOCs with additional contextual data, analysts can gain a deeper understanding of the threat landscape, which enables them to detect sophisticated, multi-phase attack campaigns. Contextual analysis adds a layer of intelligence that helps teams prioritize responses and focus on the most relevant threats.

3. Behavioral Analytics

Behavioral analytics solutions use machine learning algorithms to analyze user and entity behavior across an organization's network. These systems establish baseline activity patterns for users, devices, and applications, enabling them to detect deviations that may signal a security incident. Behavioral analytics not only improves the recognition of traditional IOCs but also enables proactive threat hunting by identifying suspicious behaviors that might not immediately align with known IOCs. This approach helps uncover threats that evolve over time or are designed to evade detection by conventional methods.

4. Endpoint Detection and Response (EDR)

Endpoint Detection and Response (EDR) solutions provide real-time visibility into endpoint activities and enable rapid response to potential security incidents. By continuously monitoring endpoint behavior, collecting forensic data, and applying behavioral analysis, EDR systems can detect IOCs indicative of endpoint compromise. These indicators might include fileless malware execution, lateral movement within the network, and attempts to escalate privileges. EDR solutions help security teams pinpoint the early stages of an attack and prevent further damage by quickly isolating or remediating affected endpoints.

5. Human Expertise

While automated threat detection systems have become more advanced, human expertise remains crucial in identifying complex IOCs and emerging threats. Security analysts bring the experience, critical thinking, and intuition needed to detect subtle signs of an intrusion that automated systems may overlook. Human analysts are essential for providing context to automated alerts, performing deeper investigations, and identifying new or sophisticated attack patterns. Through ongoing training, collaboration, and knowledge sharing, security teams can enhance their ability to recognize IOCs, adapt to new threat tactics, and respond to evolving cybersecurity risks.

By combining cutting-edge technology with human expertise, organizations can significantly improve their ability to detect and respond to IOCs. This integrated approach enables proactive threat identification, efficient incident response, and a stronger defense against the evolving landscape of cyber threats.

The Significance of Human Involvement

Automated techniques and algorithms excel at identifying known Indicators of Compromise (IOCs) and established attack patterns, but they have limitations. Cyber attackers are constantly adapting their tactics, techniques, and procedures (TTPs) to bypass traditional security measures and evade detection. This ongoing battle between attackers and defenders requires human involvement, as it brings the flexibility, creativity, and critical thinking needed to stay ahead of increasingly sophisticated threats.

1. Flexibility

Cyber attackers continuously modify their strategies to evade detection, often employing novel methods to avoid detection by traditional, rule-based systems. Automated detection tools are limited to recognizing pre-defined patterns and signatures, making it difficult for them to keep up with these evolving tactics. In contrast, human analysts possess the flexibility to adapt quickly to changing circumstances. Their ability to think critically allows them to identify subtle anomalies and deviations that may signal new or evolving attack strategies. This agility enables human analysts to detect previously unknown threats that automated systems might miss.

2. Innovation

Innovation is essential in the fight against cybercrime. Human analysts are not bound by predefined patterns or algorithms—they can approach threat detection and response with creativity and inventiveness. This creative problem-solving allows analysts to think outside the box, pursuing alternate paths or hypothetical scenarios to uncover hidden IOCs or vulnerabilities. By adopting an offensive mindset, human experts can proactively search for potential threats, anticipate attack methods, and build defenses to counteract emerging risks before they escalate.

3. Critical Thinking

Critical thinking is a cornerstone of effective cybersecurity. Analysts must navigate complex, high-pressure situations, often with incomplete or ambiguous information, and make informed decisions quickly. Human analysts bring the ability to assess IOCs in the context of an organization's specific environment and potential impact. They evaluate the intent behind suspicious activity and consider its significance, distinguishing between harmless anomalies and true signs of compromise. By conducting thorough investigations and testing hypotheses, human analysts reduce the likelihood of false positives (false alarms) and false negatives (missed threats), improving the overall effectiveness of the security response.

4. Collaboration and Knowledge Sharing

Cybersecurity thrives on collaboration, as it leverages collective intelligence and information-sharing. Security teams that actively engage with peers, researchers, and threat intelligence communities benefit from a wealth of diverse expertise and insights. By participating in forums, conferences, and threat intelligence exchanges, cybersecurity professionals can share their experiences, discuss emerging threats, and stay informed about the latest attack methods. Collaboration enhances a team's ability to recognize IOCs more effectively, build stronger defenses, and anticipate future threats based on the collective knowledge of the broader cybersecurity community.

Conclusion

While automated systems are invaluable in identifying known threats, human involvement is crucial to adapt to the ever-evolving nature of cyber attacks. Human analysts bring flexibility, creativity, critical thinking, and the ability to collaborate with others, which are essential for staying ahead of sophisticated attackers. By combining the strengths of automated tools with human expertise, organizations can better detect, respond to, and mitigate cyber threats, enhancing their overall security posture.

Frequently Asked Questions

- What is your understanding of incident response?
- What are some key strategies for effectively responding to incidents?
- What methods do you use to detect and analyze security incidents?
- What approach do you take in managing incident response?
- How do you identify signs of a potential compromise?

CHAPTER SEVEN
CYBERSECURITY CONSIDERATIONS WHEN WORKING FROM HOME

Overview

When working remotely from the comfort of your home, it's crucial to stay vigilant about cybersecurity risks. The digital space is filled with cybercriminals looking for opportunities to exploit vulnerabilities. In this chapter, we'll explore essential cybersecurity practices and precautions to take while working from home to protect yourself and your data.

Introduction to Cybersecurity Considerations

The global outbreak of COVID-19 in early 2020 marked a pivotal moment in the way people work, as the rapid spread of a highly contagious virus forced significant changes to daily life. In response, governments around the world implemented strict lockdown measures to contain the outbreak, disrupting traditional office-based work arrangements.

This sudden shift posed significant challenges, forcing businesses and employees to quickly adapt to a new work environment. One of the most notable aspects of this change was the ability of many workers to continue their jobs remotely, thanks to advances in technology over the past few decades. Unlike in previous pandemics or crises, where alternatives to in-person work were limited or nonexistent, modern technologies provided the tools needed to stay connected, productive, and operational, even while confined to home.

Video conferencing, cloud computing, and virtual private networks (VPNs) became crucial for maintaining business continuity during this time, allowing organizations to operate remotely despite the physical separation of their teams. However, this sudden and unexpected transition from office-based to remote work created a host of new challenges, particularly in the realm of cybersecurity. With little time to prepare, many organizations found themselves rushing to expand their remote access capabilities, often at the expense of security protocols.

Employees working from home brought new risks, such as unsecured home networks, the use of personal devices, and an increased vulnerability to phishing attacks and other cyber threats. These factors introduced significant security gaps that businesses had to address quickly. What was initially thought to be a temporary shift in response to the pandemic turned out to be a longer-term or even permanent change. As many organizations adopted hybrid or fully remote work models, even after lockdowns eased, the need for robust cybersecurity became more critical than ever.

The extended duration of remote work underscored the importance of ongoing cybersecurity vigilance. The weaknesses that emerged in the early days of the pandemic required continuous attention and improvement to keep pace with evolving threats.

In conclusion, the COVID-19 pandemic triggered a fundamental shift in the workplace, making remote work the new norm for many people. While technological advancements made this shift possible, the rapid and unexpected transition created significant cybersecurity challenges. The long-term nature of remote work highlighted the need for businesses to continually reassess and strengthen their security measures, ensuring they can operate safely and securely in an increasingly dispersed work environment.

Concerns about Network Security

One of the primary concerns with remote work is the security of the networks that employees use to access sensitive data. If these networks are not adequately secured, two potentially disastrous outcomes can occur:

1. **Data Theft**: Sensitive information could be stolen without either the employee or employer realizing it, putting confidential data at risk of exposure or misuse.
2. **Device Compromise**: Employees' personal devices may become targets for malware or hackers, who can exploit vulnerabilities to infiltrate corporate systems. Once inside, cybercriminals can cause significant damage, including data breaches, system disruption, or further security compromises.

What are the common security risks associated with remote-worker networks?

Businesses typically have stronger firewalls and security measures in place than consumer-grade equipment. However, it's important to recognize that many remote workers rely on inexpensive, off-the-shelf routers that may not have additional layers of protection like firewalls. Is it really wise for a company to trust a router purchased for $19.99 during a Black Friday sale five years ago? The reality is that most consumers are not equipped to properly configure their routers or firewalls, often opting for the default, minimal security settings provided by the manufacturer. While more advanced options are available, many remote workers fail to implement features like intrusion detection systems or other essential security tools in their home networks. Unfortunately, such features are rare in low-cost consumer routers.

In contrast, businesses typically deploy a variety of security solutions to safeguard their networks. For example, enterprise firewalls can restrict certain outbound requests, and data loss prevention (DLP) systems can prevent sensitive information from being accidentally emailed or shared. Remote workers, however, generally do not have access to these robust security systems through their personal routers.

This raises an important question: Do employers even know which routers their remote staff are using, let alone whether the firmware is kept up to date? Can managers effectively assess whether remote employees are conducting vulnerability scans on their devices or networks? Beyond the router's security features, employers must also consider how many have taken steps to ensure that workers' home Wi-Fi networks are properly secured. Are businesses aware of who else is accessing these networks or how those devices could pose a risk? For instance, downloading games or other non-work-related software can introduce viruses or malware that could easily spread across a network connection.

To address these risks, some suggest that businesses require remote workers to use a fully tunneling Virtual Private Network (VPN). This type of VPN would route all of the employee's internet traffic through the company's network, ensuring that all online activity is subject to the company's perimeter security measures. However, this approach also introduces its own challenges. If a virus or other security threat exists on the employee's home network, it could potentially be transferred to the company's network. Additionally, if the employer's network experiences any technical issues, remote workers may be unable to perform their duties, even from a distance.

In summary, while businesses may have strong perimeter security in place, the security of remote workers' home networks remains a significant concern. Employers need to consider whether remote workers' personal routers and Wi-Fi networks are sufficiently protected, and how to mitigate the risks of connecting those networks to the company's infrastructure.

What steps can be taken to mitigate these risks?

The ideal scenario involves your employer providing a second router that connects to your home router, creating a dedicated work network separate from your personal network. In this setup, the work network would have its own segment, ensuring that it operates independently and securely. With the right configuration, the work network can send outbound requests to the internet, but it cannot initiate any communication with the business network, providing an added layer of security.

This approach is certainly more secure than relying on a single router for both personal and work-related activities. However, it does have its limitations. While the networks are separated, there is still the potential for connectivity between the two, which could lead to vulnerabilities if not properly managed. While security measures can be implemented to mitigate risks in this design, the complexity of the configuration increases the chances of errors, which could unintentionally compromise the system's security.

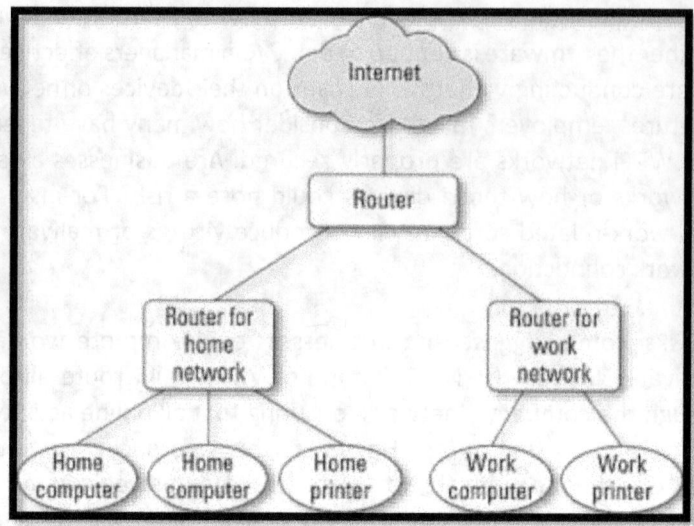

It is highly recommended that employees use devices provided by their employers for work-related tasks. This approach ensures compliance with privacy regulations and significantly reduces the risk of data breaches or leaks that could occur when corporate information is accessed through insecure personal networks or devices. Ideally, only employer-issued devices should be connected to the company's work network to maintain a secure and controlled environment.

Concerns About Device Security

Devices without proper security measures can create vulnerabilities similar to those posed by unsecured networks. These risks include data theft and the possibility of hackers infiltrating the organization to cause various types of damage. As mentioned earlier, it is strongly preferable for all work devices to be owned and managed by the employer, for several key reasons:

- **Monitoring and Control**: Employers need to be aware of the contents of employees' devices to ensure optimal productivity and prevent distractions. This also helps in identifying potential security threats early, such as unauthorized apps or malware.
- **Liability Risks**: When employers ask employees to install work-related apps on personal devices, they may inadvertently introduce security vulnerabilities or software conflicts. If these issues lead to security breaches, employers could be held liable for the consequences.
- **Data Security After Employee Departure**: If an employee leaves the company and retains work-related data on a personal device, there is a risk that the data could be exposed or misused, either accidentally or intentionally. This risk is heightened if the device is lost or stolen. In extreme cases, if an employee were to pass away, the whereabouts of sensitive work data could become a critical concern if the device is lost or inaccessible.

While providing employer-issued devices for remote work is the ideal solution, it may not always be practical. In cases where employees must use their own devices—such as laptops, tablets, or smartphones—it is essential to ensure that the necessary security software is installed, active, and regularly updated. Devices should also be equipped with features like remote wiping in the event of loss or theft. Additionally, all sensitive data stored on these devices must be encrypted and properly backed up to minimize the risk of exposure or loss.

In conclusion, while employer-issued devices offer the highest level of security, if employees are required to use personal devices for work, strong security measures—such as encryption, remote wipe capabilities, and regular updates—must be in place to protect corporate data and ensure business continuity.

Cybersecurity Location

While technology is often at the forefront of discussions about data security, it's important to remember that other factors play a crucial role as well. One of the key considerations is the **location** of systems and data access. The significance of this factor has grown substantially with the shift from in-office work to remote work. As employees increasingly work from various locations—home offices, coffee shops, or even while traveling—the risks associated with where data is accessed have become more pronounced.

Accessing company data from unsecured or public locations can expose sensitive information to a range of threats, from cyberattacks to physical theft. Whether it's an unsecured Wi-Fi network or a shared device, understanding the risks tied to location is now more critical than ever in maintaining robust security and safeguarding corporate data. As businesses adapt to the new remote work environment, they must implement measures that account for both technological and location-based vulnerabilities to ensure comprehensive protection against emerging threats.

Shoulder surfing

Employees working remotely, though a common practice, often represent an overlooked security risk to company data and privacy. One significant threat is the inadvertent exposure of sensitive information through a practice known as *shoulder surfing*, where others can view or even record what's displayed on an employee's device screen. This can lead to breaches in data confidentiality, especially in environments where others have access to the worker's physical space.

While shoulder surfing is not a new concept, it remains a persistent concern, particularly as more employees work outside of traditional office settings. The risk is especially high when workers choose to work in public spaces like coffee shops or parks, where the visibility of their screens increases the potential for exposure.

To mitigate this risk, it is crucial for remote workers to establish a dedicated, secure workspace at home, where sensitive information can be shielded from view. Ideally, this should be a private area that limits access by family members or others, especially children, who may inadvertently expose company data. Employers can support remote workers by providing ergonomic furniture or privacy equipment, such as privacy screens or office partitions, to help ensure a secure and private working environment at home.

Eavesdropping

Exercise caution when engaging in voice communication, especially in public or shared spaces. Refrain from discussing sensitive details over the phone or through any voice-based communication tool if others are nearby and may overhear the conversation. The employees on these calls appeared unaware that they were inadvertently disclosing confidential information that should have been kept private. A white noise machine can be a useful tool for maintaining privacy, particularly when working from home. Similar devices are commonly used by therapists and counselors to safeguard confidentiality in their offices.

Theft

Home offices generally have less robust security than traditional office environments, and public places like parks, libraries, and coffee shops are even more exposed in terms of safety. As a result, remote workers are at a greater risk of laptop theft compared to those who work in secure, professional office settings.

Human error

It's important to recognize that frequent interruptions can significantly increase the likelihood of mistakes, potentially leading to data breaches. To maximize productivity while working remotely, it's essential to establish a focused, distraction-free workspace. Remote work environments, especially during challenging times like a pandemic when children are home and attending school remotely, can present additional obstacles. Creating a dedicated workspace that promotes both efficiency and attention to detail is crucial, not only for productivity but also for maintaining a reasonable level of data privacy.

Ensuring Cybersecurity in Video Conferencing

The shift from in-office to remote work in 2020, driven by the COVID-19 pandemic, led to a significant surge in the use of video conferencing and call technologies. In a very short period, a growing number of people began conducting work-related video meetings from locations outside of their traditional offices. With the rapid adoption of this new and unfamiliar technology, it is crucial to acknowledge the potential risks associated with its use. In particular, the primary concerns with video conferencing are information security and privacy, which must be carefully managed.

Ensure that personal items are not visible in the camera frame

When participating in video conferences, it's essential to be mindful of what's visible in your camera's frame and avoid displaying sensitive or private information. Keep in mind that mirrors and reflective surfaces in your environment can inadvertently reveal objects outside of the camera's direct view. While these guidelines may seem obvious, there are numerous examples online of people who overlooked such precautions. Using a virtual background can be helpful, especially if you have access to a green screen, as it helps keep the focus on you and minimizes distractions in your surroundings. Many video conferencing tools also offer a blur background option, which can further protect your privacy.

It's also important to inform everyone in your household when you're on a video call, especially if your camera or microphone will be on, even for just part of the meeting. Remember that your camera and microphone are active during the call, so any noise or movement near the device can be picked up and shared with others. Sadly, there have been numerous embarrassing moments where individuals unintentionally entered the frame of a video call while not fully dressed, highlighting the need for caution and awareness in your environment.

Ensure the security of your video conferences by preventing unauthorized access

Cybersecurity in video conferencing goes beyond just keeping sensitive information out of the camera's frame. In the early months of the COVID-19 pandemic, there were significant security breaches, including unauthorized parties frequently joining Zoom meetings and causing disruptions, a phenomenon that led to the term *Zoom bombing*.

To ensure higher levels of security in your video communications, consider these best practices:

- **Avoid using video conferencing for confidential discussions.** Video conferencing systems, particularly commercial platforms, are not designed for highly sensitive communications. Like any software, they may have vulnerabilities that could be exploited by attackers.
- **Password-protect your meetings.** Setting up a password for your video calls makes it much harder for unauthorized individuals to join. Without the correct password, they won't be able to access your meeting.
- **Use unique meeting room names for each session.** While some video conferencing services allow you to reuse the same meeting room name, this increases the risk of

someone with previous access joining a future session. Always create a new room name for each meeting.
- **Enable a waiting room.** Many video conferencing platforms allow you to automatically place all participants in a virtual waiting room upon joining. As the host, you can then review and approve who enters the meeting. You can choose to admit everyone at once, or select participants individually. Pre-registered participants can be placed directly into the meeting, while unknown individuals will need to wait for your approval.
- **Lock the meeting once everyone has joined.** After all participants have entered—or if some haven't joined within a reasonable time frame—lock the meeting to prevent anyone else from joining.
- **Monitor the participant list regularly.** Periodically check the attendee list for unauthorized participants. If someone doesn't belong, remove them immediately. If an authorized person is causing disruptions, they may need to be removed as well. Once the meeting is locked, you typically only need to check the list once, but be aware that cohosts might inadvertently undo the lock.
- **Disable private chat.** If possible, turn off the option for participants to send private messages during the meeting. If someone needs to chat privately, they should use another messaging platform rather than relying on the built-in chat feature.
- **Restrict screen sharing.** If there's no specific need for a participant to share their screen, either disable screen sharing or limit it to the host and co-hosts only. This minimizes the risk of unauthorized or distracting content being shared during the meeting.

By following these guidelines, you can significantly improve the security of your video conferences and reduce the risk of interruptions or unauthorized access.

Concerns with Social Engineering

Remote workers, especially those operating in isolation away from their colleagues, may be more susceptible to certain types of social engineering attacks than those working in close proximity to their teams in a traditional office setting. In remote environments, it can be challenging to quickly verify the authenticity of a request. For example, if a CFO working from home receives a payment request from the CEO, they can't easily walk over to the CEO's office to confirm the legitimacy of the request.

Additionally, during the early days of the COVID-19 pandemic, many organizations had to transition to remote work quickly, often without adequate preparation. As a result, the security measures in place at physical office locations to mitigate social engineering risks weren't always extended to remote work environments in time.

To effectively guard against social engineering attacks, it's crucial that all remote workers recognize they could be potential targets. Those who embrace this awareness are more likely to approach situations that could lead to data breaches with greater caution. Regular training and assessments on recognizing and preventing social engineering tactics can also play a vital role in bolstering security and ensuring employees remain vigilant in a remote setting.

Regulatory Concerns

Although remote work became necessary due to the rapid spread of a dangerous virus, it's important to remember that various rules and regulations related to information security and privacy still apply. For example, businesses that fall under Europe's General Data Protection Regulation (GDPR) must continue to prioritize the protection of personal data, even when operating remotely. Similarly, healthcare organizations that allow clerical staff to work remotely—for instance, handling tasks like insurance billing—must still comply with the data protection requirements of the Health Insurance Portability and Accountability Act (HIPAA) in the United States.

In addition, companies governed by regulations from bodies like the U.S. Securities and Exchange Commission (SEC) must ensure that insider information is properly protected and not exposed, even to authorized individuals, at inappropriate times. Many other industry-specific regulations follow the same principle of safeguarding sensitive data.

It is essential to ensure that your remote work setup complies with all relevant regulatory standards to avoid legal complications for yourself or your organization.

Frequently Asked Questions

1. What are the concerns about network security?

Network security concerns are focused on protecting data as it is transmitted across networks, including the internet, private networks, and local area networks (LANs). Common concerns include:

- **Unauthorized access:** Attackers trying to gain access to your network or devices through methods like hacking, malware, or exploiting vulnerabilities in network configurations.
- **Data breaches:** The risk of sensitive or private information being exposed, stolen, or tampered with during transmission.
- **Malware and ransomware:** Software designed to damage, disrupt, or gain unauthorized access to systems. Ransomware, in particular, can lock or encrypt data, demanding payment for its release.
- **Denial of Service (DoS) attacks:** These attacks aim to disrupt the availability of services or networks, overwhelming them with traffic and making them inaccessible to legitimate users.
- **Phishing and spoofing:** Techniques used to deceive users into giving away sensitive information or clicking on malicious links.

- **Weak encryption:** Using weak or outdated encryption methods to protect data during transmission can leave it vulnerable to interception and unauthorized access.

To address these concerns, businesses typically use firewalls, intrusion detection systems (IDS), encryption, multi-factor authentication (MFA), and regular security updates and audits.

2. How do you ensure cybersecurity in video conferencing?

To ensure cybersecurity in video conferencing, several measures can be taken to protect meetings from unauthorized access and potential data breaches:

- **Use strong passwords:** Always password-protect meetings to ensure only invited participants can join. Share passwords securely, not via unprotected channels.
- **Enable waiting rooms:** Waiting rooms allow the host to screen participants before they are admitted into the meeting, ensuring only authorized users join.
- **Lock the meeting:** Once all invited participants are in the meeting, lock the session to prevent unauthorized individuals from joining.
- **Unique meeting links:** Avoid reusing the same meeting link for multiple sessions to minimize the chance of an old meeting link being used by someone unauthorized.
- **Limit screen sharing:** Restrict screen sharing to the host and designated presenters to prevent unauthorized sharing of sensitive content.
- **Disable private chat:** If possible, prevent participants from sending private messages to each other, as this can be exploited for malicious communication.
- **Keep software up to date:** Regularly update video conferencing software to ensure you have the latest security patches and fixes.
- **End-to-end encryption:** Ensure the video conferencing platform uses end-to-end encryption to protect the data during transmission and prevent unauthorized access.

3. What are the concerns with social engineering?

Social engineering is the manipulation of people into divulging confidential information or performing actions that compromise security. Common concerns include:

- **Phishing attacks:** Fraudulent emails, phone calls, or messages designed to trick individuals into sharing personal information, login credentials, or financial data.
- **Pretexting:** The attacker creates a fabricated scenario (a "pretext") to steal information, such as impersonating an IT support technician or company executive.
- **Baiting:** Offering something enticing (e.g., free software or a prize) to lure victims into performing actions that give the attacker access to systems or data.
- **Tailgating:** Gaining unauthorized physical access to secure areas by following authorized personnel without their knowledge or consent (e.g., entering a building behind someone without using a badge).

- **Impersonation:** Attackers pose as legitimate individuals (such as a colleague or superior) to gain access to sensitive information or systems, often via email, phone calls, or online communication.
- **Exploiting human emotions:** Many social engineering attacks prey on emotions such as urgency (e.g., "Your account has been compromised! Click this link to fix it now!") or fear (e.g., "Your account will be locked if you don't act immediately").

To defend against social engineering, it's essential to:

- **Educate employees** on common tactics used in social engineering attacks.
- **Verify information** through multiple channels (e.g., call the person directly if they ask for sensitive information via email).
- **Be skeptical** of unsolicited requests for sensitive information, especially those that create a sense of urgency.
- **Use strong authentication** methods, such as multi-factor authentication (MFA), to make it harder for attackers to gain access with stolen credentials.
- **Regularly train employees** to recognize red flags and implement phishing simulations to help them practice identifying these attacks.

By understanding and addressing these concerns, organizations can significantly reduce their vulnerability to cybersecurity threats in video conferencing and social engineering scenarios.

CHAPTER EIGHT
SECURING YOUR ACCOUNTS

Overview

This chapter focuses on ways to protect your accounts from cybercriminals and online threats.

Account Safety

People are often the weakest link in the cybersecurity chain, and it's important to recognize that you are usually your own biggest cybersecurity risk. Moreover, your family members can also pose a significant threat. While advanced technology and expertise are crucial for securing systems, it's equally important to acknowledge the limitations of human behavior. It's vital to understand that you are a potential target for cyber-attacks. Cybercriminals are determined to exploit vulnerabilities in your devices, online accounts, and any sensitive information they can find. Accepting this reality is crucial — even if you're already aware of the risks. People who understand the dangers of cyber threats often behave differently than those who remain unaware. A lack of skepticism can lead to serious consequences. Simply knowing that you're a target isn't enough; you need to truly internalize it to effectively protect yourself.

It's also important to ensure that your family members, including children, understand that they too could be targets, as their actions can have unintended consequences for your security. For example, there have been cases where attackers exploited remote work setups by targeting home networks used by children, which ultimately impacted employees working remotely. The risks posed by these types of attacks can be severe, particularly in today's world where remote work is common. Unlike straightforward data theft, these attacks are often designed to cause long-term damage, such as financial, political, or even military harm, benefiting the attacker while hurting the victim. The consequences of such breaches can be far-reaching, often more damaging than financial theft alone.

Ensuring the Safety of Your External Accounts

It is highly likely that computer systems operated by various corporations, organizations, and government agencies store information about every individual living in the Western world today. This data is spread across a variety of locations, including physical offices, shared data centers, and virtual servers rented from third-party vendors. Additionally, some data may be hosted on cloud platforms managed by external providers. It's important to recognize that the data — or any copies of it — may not necessarily be stored in the same country as the individuals to whom it pertains. This data is typically categorized based on specific characteristics of interest, which can vary widely.

To improve the security of this data, it can be useful to categorize it into the following groups:

- **User-established accounts and the data they contain**
- **Data related to organizations with which a user has knowingly and voluntarily interacted, but over which the user has no control**
- **Data held by organizations the user is unaware of or has no direct connection to**

Each of these categories requires a tailored strategy to address potential risks and ensure the appropriate level of protection.

Ensuring the Protection of User Account Data

When you engage in online activities like banking, shopping, social networking, or even basic web browsing, you inevitably share various types of data with the companies you interact with. By creating and maintaining accounts with banks, retailers, social media platforms, or other online services, you essentially entrust these entities with significant amounts of personal data. While you may have some control over the information you provide, you typically have little influence over the security measures in place to protect it, as the data is stored on their systems.

However, it's crucial to take proactive steps to safeguard your data without compromising the security protocols established by the companies hosting your accounts. While each situation and account may differ, there are certain measures you can implement to enhance the security of your data stored by third parties. Not all of the suggestions that follow will be applicable to every scenario, but by selecting the most relevant strategies and applying them across your various accounts and online activities, you can significantly improve your cybersecurity and reduce potential risks.

Engage in transactions with trustworthy individuals

Supporting local businesses is a commendable choice and should be encouraged. While it's true that many large corporations have experienced significant security breaches, it's important to remain cautious when encountering lesser-known businesses offering steep discounts, especially on high-tech gadgets. While some deals may be legitimate, others could be scams. Before making any purchases, take the time to thoroughly check the websites of the companies you're considering. If anything seems off or too good to be true, proceed with caution. Always trust your instincts and ensure the site appears trustworthy before sharing any personal or financial information.

Use official apps and websites

There have been instances of counterfeit versions of official apps being found in various app stores. When downloading banking, credit card, or shopping apps, it's essential to ensure you're getting the official version to avoid falling victim to malicious imitators. Always download apps from trusted sources like Google Play, the Apple App Store, or the Amazon Appstore to minimize the risk of downloading fraudulent or harmful apps.

Avoid installing software from untrusted sources

Malware has the ability to steal sensitive information from various programs and web sessions on an infected computer. Therefore, it's crucial to exercise caution when encountering websites that offer free downloads of movies, software, or other typically paid content. These offerings could be unauthorized or pirated, and it's important to question how the website operators are making money. In many cases, the revenue may come from distributing malware or other malicious activities, putting your security at risk. Always be wary of "free" content, especially when it seems too good to be true.

Avoid rooting your phone

If you have an Android phone, you might be tempted to root it for greater control over your device. While rooting can provide more customization options, it's important to be aware that it can also compromise your phone's security. Rooting may make your device more vulnerable to malware and other threats, potentially exposing sensitive information and increasing the risk of account breaches. Always weigh the benefits against the security risks before deciding to root your smartphone.

Avoid sharing unnecessary sensitive information

It's essential to be cautious when sharing personal information and only disclose it to those who genuinely need it. For example, avoid sharing your Social Security number with online stores or medical professionals unless it is absolutely required. Although it may be requested, it's often not necessary. By limiting the personal information you share, you can reduce the risk of data breaches and prevent your information from being aggregated in ways that could compromise your privacy and security.

Use payment services that eliminate the need to share credit card numbers

Payment systems like PayPal, Samsung Pay, Apple Pay, and similar services offer a secure way to make online payments without directly sharing your credit card information with retailers. If a vendor experiences a data breach, the risk of your account details being stolen and misused for identity theft is much lower compared to retailers that store actual credit card data. In addition, reputable payment providers employ dedicated teams of skilled cybersecurity professionals who work continuously to safeguard their systems — expertise that often surpasses the security capabilities of individual merchants.

Many businesses have also adopted Near-Field Communication (NFC) technology, which allows for quick, contactless payments. With NFC, you can make wireless payments by simply holding your phone near a payment terminal, offering a higher level of security than the traditional method of handing over a physical credit card. This method not only enhances cybersecurity but also reduces potential health risks associated with handling cash or credit cards that may carry germs.

Consider using one-time, virtual credit card numbers when it is suitable

Some financial institutions offer a feature that allows users to generate temporary virtual credit card numbers through an app or website. These virtual numbers can be used for online purchases, linked to your actual credit card account, but without exposing your real card number to the merchant. This adds an extra layer of security, reducing the risk of fraud and unauthorized transactions.

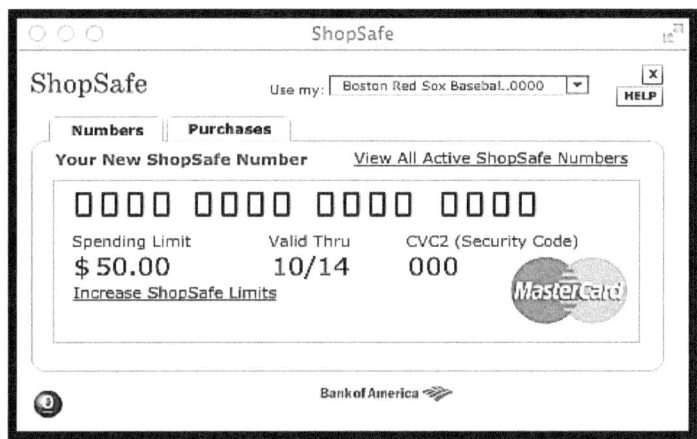

While generating one-time virtual credit card numbers may seem unnecessary, especially when dealing with trusted vendors that have strong security measures, these numbers provide vital protection against fraud. They are particularly useful when interacting with unfamiliar or new merchants. Beyond minimizing the risk of dealing with fraudulent suppliers, virtual credit card numbers offer additional security benefits.

For example, if a vendor is hacked and criminals gain access to your virtual card number, they won't be able to make any unauthorized charges. This added layer of security makes it more difficult for fraudsters to use your information. Furthermore, any attempts to misuse the virtual number could help law enforcement and forensic teams trace the breach, potentially identifying the source of the compromised data.

Keep a close eye on your accounts

Regularly monitor your payment, banking, shopping, and other financial accounts for any suspicious activity. Make it a habit to carefully review your online transaction logs and monthly statements, whether they're delivered electronically or in paper form. Pay close attention to any unauthorized charges or unfamiliar transactions, as early detection can help you address potential issues before they escalate.

Report any suspicious activity as soon as possible

Reporting fraud quickly to the appropriate authorities boosts the chances of reversing the damage and preventing further misuse of the involved resources. Additionally, prompt reporting increases the likelihood of identifying and apprehending those responsible. Timely reporting of fraud or any suspicious activity is essential to ensure a swift response and effective resolution.

Use a well-thought-out password strategy

While it's widely believed that complex passwords are necessary for all systems, this approach often proves ineffective in practice. It's important to adopt a robust password strategy that balances complexity with usability and security.

Use multi-factor authentication

Multi-factor authentication (MFA) requires users to verify their identity using at least two different methods. These methods typically fall into three categories:

- **Something the user knows** (e.g., a password or PIN)
- **Something the user has** (e.g., a fingerprint or hardware token)
- **Something the user is** (e.g., biometric data)

To enhance security, it is recommended to use authentication methods that go beyond just passwords, especially for systems that store sensitive information. Here's an overview of various authentication techniques:

- **Biometrics**: This method uses unique physical or behavioral characteristics to verify identity. Examples include fingerprints, facial recognition, iris scans, voiceprints, and even typing patterns.
- **Digital Certificates**: These certificates authenticate the identity of a user or device by linking a public key to its owner. The ability to decrypt messages encrypted with the public key proves that the user possesses the corresponding private key, which should only be held by the rightful owner.

- **One-Time Passwords (OTPs)**: These are temporary passwords used for a single session or transaction. OTPs can be generated by apps, provided through SMS, or retrieved from a list of codes.
- **Hardware Tokens**: Small electronic devices generate unique codes used for authentication. While smartphone apps can replicate some of these functions, hardware tokens are generally considered more secure, especially in high-risk environments, as smartphones are vulnerable to certain security threats that dedicated hardware tokens are not.
- **Knowledge-Based Authentication (KBA)**: This approach relies on answers to personal questions, like "What is your mother's maiden name?" However, it's important to note that KBA, when used alongside passwords, does not count as multi-factor authentication, since both are based on "what the user knows." For better security, it is essential to choose difficult-to-guess questions.

Using multi-factor authentication (MFA) is highly recommended, especially by financial institutions, social media platforms, and major online retailers. However, it's important to be aware that delivering OTPs via SMS may not be as secure as assumed. While SMS-based verification confirms that the user has access to a particular phone, this method can be vulnerable to attacks, such as SIM swapping or interception of text messages, potentially compromising security. Therefore, it is crucial to consider more secure alternatives where possible.

Remember to log out once you're done

Relying on automated timeouts, browser closures, or machine shutdowns to log out of accounts is not recommended. It's important to manually log out of your accounts every time you're finished using them. This ensures that your sessions are properly terminated, especially when using a device you trust for security. Always make it a habit to log out to protect your accounts from unauthorized access.

Use your personal computer or phone

Always consider the security of devices you don't control. For example, a computer could be infected with malware that compromises your passwords and sensitive information, or even hijacks your sessions to perform malicious actions. Additionally, some applications and websites store data on the devices used to access them, which can create serious security risks. To protect your privacy, make sure that your sessions don't leave behind any traces or sensitive data that could be accessed by others. Always take extra precautions to ensure that no information is left exposed after using a shared or potentially insecure device.

Lock your PC

It's essential to secure any computer used to access sensitive accounts. Always lock the computer when you're not using it, and ensure it remains physically secure to prevent unauthorized access. Taking these simple steps can significantly reduce the risk of your sensitive information being compromised.

Using a separate, dedicated computer for sensitive tasks

It's recommended to use a dedicated computer exclusively for online banking and other sensitive activities. Although having a second computer may not be feasible for everyone, there are distinct security advantages to reserving a separate device for tasks such as checking email, using social media, and web browsing.

Use a separate browser solely for tasks that require a higher level of security

If having a separate computer isn't an option, consider using a different browser for sensitive tasks. You can designate one browser for activities like reading the news, browsing social media, checking blog posts, and other routine online activities, while reserving another for more secure tasks.

Ensure the security of your access devices

It's essential to install security software on all devices that access secure networks. This software should be properly configured to perform regular scans of newly installed apps as well as periodic full system checks. Additionally, keeping the security software up to date is crucial, as antivirus programs are much more effective at defending against new types of malware when they are regularly updated.

Ensure that your devices are always kept up to date

Make sure to regularly update both your security software and your operating system, along with any program updates. This helps reduce the risk of exposure to vulnerabilities. Using tools like Windows AutoUpdate or similar features on other platforms can make keeping everything up to date much easier.

Avoid conducting sensitive tasks while connected to public Wi-Fi networks

It's recommended to perform sensitive tasks in a location with cellular network access rather than relying on public Wi-Fi. Public Wi-Fi poses a variety of security risks that can expose your data to potential threats.

Avoid using public Wi-Fi in high-risk locations

Avoid connecting devices used for sensitive tasks to Wi-Fi networks in locations known for cyber threats, such as areas with high hacking activity or those associated with virus distribution. High-risk environments include hacker conventions and countries with reputations for cyber espionage, like China. Many cybersecurity experts recommend powering off your primary computer and phone and using a separate set of devices when operating in these risky environments. This advice was frequently shared in the media leading up to the 2022 Winter Olympics in Beijing, with journalists and athletes discussing their strategies for mitigating potential security threats.

Make sure to access your accounts in secure locations

Exercise caution when using a private network, especially in public spaces. Avoid entering passwords or carrying out sensitive tasks where others may easily observe your actions.

Use suitable devices

When it comes to equipment, prioritize safety over cost. Avoid purchasing electronics from overseas sellers or using unbranded networking devices that lack certification from U.S. authorities, as these devices could potentially contain compromised hardware.

Establishing suitable boundaries

Many online platforms allow you to set transaction limits for added security. These limits can include the maximum amount that can be transferred from a bank account, the highest charge allowed on a credit card without physical use (such as for online purchases), or the maximum number of items that can be purchased in a single day.

Use alerts

It is highly recommended to take advantage of the text or email alert services offered by your bank, credit card provider, or preferred retailers. Ideally, receiving an alert for any activity on your account would be ideal. However, if constant notifications feel overwhelming and cause you to overlook important updates (which is common), you can set alerts for transactions above a certain dollar amount. This threshold can be customized for specific merchants, accounts, or any transactions that seem unusual to the issuer.

Regularly monitor access device lists

Many websites and apps, especially those linked to financial institutions, offer the option to see which devices have accessed your account. Checking this list regularly when you log in can help you quickly spot any potential security concerns.

Review the most recent login information

When you log in to certain websites and apps, especially those related to financial institutions, you may find a record of your previous login sessions, including details like time and location. It's a good practice to review this information whenever it's available. If there's any suspicious activity or an unauthorized login, it should be easy to spot.

Make sure to respond promptly to any fraud alerts

If you receive a call about potential fraud on your account from a bank, credit card company, or retailer, it's crucial to respond quickly. However, avoid discussing the matter with the caller directly. Instead, contact the organization yourself using a verified phone number from its official website to ensure you're speaking with the right person.

Avoid sending sensitive information over an unencrypted connection

When browsing websites, always look for the padlock icon in the address bar, which indicates the site is using encrypted HTTPS. HTTPS is now widely adopted, even by sites that don't require you to enter sensitive information. If the padlock is absent, the site is using unencrypted HTTP, which could pose a security risk. In such cases, avoid entering personal details or logging in. It's particularly concerning if a site that asks for a username and password or handles financial transactions lacks the padlock, as this could signal a potential problem. However, it's important to remember that the presence of a padlock doesn't guarantee complete security—it's just one indicator.

Be cautious of social engineering attacks

In cybersecurity, social engineering refers to the manipulation of individuals by cybercriminals who use psychological tactics to trick victims into taking actions or revealing personal information they normally wouldn't. Many data breaches occur as a result of successful social engineering attacks. It's essential to stay vigilant when interacting with any unsolicited communication, whether it's emails, text messages, phone calls, or social media messages, especially those claiming to be from banks, credit card companies, healthcare providers, retailers, or other entities. These may be fraudulent, so always proceed with caution. Avoid clicking on any links in such messages. Instead, directly visit the official website by typing the URL into your browser's address bar to ensure you're connecting with the legitimate organization.

Set up voice login passwords

Criminals can also gain unauthorized access to your accounts through methods beyond just online attacks. Some may conduct research online and then use this information to manipulate customer service representatives into granting access to your account. To improve security, it's recommended to set up a voice login password for your accounts. This unique password is required when interacting with customer service to access your account or make changes. While many companies offer this feature, it's surprising how few people actually take advantage of it.

Ensure the security of your cell phone number

For enhanced security, consider adding a forwarding phone number to your mobile device and using that number whenever you share your contact details. This adds an extra layer of protection to your strong authentication via SMS. By doing so, you significantly reduce the risk of hackers intercepting one-time passwords sent to your phone and minimize the chances of other attacks. For instance, services like Google Voice allow you to create a separate phone number that forwards calls to your mobile. This way, you can provide a different number for public use while keeping your actual mobile number private for authentication purposes.

Avoid clicking on links in emails or text messages

Links can easily mislead unsuspecting individuals to fraudulent websites, diverting them from their intended destination. Phishing emails and similar tactics are common examples of social engineering attacks designed to deceive users into visiting these malicious sites.

Ensuring the Security of Data Shared with Parties You've Interacted With

When engaging in online activities, it's important to remember that you don't have full control over the data associated with your actions. When you browse a website using default settings on your browser, that site can track your behavior. Due to content syndication, websites can also monitor your activities across different sites, especially those connected to advertising networks. To understand how this works, imagine two separate companies with their own websites, but both using the same advertising network. Each business embeds code on their site that loads ads from the network. When you visit the first site, the ad network may place a cookie on your device. Later, when you visit the second site, the ad network can read that cookie because both sites share the same network. Even if you haven't shared any personal information, websites that track and syndicate content can gather a lot of data about you, including your browsing habits. They can use this data to build a profile for marketing purposes. This can happen even if you don't have an account or log in, and your identity is not explicitly known. However, if you do log in to any of these sites later, the profiles they've created may be linked to your real identity.

Protecting data that belongs to others and is beyond your direct control can be more challenging than safeguarding information stored in your own accounts. However, this doesn't mean you are powerless. Interestingly, many data owners, such as companies, often do a better job of securing personal information than individuals do. If using Tor seems too complex, a reliable VPN service can offer similar benefits by protecting your online privacy. VPNs make it more difficult for websites to track your browsing behavior, reducing the chances of creating detailed profiles of you and minimizing the amount of sensitive data that could be exposed. Additionally, some websites may simply choose not to create profiles about you in the first place. While private browsing mode on most browsers can help limit tracking, it does not guarantee full privacy and has significant limitations compared to solutions like Tor or VPNs.

Securing Data at Parties You Haven't Interacted With

It's startling how much personal information organizations can gather about you, often without your knowledge or consent. For instance, some social networking platforms create profiles for individuals who haven't even registered for an account. These profiles are built from interactions such as comments made by others or your activities on websites that use social media widgets or similar tracking tools. These companies can then use these profiles for targeted marketing, sometimes without ever knowing your real identity or understanding the behind-the-scenes tracking taking place. Similarly, many data brokers compile information from a variety of public sources to create detailed profiles. These profiles may contain data you didn't realize was publicly accessible. Genealogy websites, for example, often collect and share public records, allowing users to update and add information about individuals. In some cases, people with trial memberships or regular users may gain access to private details about you without your consent, leading to potential privacy concerns. These platforms make it easier to discover sensitive data, such as your mother's maiden name or your birthday, which could compromise security measures used by banks or other institutions.

Beyond genealogy sites, other platforms, like professional networking sites, document and display your career history, publications, and other personal details. Credit bureaus also maintain extensive records on your financial history, which are supplied by banks, lenders, collection agencies, and others. While the Fair Credit Reporting Act regulates how these bureaus handle your credit information, it doesn't address how other sources, such as old news articles, may retain personal data about you. These articles can sometimes be used to answer security questions or challenge authentication measures, potentially exposing you to security risks. If you find personal information in such sources that you want removed, it may be worth contacting the organization holding the data to request deletion, though they may not always comply.

Additionally, certain companies, including insurance providers and pharmacies, maintain sensitive medical records, often without your direct oversight or control. These types of personal information, which may be outside your immediate influence, can still have significant consequences.

While businesses are responsible for safeguarding your data, they often fail to do so adequately. The Federal Trade Commission, for example, reported that in 2017, a massive data breach at Equifax exposed the personal information of 143 million Americans. When you're unable to directly update or request changes to these records, your options for protecting your data are limited.

Ensuring Data Security by Avoiding Connection with Hardware of Uncertain Origins

While technology has advanced significantly since the 1980s, the risks associated with connecting unknown or untrusted data storage devices to computers remain largely unchanged. For example, plugging in a USB drive that contains malware can easily infect your laptop or any other device it's connected to. The contents of an infected memory card can also pose serious cybersecurity threats to any system it is inserted into.

When you connect a hardware device to a computer via USB, the devices can communicate with one another. This is facilitated by Plug and Play, which allows for the automatic execution of specific code when a USB device is connected. However, if this code is compromised, it opens the door for hackers to gain access to the system. This same vulnerability exists with other USB devices, which could potentially expose your computer or network to various types of attacks.

The risks are not limited to data breaches alone. Certain USB devices are designed to draw power from the computer's USB port to charge themselves, storing energy in a capacitor. If the stored energy is suddenly released all at once, it can deliver a powerful surge that may permanently damage the connected electronics in less than a second. This kind of issue can arise with phone chargers and similar devices. Essentially, any USB-enabled device has the potential to interact with and potentially harm the computer or network it's connected to, especially if it overloads the system with excessive power.

Therefore, it's crucial to exercise caution when handling USB devices, chargers, and memory cards. Always ensure that you know the origin of any device before plugging it into your computer or network to avoid exposing yourself to unnecessary security risks.

Frequently Asked Questions

Ensuring the safety of your external accounts, protecting user account data, and securing accounts in general involves several best practices. Here's how you can address these concerns:

1. How do you ensure the safety of your external accounts?

- **Use Strong, Unique Passwords**: For each external account (email, social media, banking, etc.), use complex passwords that are difficult to guess. Avoid reusing passwords across different sites. A combination of uppercase and lowercase letters, numbers, and special characters is recommended.
- **Enable Two-Factor Authentication (2FA)**: Whenever possible, enable 2FA, which adds an additional layer of protection. This requires you to provide a second piece of information (like a code sent to your phone) when logging in, even if someone knows your password.
- **Monitor Account Activity**: Regularly check your account activity for any suspicious logins or changes. Many services offer security notifications or alerts that inform you of unusual activity, like logins from unknown locations.
- **Keep Your Software Up to Date**: Ensure that the apps and software you use for accessing these accounts (e.g., browsers, email clients, and apps) are up to date with the latest security patches.
- **Use a Password Manager**: A password manager can securely store and generate strong passwords for all your external accounts, helping you avoid password fatigue and reducing the chances of weak passwords.

2. How do you ensure the protection of user account data?

- **Encryption**: Always encrypt sensitive data, both in transit and at rest. Use HTTPS for secure browsing, and ensure that any data stored in databases is encrypted.
- **Access Controls**: Implement role-based access controls (RBAC) to ensure that only authorized personnel can access sensitive user data. Limit the scope of access to what's necessary for the task at hand.
- **Data Minimization**: Only collect and store the data necessary for your service, and ensure you have processes in place to securely delete any data that's no longer needed.
- **Regular Audits and Monitoring**: Regularly audit data access logs to ensure no unauthorized access has occurred. Monitoring systems can help flag suspicious activities related to account data.
- **User Education**: Educate users on how to protect their accounts (e.g., using strong passwords and recognizing phishing attempts) to reduce the risk of data exposure from social engineering attacks.

3. How do you secure your accounts generally?

- **Multi-Factor Authentication (MFA)**: Implement MFA on all critical accounts (including email, financial accounts, and cloud services). This can include something you know (password), something you have (a phone or token), or something you are (biometrics).
- **Regular Password Changes**: Encourage regular password updates, particularly for high-value accounts or in case of a potential breach. Use password policies to enforce this where necessary.
- **Security Questions and Recovery Options**: Be cautious with security questions and answers. Ensure the questions are not easily guessed, and regularly update recovery email addresses or phone numbers to ensure they are up to date.
- **Account Lockout Mechanisms**: Implement account lockout or rate-limiting mechanisms to prevent brute-force attacks. After several failed login attempts, the account should be temporarily locked to thwart further attempts.
- **Avoid Public Wi-Fi for Sensitive Access**: If you need to access your accounts while on the go, avoid using public Wi-Fi for transactions or logins. Use a VPN (Virtual Private Network) to secure your connection when accessing sensitive data over untrusted networks.
- **Use Antivirus and Anti-Malware Software**: Protect your devices with reputable antivirus software to detect and block malware that could compromise your accounts, such as keyloggers or phishing attempts.

By combining these strategies—strong passwords, multi-factor authentication, regular monitoring, and encryption—you can significantly reduce the risks associated with external accounts and improve the overall security of your user data and online activities.

CHAPTER NINE
COMPUTER SECURITY TECHNOLOGY

Overview

Chapter nine will cover the different types of computer security technologies.

Computer Security Technology Overview

Hackers commonly use a range of tools to launch attacks on networks or systems. These tools can also be employed to assess and identify potential vulnerabilities in a system or network. During the development and testing phases, these tools help evaluate system performance and uncover weaknesses. While hackers are often considered highly skilled IT professionals, compromising a private computer or network is typically more complex than designing one. The term "hacking" refers to unauthorized access to a system to steal sensitive data or damage computer systems and networks. Hackers possess a deep understanding of how systems function, how they are developed, and their architectural design, which allows them to bypass security measures and gain access to critical information. Hacking can also involve privacy breaches, illegal access to corporate data, internet fraud, and other forms of deception. Understanding the technologies used in hacking can provide valuable insights into network and system vulnerabilities, helping to better protect against such threats.

EtherPeek

This software is a highly efficient and compact tool, specifically designed for analyzing an MHNE (Multiprotocol Heterogeneous Network Environment). It works by analyzing data packets within the network, supporting a range of network protocols, including IP, IP ARP, AppleTalk, TCP, NetWare, UDP, NBT packets, and NetBEUI.

QualysGuard

This software package offers integrated solutions designed to enhance network security operations while reducing associated costs. The system comprises several modules that work in tandem to complete the entire testing process, starting with the initial phase of mapping and assessing attack surfaces to identify security vulnerabilities. It effectively manages, detects, and isolates global networks to strengthen network security. Additionally, the software provides valuable security intelligence and streamlines the auditing, monitoring, and protection of both network infrastructure and online applications.

SuperScan

SuperScan is an excellent tool for network administrators, designed to scan and analyze TCP ports and resolve hostnames. Its user-friendly interface makes it easy to navigate and highly intuitive. SuperScan performs the following functions: it scans a predefined list of ports or any custom range specified by the user, evaluates the responses received from networked hosts, conducts ping scans and port checks across multiple IP ranges, combines port lists to create new ones, and connects to any open or accessible ports.

WebInspect

This web-based security assessment tool is designed to help developers identify both known and unknown vulnerabilities within the web application layer. The system consists of multiple modules that collaborate to complete the entire testing process, starting with mapping and evaluating attack surfaces to uncover security weaknesses. The assessment includes analyzing web server configurations and testing for issues such as parameter injection, directory traversal, and cross-site scripting (XSS).

LC4

This program is commonly used in computer networks for password recovery and is often referred to as "L0phtCrack." Its primary function is to analyze password strength and recover Microsoft Windows passwords. The tool employs various techniques, including directory searches, hybrid attacks, and brute-force methods. The system is made up of several modules that work in unison to execute the complete testing process, starting with mapping and evaluating attack surfaces to identify potential security vulnerabilities.

NMAP

This tool, called "Network Mapper" (often referred to as Nmap), is a powerful open-source utility used for network discovery and auditing. It was primarily developed to scan enterprise networks, track network inventory, monitor network hosts, and manage network service schedules. Nmap helps answer key questions such as: What types of hosts are present on the network? What services do they provide? What is the operating system running on those hosts?

Metasploit

Metasploit is widely regarded for its powerful capabilities in the field of exploitation. It offers various versions, each with unique features. This versatile tool can be used through both the command line and a user-friendly web interface to perform a wide array of tasks. These include penetration testing for small businesses, exploring and analyzing network data, and testing exploits using its extensive library of exploit modules. It allows users to thoroughly assess and test vulnerabilities across network hosts.

Burp Suite

Burp Suite is widely regarded as one of the leading tools for conducting security tests on web applications. The platform consists of several modules that work together to carry out the full testing process, beginning with mapping and analyzing attack surfaces to identify potential security weaknesses. Its user-friendly interface allows administrators to easily navigate the system, and they have the option to perform manual tests using a variety of techniques to assess vulnerabilities.

Angry IP Scanner

This tool is designed to detect IP addresses and scan a broad range of ports across multiple platforms. It is readily available on the Internet. Using a multithreaded approach, administrators can efficiently scan large ranges of IP addresses by combining multiple scanners. The tool performs checks on individual IP addresses to identify open ports and potential vulnerabilities.

Frequently Asked Questions

1. What do you understand by computer security technology?

Computer security technology refers to the tools, systems, protocols, and methods designed to protect computer systems, networks, and data from unauthorized access, attacks, theft, or damage. These technologies are aimed at ensuring the confidentiality, integrity, and availability of information and resources, preventing cyber threats such as hacking, malware, and data breaches. Computer security technology involves both hardware and software components, and it is an essential part of IT infrastructure to safeguard against security risks in the digital world.

2. What are the different computer security technologies?

There are various computer security technologies that provide protection at different layers and aspects of computing. Some of the key technologies include:

1. **Encryption**: This technology uses algorithms to encode data so that it can only be read or decrypted by authorized parties. It helps protect sensitive information during transmission (e.g., SSL/TLS for secure web browsing) or when stored on devices.
2. **Firewalls**: Firewalls act as a barrier between a trusted internal network and untrusted external networks, such as the internet. They filter incoming and outgoing traffic based on predefined security rules to prevent unauthorized access.

3. **Intrusion Detection and Prevention Systems (IDS/IPS)**: These systems monitor network traffic for signs of malicious activity or security policy violations. An IDS alerts administrators to potential threats, while an IPS can actively block malicious actions.
4. **Antivirus and Anti-malware Software**: These tools detect, prevent, and remove malicious software (malware), including viruses, worms, ransomware, and spyware, protecting systems from known and emerging threats.
5. **Access Control Systems**: These technologies restrict access to resources based on user credentials, roles, and permissions. They ensure that only authorized users can access certain data or systems, often using mechanisms like multi-factor authentication (MFA), passwords, biometrics, or smart cards.
6. **Virtual Private Networks (VPNs)**: VPNs create a secure, encrypted connection over a public network (such as the internet) to protect data while it is being transmitted. VPNs are commonly used by remote workers to securely connect to an organization's internal network.
7. **Security Information and Event Management (SIEM)**: SIEM systems collect and analyze data from various sources, such as firewalls, IDS/IPS, and servers, to identify and respond to security incidents in real-time. They provide centralized monitoring and alerting.
8. **Data Loss Prevention (DLP)**: DLP technologies are used to monitor and prevent the unauthorized transfer or leakage of sensitive data outside the organization, ensuring that critical information is not exposed.
9. **Endpoint Security**: This includes the protection of devices such as desktops, laptops, smartphones, and servers from security threats. Endpoint security software typically includes antivirus, encryption, and device management tools.
10. **Identity and Access Management (IAM)**: IAM systems help manage users' digital identities and control access to resources across the network. This includes user authentication, authorization, and identity verification.
11. **Patch Management**: Keeping software up-to-date with the latest security patches is critical for protecting against known vulnerabilities. Patch management tools automate the process of detecting and installing security updates.
12. **Backup and Disaster Recovery**: Regular backups and disaster recovery technologies ensure that critical data can be restored in case of a security breach, hardware failure, or other catastrophic events.

These technologies work together to form a comprehensive defense strategy that helps safeguard systems, networks, and data from a variety of cyber threats.

CHAPTER TEN
CYBERSECURITY FOR BUSINESSES AND ORGANIZATIONS

Overview

In this chapter, you will discover how implementing cybersecurity can provide advantages to businesses and organizations, both in the present and in the near future.

Ensuring Effective Leadership

When managing a network with multiple users, the responsibility for computer security becomes more complex. It's essential that someone in the organization takes full accountability for information security. This person could be you, the business owner, or another designated individual, but they must fully understand the extent of their responsibilities. Many small businesses choose to outsource certain day-to-day security tasks, allowing the person in charge to focus on other critical aspects of cybersecurity. Regardless of this, the ultimate responsibility still lies with that individual to ensure essential actions—such as timely security updates—are carried out. In the event of a breach, claiming, "I thought so-and-so was handling that security task," is no longer a valid excuse. Unfortunately, this is a common defense, but it holds little weight when it comes to accountability.

Keeping an Eye on Employees

Small businesses often struggle with managing the cybersecurity risks posed by their employees. Human error is frequently a major cause of data breaches, making employee education a top priority for business owners. This education should focus on three key areas:

- **Recognizing Potential Risks**: Employees need to understand that both they and the organization are potential targets for cybercriminals. Those who acknowledge the threat of hackers trying to access their computers, phones, and data tend to exhibit more cautious behaviors. While formal, ongoing training is ideal, even a brief discussion at the start of employment, followed by periodic reminders, can be highly effective in raising awareness.
- **Foundational Information-Security Training**: Every employee should have a basic understanding of information security principles. This includes recognizing risky behaviors such as opening attachments or clicking on links in unsolicited emails, downloading files from unreliable sources, using public Wi-Fi inappropriately, or purchasing from unfamiliar online stores that offer unusually low prices and lack a physical address. While various online training resources are available, it's important to note that training alone isn't a

foolproof defense. Many people, even after receiving training, still make poor decisions, and training doesn't address the risk posed by employees who might intentionally undermine security.
- **Practical Experience**: Information security training should be interactive and hands-on. Employees should be given opportunities to practice what they've learned, such as identifying and responding to phishing attempts. This allows them to reinforce their knowledge and become more confident in handling real-world security challenges.

By prioritizing these components, small businesses can significantly reduce the risk of cybersecurity threats stemming from human errors.

Motivate your staff

It's important not only to address employees' mistakes but also to acknowledge and reward their efforts in maintaining a secure cyber environment and practicing good cyber hygiene. Positive reinforcement is generally more effective and better received than negative feedback. In addition, many organizations have successfully implemented reporting systems that allow employees to confidentially report suspicious activities or potential security threats, such as insider risks or system vulnerabilities. While such programs are common in larger companies, they can also be valuable for small businesses and other organizations, helping to foster a proactive security culture and enabling early detection of potential issues.

Be cautious about sharing sensitive information

There are numerous examples where employees' mistakes have allowed hackers to gain access to an organization's systems, as well as cases where disgruntled employees have stolen data or sabotaged systems. Such incidents can have catastrophic consequences, especially for small businesses. To protect your organization from these risks, it's essential to establish a robust information security infrastructure.

How can this be achieved? First, ensure that employees have access only to the systems and data necessary for them to perform their jobs effectively. At the same time, implement strong security controls to prevent unauthorized access to sensitive information. A key strategy is to restrict system access based on job roles. For instance, programmers should not have access to the company's payroll system, and accountants should not have permissions to the version control system that stores proprietary software code.

By carefully controlling access, you can significantly limit the potential scope of a data breach if an employee becomes compromised or untrustworthy. Many companies have learned this lesson the hard way through unfortunate security incidents. Don't let your business become one of them—take proactive steps to safeguard your systems and data.

Provide each individual with their own set of login credentials

Every employee should have unique login credentials for all systems used by the company. Sharing login details is strictly discouraged. This approach not only enhances the ability to audit actions in the event of a data breach or cybersecurity incident, but it also encourages employees to be more mindful of their passwords, knowing that any misuse will be promptly addressed by management. When employees understand they will be held accountable for their security practices, it can motivate them to adopt a more proactive approach to safeguarding their accounts. Additionally, it's crucial that every individual has access to multi-factor authentication (MFA), such as a physical token or a code generated on their smartphone, to further strengthen security.

Limit the access of administrators

System administrators often have superuser privileges, giving them the ability to view, modify, delete, and access data across the organization. As a result, it is crucial for business owners to implement controls that monitor administrators' actions, particularly when there are multiple superusers. One effective approach is to log administrator activities on a separate system that the administrators cannot access, providing an additional layer of oversight. Alternatively, restricting access to specific devices or locations can also help, although this may not always be feasible due to business needs. In such cases, an additional measure could involve installing surveillance cameras to monitor the administrator's activities on those systems, ensuring there is accountability and visibility into their actions.

Restrict access to corporate accounts

Your business likely manages multiple accounts, including social media profiles (e.g., Facebook, Instagram, Twitter), customer service, email, phone, and utility accounts. It's essential to limit access to these accounts to only those who truly need it, as discussed earlier. Moreover, every individual granted access must be traceable so you can easily identify who made changes or modifications to any account.

For platforms like Facebook, controlling access is straightforward. For example, you could manage the company's Facebook Page and invite others to contribute to it. However, granular control may not always be available, especially on social media platforms, so you may have to decide between giving multiple people direct access to a single account or having them submit content to one designated person (perhaps yourself), who then posts it.

When sensitive accounts require multi-factor authentication (MFA) for protection, managing access becomes more challenging. While MFA is a crucial security measure, it can complicate the process when multiple people need access to the same social media account. Some systems offer MFA with the ability for multiple users to have auditable access, but others may not integrate well into multi-user scenarios. For instance, MFA may allow a single phone number to receive one-time passwords (OTPs) via SMS, which could be shared across several users. In such cases, you'll need to weigh your options:

- **Use MFA with a workaround**: For example, you could use a VOIP number (such as Google Voice) to receive SMS OTPs and set up email forwarding so multiple parties can access the messages. This method is free and can be effective, but it's not ideal for every situation.
- **Stick with MFA without exceptions or workarounds**: Adjust the settings on users' devices so they don't bypass MFA. This ensures a higher level of security but may reduce convenience for users.
- **Choose a multi-factor authentication system that supports multiple users**: Some systems allow different users to authenticate separately using unique credentials while still accessing the same account. This provides security without the need for workarounds.
- **Use a shared MFA method**: Some systems allow users to authenticate separately, but still use the same one-time code generator, ensuring they generate identical OTPs simultaneously. This could be done with a shared device or a one-time code generator set with the same seed.
- **Skip MFA and rely only on strong passwords**: While this option may seem easier, it is not recommended as it significantly weakens your security.
- **Explore alternative solutions**: You might adjust your processes, procedures, or technologies to make access management more efficient and secure.
- **Incorporate third-party security solutions**: Many content management systems (CMS) are designed to handle multiple users with strong authentication and provide auditable access. This is a highly recommended approach, particularly for businesses that need to ensure transparency and security across multiple social media accounts. While larger companies often adopt this strategy due to security and administrative concerns, small businesses may opt for simpler, less secure methods.

Given that implementing third-party security products often involves minimal cost and effort, it's highly advisable to explore these solutions rather than relying on workarounds or weaker security measures. Investing in robust security now can save you from costly and potentially damaging breaches down the line. If you ever face a situation where an employee with access to your company's social media accounts is either disgruntled or compromised (e.g., through hacking), you will quickly realize how crucial it is to have strong, auditable security controls in place.

Implementing employee policies

Every business, regardless of its size, should have a comprehensive employee handbook that clearly defines the rules and regulations related to the use of company technology and data. Below are some essential guidelines to include:

- **Proper Use of Technology**: Employees are expected to use company-provided equipment, Internet access, and email systems for work-related tasks. Personal use is permitted, but it should not interfere with job responsibilities and must comply with company guidelines.
- **Maintenance of Company Equipment**: Employees are responsible for the upkeep of company-issued devices and software, and must take steps to prevent theft, loss, or damage. This includes safeguarding company accounts and ensuring that all access remains secure. Employees must also keep authentication materials, such as passwords, PINs, and hardware tokens, confidential and not share them with others.
- **Network Access Restrictions**: Employees are prohibited from connecting unauthorized networking equipment (e.g., routers, access points) to company networks unless specifically authorized by the CEO. Personal devices, including Internet of Things (IoT) devices, must not be connected to company networks unless permitted under the firm's Bring Your Own Device (BYOD) policy, which outlines specific conditions for using personal devices on the company's Guest network.
- **Security Software & Updates**: Security software must be active and operational on all company devices. Employees are not allowed to disable or tamper with security systems, and any issues must be reported to the IT department immediately. Employees must ensure their devices are regularly updated, including security software, operating systems, drivers, and applications. Auto-update features on company-issued smartphones must not be disabled.
- **Legal Compliance**: Employees must comply with all applicable laws—federal, state, and local—regardless of where they are or when they are working. Additionally, employees are prohibited from storing or transmitting copyrighted content that does not belong to the company unless written permission has been obtained from the copyright holder. Only properly licensed materials may be transmitted via company systems.
- **Prohibited Activities**: Sending unsolicited bulk emails (spamming) is strictly forbidden, as is using company resources for personal or non-business-related tasks, even if those actions are not illegal. This includes accessing or sharing inappropriate content such as explicit material, hate speech, libelous or discriminatory content, violent imagery, or any activity related to hacking. Employees working in roles that require handling such content (e.g., configuring email filters) are exempt from this restriction as long as it is necessary for their job duties.
- **Wi-Fi and Device Restrictions**: In certain countries, such as China or Russia, employees must obtain written approval from the CEO before using devices with Wi-Fi or cellular capabilities. Employees traveling to these locations will be provided with company loaner devices, and personal devices may not connect to any company network, including the Guest network.
- **Public Wi-Fi Usage**: When accessing public Wi-Fi with company devices, employees must follow the company's public Wi-Fi policy, which ideally restricts such usage except in exceptional circumstances. Employees are also required to back up their devices using

the company's approved backup system and must not use personal storage solutions (e.g., external hard drives or cloud storage) for work-related data.
- **Password Security**: All passwords must be unique to the systems they protect and should not be reused across different accounts. To strengthen password security, employees should use a combination of three or more words, at least one of which should not be found in the English dictionary. These words can be joined with numbers or special characters. Alternatively, passwords must meet the following criteria:
    o   At least eight characters long, including one uppercase letter
    o   At least one lowercase letter
    o   Include at least one number
    o   Exclude any words that appear in the English dictionary
    o   Avoid using names of family members, friends, or colleagues
- **Data Encryption**: Any data removed from the workplace for business purposes must be encrypted, whether it is stored on physical media (e.g., hard drives, USBs, DVDs) or transmitted online. Storing or transferring work-related documents to personal cloud storage accounts (e.g., Google Drive, Dropbox) is not authorized. All data must be returned or securely destroyed following remote use or termination of employment.
- **Communication During a Crisis**: In the event of a breach, cybersecurity incident, or any disaster (natural or man-made), only the company's designated spokesperson is authorized to communicate with the media on behalf of the business.
- **Prohibited Devices**: Devices flagged by U.S. federal agencies, such as the FBI or FCC, as potentially unsafe or involved in espionage, must never be connected to company networks or brought into company offices. Storing or processing company data on such devices is prohibited.

These policies are essential for ensuring that company technology and data remain secure, and that employees understand their responsibilities in safeguarding both. Clear, concise rules help mitigate risks and protect both the business and its employees from legal and security threats.

Implement and uphold social media policies

Having well-defined, effectively implemented, and strictly enforced social media policies is crucial for any business. Incorrect or careless posts, whether made by employees or management, can lead to significant harm, including reputational damage, legal penalties, and security risks. Mishandling social media could result in the exposure of sensitive information, violations of compliance laws, or give criminals an opportunity to exploit social engineering tactics to attack your business. The consequences may include boycotts, lawsuits, and other negative repercussions.

It's essential that all employees understand the boundaries of acceptable and inappropriate social media behavior. When developing these guidelines, seeking legal counsel is advisable to ensure compliance with freedom of expression laws and to avoid unintended legal risks. Additionally, businesses can leverage technology to help manage social media usage, ensuring it doesn't spiral into a marketing or security nightmare.

Keep track of employees

Companies should inform employees about their right to monitor technology usage, even if they do not intend to actively monitor. Clearly communicating this right is important to ensure that any evidence, particularly in cases of employee misconduct or illegal activities like data theft, remains admissible in legal proceedings. Educating employees about the potential for monitoring can also act as a deterrent, as it makes them aware that their actions may be observed.

Monitoring should be confined to company-issued devices and networks. The organization has the right to monitor and manage all electronic communications, data, and network activities conducted through its systems, whether employees are on-site or working remotely. This includes both company-owned and leased or licensed equipment, as well as any systems with usage rights granted to the business. Additionally, all forms of electronic communication—such as email, text messages, and voicemail—are considered official corporate records. These communications could be subject to legal discovery or disclosure requests from regulators or other authorities.

Managing a Remote Workforce

Although remote work is not a new concept, the COVID-19 pandemic in early 2020 significantly accelerated its adoption, leading to a dramatic increase in the number of people working from home. The pandemic became the primary catalyst for this shift, transforming the workplace landscape. What was once a time when most employees were confined to their office locations quickly evolved into a period where a large portion of the workforce was working entirely from home.

While many businesses have gradually resumed in-office work post-pandemic, a significant number of employees continue to work remotely, either full-time or part-time. Remote work during a global health crisis offers protection from invisible health risks and provides businesses with potential productivity gains and cost savings. However, this shift also introduces substantial cybersecurity risks. The need for remote workers to access sensitive company data and systems from unmonitored, uncontrolled environments presents unique challenges to safeguarding critical information and maintaining secure operations.

Use work devices and separate work networks

When employees use their personal devices to access company networks, systems, or data, it exposes the business to significant cybersecurity risks. These risks include potential malware infections, insecure data storage, unauthorized access by malicious actors, and a range of other security concerns. To mitigate these risks, it is strongly recommended that employees conduct remote work using company-issued devices. Ideally, access to company systems should be done through Internet connections and networking equipment provided and managed by the employer.

Personal devices should not be used to access company networks or systems. If employees must use their personal devices, employers should have the ability to remotely monitor or wipe these devices in case they are lost or stolen. However, in many cases, such control may not be feasible, so alternative security measures must be considered.

One way employers can enhance security is by providing employees with a dedicated network router. This device can be connected to the employee's home router, effectively segregating company equipment and data from the personal network traffic in the home. It is essential that employees refrain from connecting personal devices to company networks, but if this policy is not strictly enforced, it is vital to ensure that all devices connected to the employer's network have up-to-date security software.

Employers should also manage software installations and ensure that any required software is compatible with employees' devices. If technical issues arise due to company-required software, it is the employer's responsibility to address and resolve these problems. Additionally, employers should refrain from monitoring employees' activities on their personal devices, respecting their privacy while still ensuring the security of company systems.

Establish virtual private networks

A Virtual Private Network (VPN) offers significant security benefits for remote workers, particularly in protecting sensitive data. By encrypting the Internet connection, a VPN prevents unauthorized third parties from accessing the user's online activity and the content of their transmissions. It also safeguards the user's information from being read by others on the local network or by the Internet Service Provider (ISP).

When setting up a VPN for remote workers, connecting a separate network router to the business network via the VPN can be beneficial. This configuration, known as a **demilitarized zone (DMZ)**, creates a network that is not fully trusted by the company but is also not open to the public. It is particularly useful when remote workers need to access multiple company devices or when several employees are working from the same location.

For situations where a network-to-network VPN setup is not feasible—such as when only one remote employee is using a single device—a direct VPN connection between the employee's device and the company network may be appropriate. However, both types of VPN connections can present cybersecurity risks if not properly configured and managed. This is why it's crucial that the employer has the right expertise and resources to ensure the VPN is set up and maintained securely.

Even when using a VPN, it is strongly recommended that work devices be kept separate from personal devices by using different networks, particularly in remote locations. This separation helps reduce security risks, even if a VPN is not employed.

While consumer-grade VPN services are widely available, they may not be the best option for remote work. Unlike a secure VPN tunnel that connects the remote worker directly to the employer's network, these services first route traffic through the VPN provider's servers before reaching the destination. This introduces the risk of potentially insecure transmissions, as the data passes through an intermediary. Employees should avoid using these services to connect to their company's network. Allowing employees to use unsecured or consumer-level VPNs to access company systems can lead to serious cybersecurity issues and potentially catastrophic breaches.

Develop standardized communication protocols

When making decisions regarding remote work and virtual communication tools, security should be a top priority. It's essential to establish clear policies that protect sensitive information and maintain the integrity of virtual meetings. Some key security measures to implement include:

- **Password Protection for Video Calls**: Require that all video calls are secured with strong passwords. This adds an extra layer of protection against unauthorized access, ensuring only invited participants can join the meeting.
- **Use of Virtual Waiting Rooms**: Implement virtual "waiting rooms" to control who can enter the meeting. This allows the host to screen participants before granting access, preventing unwanted guests or intruders from joining the call.
- **Restrict Access to Authenticated Users**: Ensure that non-public meetings are only accessible to authenticated and signed-in users. By requiring attendees to log in, you can verify their identity and limit access to only those who are authorized to participate in the discussion.

By incorporating these configuration requirements into your virtual meeting policies, you can significantly reduce the risk of unauthorized access and protect sensitive company information during online communications.

Use a familiar network

When working from home, it's crucial to ensure that any wireless network you connect to is properly encrypted and secured with a strong Wi-Fi key, such as WPA2 or better. This is essential for protecting your communications and ensuring you're connecting to the correct access point or router.

One of the risks to be aware of is the potential for hackers to set up "evil twin" networks—malicious access points designed to mimic legitimate networks. If your device automatically connects to one of these fraudulent networks, especially if its signal is stronger, your data could be intercepted. By using strong Wi-Fi security, such as WPA2 encryption, you significantly reduce the likelihood of this happening, as it is highly unlikely that an attacker would have the correct encryption key to decrypt your traffic.

However, if an attacker were somehow able to obtain your Wi-Fi key, it would present much more serious security risks than just this one connection issue. Therefore, maintaining strong network encryption and being cautious about which networks you connect to is key to safeguarding your data and privacy.

Find out how backups are managed

A comprehensive backup strategy is essential for remote workers' computers and data, and it is the employer's responsibility to implement, monitor, and manage backups. Relying on employees to back up corporate data on their own is not advisable, as it introduces unnecessary risks. It's important to have a consistent, automated backup system in place that ensures all critical data is regularly saved and protected from loss.

In addition to technical considerations, working from home may present security challenges that are not as prevalent in a traditional office environment. These challenges are not only related to technology but also to the physical environment in which remote work takes place. For example, "shoulder surfing"—whereby unauthorized individuals view or overhear sensitive information—becomes a risk when employees work in public or shared spaces.

To mitigate this risk, remote employees should ideally work from secure, controlled environments, such as their homes, where access to sensitive information can be better managed. Working in public spaces like coffee shops, airports, libraries, parks, or restaurants should be avoided whenever possible. These locations increase the likelihood of sensitive information being seen or overheard, especially in the case of phone calls or video conferences.

Another concern is the possibility that family members or others in the household may unintentionally gain access to confidential information. To safeguard against this, companies should encourage employees to maintain strict physical privacy while working remotely. Solutions like **privacy screens** for laptops can help prevent others from viewing the contents of the screen, while **white noise machines** or background sound devices can create a barrier to help protect conversations from being overheard. These practices can contribute to creating a more secure work-from-home environment and protect sensitive business information from unauthorized access.

Remain highly cautious when it comes to social engineering tactics

Cybercriminals recognize that remote workers are prime targets due to the combination of technological vulnerabilities in home-office setups and the potential for exploiting human weaknesses. Unlike their office-based colleagues, remote workers often lack the immediate, in-person access to colleagues or IT support that can help verify suspicious requests or resolve uncertainties. This makes remote workers more susceptible to falling victim to phishing and other social engineering attacks.

Additionally, remote workers tend to have more flexible work schedules, often working outside of traditional office hours. While this flexibility can be advantageous, it also means that remote employees may not always have the same access to advanced security tools or resources that in-office employees do, particularly when it comes to protection against phishing scams or social engineering tactics.

As a result, remote workers are more vulnerable to falling for malicious communications, clicking on harmful links, or unknowingly complying with fraudulent requests. Cybercriminals often exploit the fact that remote workers are working alone, without immediate colleagues or security systems in place to catch suspicious activities.

Given these risks, it is crucial for remote workers to be extra vigilant about social engineering threats. They need to be educated about the tactics used by criminals—such as phishing emails, fraudulent phone calls, and fake messages—and understand how to recognize and respond to these attacks. Awareness and caution are essential to protecting both personal and company data when working remotely.

Exploring Cybersecurity Insurance

If you believe your company could face catastrophic losses or even collapse as a result of a cybersecurity breach, investing in cybersecurity insurance may be a worthwhile consideration—even if the cost seems prohibitive for many small businesses. However, it's important to remember that most cybersecurity insurance policies come with exclusions or limitations, so it's crucial to fully understand what is and isn't covered under the terms of the policy.

For instance, if your business suffers a significant breach and is forced to shut down, relying on insurance that only covers a minimal amount of expert data restoration (e.g., two hours of recovery time) may not provide sufficient support. Before purchasing a policy, thoroughly review the coverage details to ensure it addresses the scale of potential damages your company could face.

Insurers often require businesses to meet certain cybersecurity standards in order to qualify for coverage. These may include maintaining up-to-date security systems, employee training programs, and other preventative measures. If your company fails to meet these requirements and a breach occurs, the insurer might deny a claim, citing negligence or failure to adhere to the agreed-upon policy conditions. Therefore, it is essential to not only secure insurance but also ensure your business complies with the necessary cybersecurity protocols to avoid being left without support in the event of an attack.

Ensuring the security of employee data

Protecting sensitive employee information is crucial for the security and integrity of your business. Failure to adequately safeguard this data can lead to severe consequences for your organization, employees, and potentially even the public. Mishandling employee information can result in legal liabilities, regulatory penalties, and reputational damage.

For physical data storage, it's recommended to implement a double-locking system. This means storing paper files in a locked cabinet located in a secured room, with separate keys for each lock to enhance security. For electronic files, these should be stored in encrypted and password-protected folders, disks, or virtual drives to ensure confidentiality. While these measures are essential, they may not be sufficient in all cases, so it's wise to seek legal advice to ensure full compliance with data protection laws.

The consequences of failing to secure employee data can be dire. In the event of a data breach where a criminal gains access to confidential information, your business could face legal action from affected employees and former staff. Additionally, government regulators may impose hefty fines on your company for failing to comply with privacy regulations. The costs associated with remediation efforts often exceed what could have been spent on preventative measures. Furthermore, the negative press resulting from a data breach can severely damage your company's reputation and sales, possibly even leading to its downfall.

Certain types of employee information, such as personnel records, W2 forms, Social Security numbers, I-9 forms, home addresses and phone numbers, medical records (including COVID-19 test results and vaccination records), and family leave data, are particularly sensitive and private. As a best practice, if you're unsure about the sensitivity of certain information, it's always better to err on the side of caution and treat it as confidential.

PCI DSS

The **Payment Card Industry Data Security Standard (PCI DSS)** is a crucial set of guidelines designed to protect credit card information and secure payment transactions. Businesses that store, process, or transmit credit card data are required to comply with these standards to ensure that sensitive information is protected from cyber threats, fraud, and breaches.

PCI DSS compliance is not only about adhering to security best practices but also about maintaining customer trust and avoiding costly penalties. Compliance levels are based on the number of credit card transactions a business processes annually and the associated risks. The standards and requirements vary depending on the volume of transactions handled.

The Four PCI Compliance Levels:

1. **PCI Level 4:**
   - **Criteria**: Businesses processing **fewer than 20,000 credit card transactions** per year.
   - **Requirements**: These businesses typically must complete a self-assessment questionnaire and may be subject to annual scans by an Approved Scanning Vendor (ASV).
2. **PCI Level 3:**
   - **Criteria**: Businesses processing between **20,000 to 1,000,000 credit card transactions** annually.
   - **Requirements**: This level may require businesses to submit an annual self-assessment report, along with quarterly vulnerability scans by an ASV.
3. **PCI Level 2:**
   - **Criteria**: Businesses processing **1,000,000 to 6,000,000 credit card transactions** per year.
   - **Requirements**: Businesses at this level typically must submit a self-assessment questionnaire and, in some cases, undergo an on-site assessment by a Qualified Security Assessor (QSA).
4. **PCI Level 1:**
   - **Criteria**: Businesses processing **over 6,000,000 credit card transactions** annually.
   - **Requirements**: This level has the most stringent requirements, including an annual on-site assessment by a QSA and quarterly vulnerability scans by an ASV. The company must also submit an annual Report on Compliance (ROC).

Key Requirements Under PCI DSS:

Regardless of your business's PCI compliance level, here are the fundamental requirements of the PCI DSS standard:

1. **Protect Cardholder Data:**
   - Use strong encryption and masking techniques to protect credit card data both in transit and at rest.
2. **Maintain a Secure Network:**
   - Ensure that firewalls, routers, and other network protections are in place to protect cardholder data.
3. **Access Control:**

- Restrict access to cardholder data to authorized personnel only, and use multi-factor authentication for sensitive systems.
4. **Monitor and Test Networks:**
    - Regularly test and monitor networks to identify vulnerabilities and ensure security measures are effective.
5. **Maintain an Information Security Policy:**
    - Have a documented security policy that covers security procedures, risk management, and training for all staff.

Steps to Achieve PCI DSS Compliance:

1. **Determine Your PCI Compliance Level:**
    - Assess how many credit card transactions you process each year and determine which level of compliance applies to your business.
2. **Understand the Requirements:**
    - Based on your compliance level, familiarize yourself with the specific requirements, including completing self-assessments, submitting security scans, or undergoing an on-site audit.
3. **Engage a PCI DSS Expert or Consultant:**
    - For small businesses, consulting with a PCI DSS expert can help ensure you meet all the necessary compliance requirements. Credit card processors often have relationships with compliance consultants who can assist.
4. **Implement Security Measures:**
    - Once you've understood the requirements, implement the necessary security measures to safeguard cardholder data, such as encryption, firewalls, secure access control, and regular vulnerability scans.
5. **Maintain Compliance:**
    - PCI DSS compliance is an ongoing process. Businesses must continue to meet security standards, conduct regular vulnerability scans, and review their compliance status annually to avoid penalties.

Why PCI Compliance Is Important:

- **Avoid Penalties and Fines:** Non-compliance with PCI DSS can result in substantial fines from credit card processors and banks.
- **Protect Customers and Build Trust:** Ensuring the security of credit card data helps build trust with customers and prevents fraud and identity theft.
- **Minimize the Risk of Breaches:** Compliance significantly reduces the likelihood of data breaches that could expose sensitive information, leading to financial loss, legal liabilities, and reputational damage.
- **Secure Payment Processes:** Compliant businesses benefit from stronger, more secure payment systems that protect both the organization and its customers.

If your business processes or stores credit card data, it is critical to understand your PCI compliance requirements and take appropriate action to ensure you meet the necessary standards. In many cases, credit card processors or payment service providers can offer advice or resources to help you achieve and maintain compliance.

Laws regarding the disclosure of breaches

Several jurisdictions have recently introduced breach disclosure requirements that mandate companies to publicly report any suspected data breaches that could have compromised certain types of sensitive information. These regulations can vary significantly depending on the country. Surprisingly, small businesses may also be subject to these rules under certain circumstances. It's essential to have a clear understanding of the laws that apply to your organization, so that in the event of a breach, you are not penalized for mishandling the situation. Keep in mind that many small businesses struggle or fail after experiencing a breach. Government involvement in these cases can greatly impact your company's chances of recovery following a successful cyberattack. The relevant laws may not only pertain to the jurisdiction where your business is located but also to the regions where the individuals whose data you manage are based.

GDPR

The General Data Protection Regulation (GDPR) is a sweeping European privacy law that took effect in 2018, fundamentally reshaping how businesses around the world handle the personal data of European Union (EU) residents. The regulation mandates that any business—regardless of size, industry, or location—that processes the personal data of individuals within the EU must comply with strict data protection standards. Importantly, this obligation applies even if the EU resident is outside the EU at the time the data is processed, meaning the reach of GDPR extends well beyond European borders.

For businesses, particularly those based in places like New York that engage in e-commerce with EU residents, GDPR compliance is not optional. The regulation imposes severe penalties for non-compliance, with violators facing hefty fines. The high-profile fines against British Airways and Marriott by the UK's Information Commissioner's Office (ICO) in 2019 underscore the regulation's robust enforcement. British Airways was fined around $230 million, while Marriott faced a penalty of approximately $123 million, both for data breaches that exposed the personal information of millions. These cases highlight the GDPR's strong commitment to holding businesses accountable for protecting consumer data.

Given the complexities of the GDPR, it is crucial for businesses that may be subject to its jurisdiction to seek expert legal counsel. A lawyer with expertise in GDPR can provide essential guidance on how to achieve compliance, helping businesses avoid costly legal consequences and fines. While some small businesses in the U.S. may feel that the risk of enforcement is low—

particularly if they do not have a physical presence in Europe—it's important to understand that GDPR enforcement is not restricted by a company's location.

There is a tendency among some small U.S. businesses to downplay the urgency of GDPR compliance, particularly since EU enforcement has thus far focused more on larger, more prominent companies. However, this attitude could lead to complacency. Although EU enforcement agencies have limited resources and may prioritize large corporations or those with operations in Europe, smaller businesses are not exempt from scrutiny.

As privacy rights gain global attention and regulatory landscapes continue to evolve, U.S. small businesses could eventually face enforcement actions under the GDPR. Even if immediate compliance is not actively enforced, it remains a prudent strategy for small businesses to understand and prepare for GDPR requirements. By doing so, they can avoid potential legal challenges and demonstrate a commitment to safeguarding the personal data of their customers, a practice that is becoming increasingly critical in today's global economy.

HIPAA

Protecting individuals' medical information is a critical priority under U.S. federal law. Entities that handle healthcare data are obligated to safeguard it appropriately. The Health Insurance Portability and Accountability Act (HIPAA), enacted in 1996, establishes strict penalties for the improper handling of such data. It is essential to assess whether HIPAA applies to your organization and, if it does, ensure that you are securely managing the data in compliance with industry standards or more stringent requirements. Many countries and regions have laws similar to HIPAA to protect personal health information.

Biometric data

If you use any forms of biometric authentication or store biometric data for any reason, you may be required to comply with privacy and security laws that govern such data. Several states have already passed laws on this matter, and it is expected that more will do the same.

Laws regarding the prevention of money laundering

Anti-money laundering (AML) laws are designed to prevent criminals from disguising illegally obtained money as legitimate earnings. Individuals involved in cryptocurrency transactions must understand and follow these laws, even if they are not part of traditional financial institutions. By doing so, they help ensure that their dealings with unfamiliar parties remain within the confines of the law.

Global restrictions

Paying ransomware ransoms can present legal challenges, particularly if the recipients of the payments are subject to penalties, as any financial transactions with them could be considered a federal crime. While individuals who have paid ransoms have not yet been penalized by the US government for violating these laws, there are signs that leniency toward such violations may be decreasing.

Managing Internet Access

Small businesses face distinct challenges when it comes to internet access and information systems, making it essential for them to take proactive steps to protect against potential risks.

Separate Internet access for personal devices

It's a good idea to establish a separate network for internet access at your business location. This helps keep your primary business network secure and isolated from potential risks. Many modern routers offer this capability, often referred to as a "Guest network," which can be easily set up through the router's configuration settings.

Implement policies for employees to bring their own devices (BYOD)

It's important to establish clear standards and implement appropriate technologies to protect company data when employees use personal computers or mobile devices for work. Relying solely on policies is not enough. Without proper rules and technological safeguards, small businesses risk catastrophic data loss due to employee mistakes or malicious actions. While the convenience of a Bring Your Own Device (BYOD) policy might seem appealing, it's best for small businesses to avoid it. In many cases, businesses fail to secure data effectively when employees use their personal devices for work. This can lead to complications, especially when an employee leaves the company, particularly under less-than-ideal circumstances.

One specific concern is that certain devices, such as Android phones, can track typing activity. While this feature can improve things like spelling and word prediction, it poses a risk that sensitive company data might be retained in the device's memory, even after an employee departs.

If a BYOD policy is implemented, it's essential to have clear procedures in place to manage and protect business data. This includes setting standards for the use and decommissioning of work-related technology on personal devices, as well as procedures for securely erasing company data when an employee leaves.

A comprehensive mobile device security plan should cover the following:

- Remote wipe capabilities to erase company data remotely if needed
- Strict password protection requirements
- Safeguarding sensitive data through encryption or secure storage methods (e.g., sandboxing)
- Installation and regular updating of mobile security software
- Prohibiting the use of public Wi-Fi for work-related activities that involve sensitive information
- Restricting access to sensitive systems and data based on device security status

By taking these steps, businesses can significantly reduce the risks associated with employees using personal devices for work.

Ensure efficient management of inbound access

The internet treats individuals and businesses differently when it comes to the need for granting inbound access to untrusted parties. For businesses, it's essential to allow external parties to connect with internal systems. For example, if a company wants to sell products online, it must enable untrusted visitors to access its website and make transactions. These visitors, regardless of their trustworthiness, must interact with systems like payment processors and internal order tracking.

In contrast, individuals typically aren't required to provide any inbound access to their personal devices or networks. This creates a significant difference between businesses and individuals regarding the need for incoming connections.

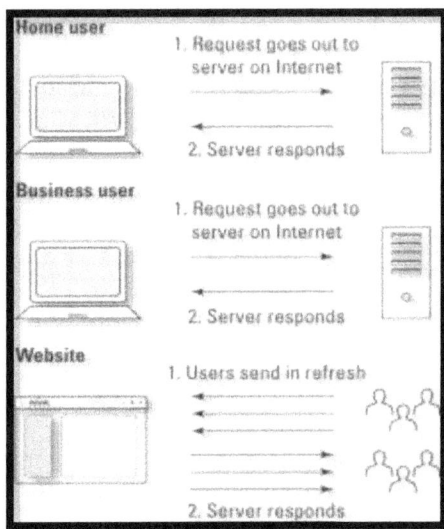

While small businesses can secure their web and email servers, the reality is that very few have the resources or expertise to do so effectively—unless they specialize in cybersecurity. Therefore, small businesses should consider leveraging third-party software and infrastructure, managed by experts, to host any systems that require inbound access.

Here are a few options small businesses can consider:

1. **Sell through a Major Retailer's Website**: If your business primarily sells through established platforms like Amazon, Rakuten, or eBay, these sites provide a strong security layer between your company's internal systems and external threats. Their security teams work to protect customer-facing systems from attacks. Additionally, this model reduces your exposure to incoming messages from the general public, as any communications will typically come through the retailer's systems. However, it's important to weigh the security benefits against the high fees these platforms often charge.
2. **Use a Third-Party Hosted Retail Platform**: With this approach, a third-party service manages most of the infrastructure and security, allowing you to focus on customizing and managing your online store. While this method may not isolate your business entirely from external threats, it still offers better protection against attacks compared to hosting and securing your own platform. Shopify, for example, is a widely used third-party platform that provides these services.
3. **Use a Platform Operated and Secured by a Third Party**: This option offers enhanced security compared to self-managed platforms. The third-party provider is responsible for securing the infrastructure, but you'll still need to manage your online store's content and some aspects of security. This model offers a good balance between convenience and protection, although it doesn't entirely shield your business from potential external threats.
4. **Host Internally or Externally with Managed Security Services**: If you choose to host your systems either in-house or with an external provider, you can enlist a managed services provider (MSP) to handle security. However, it's crucial to understand that you remain fully responsible for the security of the platform and infrastructure. The MSP will take care of key security functions, but the overall responsibility for securing your business rests with you.

In all cases, small businesses should carefully assess the security risks, costs, and benefits of each approach, balancing the need for protection with the resources available to manage and maintain those systems.

Defend your system from denial-of-service attacks

It's essential to implement security measures to protect your internet-facing sites from potential denial-of-service (DoS) attacks. If you're selling through a major retailer, they likely already have these protections in place. Similarly, if you're using a third-party cloud platform, the provider may offer built-in DoS protection. However, if you're managing the site independently, securing your own protection is crucial to prevent disruptions that could negatively impact your site and business. There are several companies that specialize in providing this type of security to help mitigate the risk of such attacks.

Consider using HTTPS

For businesses with websites, it's essential to have a valid TLS/SSL certificate installed. This ensures that communication between users and your site is encrypted, safeguarding sensitive data, and provides users with confidence that the site is legitimately owned by your business. Many security systems designed to protect against DoS attacks often include a TLS/SSL certificate as part of their package, offering both security and authentication in one solution.

VPN

When it comes to remote access, your VPN should create a secure tunnel between remote users and your business, rather than between users and a VPN provider. This tunnel ensures that communications are encrypted and secure, allowing remote users to access business resources as if they were physically in the office, while keeping sensitive data safe from external threats.

Conduct penetration tests

Many individuals and small businesses overlook testing their systems for vulnerabilities to hackers. However, conducting these tests can be highly beneficial, especially when introducing a new system or upgrading network infrastructure. Identifying potential weaknesses before they can be exploited is a crucial step in strengthening security.

Exercise caution when using IoT devices

Many businesses today rely on connected devices such as cameras, alarms, and other security systems. It's crucial to designate someone to oversee the security of these devices. Additionally, these devices should operate on separate networks or virtual segments, distinct from those used by business computers and operations. Implement strict access controls for these devices, and prohibit employees from connecting unauthorized IoT devices to the company network. When purchasing IoT devices, always choose products from reputable vendors. For instance, opting for the cheapest connected cameras available online without considering the manufacturer's reputation or the device's origin could expose your business to significant security risks.

Use multiple network segments

Depending on the size and nature of your business, it may be a good idea to segment individual PCs into separate network segments. For example, a software development company should have distinct networks for developers and operational staff. This separation ensures that sensitive processes like payroll and accounts payable don't interfere with the coding or development environment. The same principle applies to remote workers. It's essential to keep personal and professional networks separate, ensuring that work-related activities are isolated from personal use, thus minimizing potential security risks.

Exercise caution when using payment cards

If your business accepts credit and/or debit cards and you're not selling through a major retailer's website, it's important to have a conversation with your payment processor about the various anti-fraud technology options available to you. These tools can help protect your business from fraudulent transactions and minimize the risk of chargebacks or data breaches. Be sure to explore solutions such as address verification systems (AVS), 3D Secure, and other fraud detection services that can enhance the security of your payment processing.

Addressing Power Problems

It is highly recommended to use an uninterruptible power supply (UPS) for systems that need to run continuously without interruption. Be sure to test the UPS to ensure it can handle the total load of all connected devices without being overwhelmed. Additionally, the UPS should be capable of powering your systems for a sufficient amount of time to cover any potential power outages. For businesses that offer products and services through online shopping, even a brief period of downtime can severely impact your ability to make sales. This can lead to immediate revenue losses and long-term damage to your reputation.

Frequently Asked Questions

1. How do you think businesses and organizations should keep off cyber criminals?

To keep cybercriminals at bay, businesses and organizations should take a proactive, multi-layered approach to cybersecurity. This includes:

- **Implementing Strong Access Controls**: Ensure that only authorized personnel can access sensitive information or systems. Use multi-factor authentication (MFA), strong passwords, and role-based access controls.
- **Regularly Updating Software**: Keep all software, operating systems, and security tools up to date with the latest patches to close any vulnerabilities that cybercriminals could exploit.

- **Employee Training and Awareness**: Educate employees about common cyber threats such as phishing, social engineering, and malware. Conduct regular security awareness training and simulated phishing campaigns to help employees recognize and avoid potential threats.
- **Network Segmentation and Firewalls**: Use network segmentation to isolate sensitive data and limit the spread of potential breaches. Implement firewalls and intrusion detection systems (IDS) to block unauthorized access.
- **Endpoint Protection**: Secure all devices connected to the network, including laptops, desktops, mobile phones, and IoT devices, with antivirus software, encryption, and device management tools.
- **Regular Backups**: Implement regular data backups and ensure that backup systems are secure and tested. In case of ransomware or other attacks, having secure backups allows the business to recover without paying a ransom.
- **Incident Response Plan**: Develop and test an incident response plan so that if an attack occurs, the business can respond quickly and minimize damage.
- **Security Audits and Penetration Testing**: Regularly assess the security of your systems through audits and penetration testing to identify weaknesses before attackers do.

2. What do you understand by cybersecurity insurance?

Cybersecurity insurance, also known as cyber insurance, is a type of insurance designed to protect businesses from the financial losses associated with cyberattacks and data breaches. This insurance typically covers:

- **Data Breaches**: Costs related to breach notification, credit monitoring for affected customers, and legal fees.
- **Ransomware Attacks**: Costs associated with paying ransom (in some cases), recovery, and business interruption caused by the attack.
- **Business Interruption**: Losses caused by a cyberattack that causes downtime or disrupts business operations.
- **Legal and Regulatory Fees**: Costs for compliance with privacy laws and regulations, including potential fines and penalties.
- **Forensic Investigation**: Expenses related to investigating the breach, including hiring experts to determine the scope of the attack and how it happened.
- **Public Relations and Reputation Management**: Expenses for managing the public fallout from a breach, including hiring PR firms to handle media relations and minimize brand damage.

Cybersecurity insurance can help mitigate the financial impact of a cyberattack, but it's important to note that it does not replace the need for strong cybersecurity practices—it's a safety net, not a substitute for prevention.

3. How do you manage internet access in cybersecurity?

Managing internet access in cybersecurity involves several strategies to ensure that only authorized users and systems can connect to the network while minimizing potential vulnerabilities. Key practices include:

- **Firewalls**: Use firewalls to filter incoming and outgoing traffic, allowing only authorized traffic to access internal systems while blocking malicious traffic.
- **Access Controls**: Implement role-based access control (RBAC) and least privilege principles to ensure that users only have access to the resources they need. Use strong authentication methods such as multi-factor authentication (MFA) to prevent unauthorized access.
- **Network Segmentation**: Divide the network into separate segments to isolate sensitive data and limit the impact of a potential breach. For example, separating financial systems from other operational systems or isolating guest Wi-Fi networks from internal business networks.
- **VPNs for Remote Access**: Use Virtual Private Networks (VPNs) to secure remote access to the network. VPNs encrypt traffic, ensuring that data transmitted between remote users and the business network remains secure.
- **DNS Filtering**: Use Domain Name System (DNS) filtering to block access to known malicious websites or suspicious domains. This helps prevent users from accessing harmful sites and reduces the risk of malware infections.
- **Proxy Servers**: Use proxy servers to manage and monitor internet traffic, allowing businesses to filter and control the websites that employees can access, while also logging activities for auditing purposes.
- **Bandwidth Management**: Implement measures to control and monitor internet bandwidth usage to ensure that the network isn't overwhelmed by excessive traffic, particularly in the case of DoS (Denial-of-Service) or DDoS (Distributed Denial-of-Service) attacks.
- **Monitoring and Logging**: Continuously monitor internet traffic and log all access to network resources. Use intrusion detection/prevention systems (IDS/IPS) to detect and block malicious activities in real-time.
- **Secure Wi-Fi Networks**: Ensure that Wi-Fi networks are secured with strong encryption protocols (e.g., WPA3) and require authentication to prevent unauthorized devices from connecting.

By managing internet access effectively, businesses can minimize the risk of cyberattacks and ensure that only legitimate, authorized traffic can interact with their systems.

CHAPTER ELEVEN
Wireless Network Pirating

When it comes to defending against black hat attacks, wireless internet introduces a unique set of challenges for users. The main difference between wireless and wired networks is that wireless networks are, well, wireless. Rather than transmitting data through physical cables, wireless networks use radio waves to send information between devices. As Phil Collins' 1981 song suggests, the data is "in the air tonight."

But humor aside, the wireless internet can be much more vulnerable to attacks than wired networks. One key reason is that wireless networks lack the physical isolation that serves as a primary defense in wired networks. For instance, securing a wired network can be as simple as locking the doors to a building to prevent unauthorized access. Unfortunately, this tactic doesn't work for wireless networks, since the signals from wireless devices can pass through walls and other barriers, making them detectable from the outside.

In this guide, we'll explain how wireless networks function and what makes them unique. After covering the basic principles of wireless communication, we'll explore how attackers take advantage of these features to breach networks and steal sensitive data. Lastly, we'll discuss several important security measures you can use to protect your wireless network, whether you're at home or in the office. As part of the activity, you'll learn how to secure a typical wireless router.

How Wireless Networks Work

Wireless networks do not rely on physical cables to transmit data. Instead, devices use antennas to emit and receive wireless signals. These antennas can be external, sticking out from the device like "alien ears," or internal, as seen in many laptops and smartphones. Modern wireless devices typically employ multiple antennas to improve signal strength and increase the amount of data they can handle simultaneously.

In a wireless network, devices communicate with a central unit called a **Wireless Access Point (WAP)**, which is often your router or a switch. The WAP manages the data flow between devices, either sending the signal to another wireless device or forwarding it to a wired network.

There are two primary configurations for wireless networks:

1. **Infrastructure mode** – In this setup, the WAP acts as both a router and a switch, providing internet access to the entire network. In some cases, WAPs may lack full routing or

advanced switching capabilities, simply passing data between the wireless and wired networks.
2. **Ad-hoc mode** – This configuration does not require a central WAP. Instead, devices communicate directly with one another over wireless signals. Each device establishes a direct connection to the other device it's linked with. A common example of an ad-hoc network is Bluetooth, which is used for short-range communication, such as connecting a phone to a car's stereo system to play music.

The first diagram typically illustrates how each of these network configurations is set up.

Devices in a wireless network can identify and distinguish different networks by the **Service Set Identifier (SSID)**, a unique name associated with each WAP. The SSID is essentially the "name" of the wireless network, and it's what you see when you connect your device to a network. Most WAPs broadcast their SSID, making it visible to any device looking for a wireless connection. However, some WAPs may choose to hide their SSID, requiring users to know the specific ID in order to join the network.

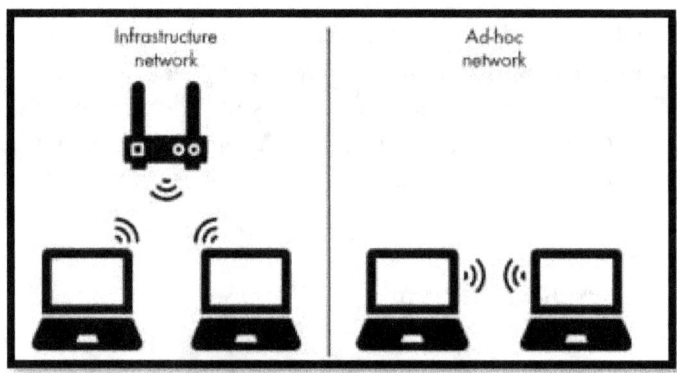

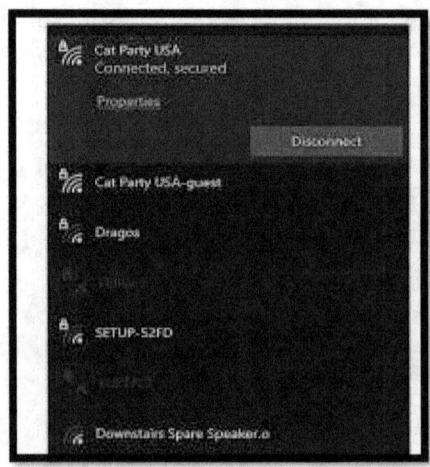

Once you've selected a wireless network, your device connects to it through a process called **affiliation**. Typically, a device like a laptop or smartphone can only be connected to one network at a time, whereas a **Wireless Access Point (WAP)** can handle multiple devices simultaneously. The WAP manages traffic between all connected devices, ensuring that each one gets its fair share of the signal without causing interference with the others.

Modern wireless networks are capable of supporting many connected devices. However, as the number of devices increases, the network may become congested, resulting in slower speeds or even dropped connections. Because of this, it's important to consider your network usage before setting up your WAP. In a small home, one central access point is usually sufficient to handle the traffic. In larger environments, like office buildings or expansive areas, multiple access points may be necessary to distribute the load and ensure no single device or access point becomes overloaded.

Using multiple access points, however, can create challenges, especially if a device struggles to seamlessly switch between different networks when moving through the area. This issue can be resolved by setting up a **mesh network**. A mesh network links several WAPs together to create a unified, large wireless network with a single SSID. This allows devices to roam freely between access points without losing their connection, as long as they stay within the mesh network's coverage area.

Wireless Standards

The widespread success of wireless technology is largely due to the development of universally accepted standards that enable devices to communicate seamlessly with each other. **Interoperability** in this context means that a wireless-enabled device can easily connect with almost any other wireless device, regardless of the manufacturer. This is a key achievement of the **Wi-Fi Alliance**, which plays a major role in promoting wireless standards. Essentially, if a device meets specific criteria, it can be labeled as "Wi-Fi enabled."

One of the most common and widely adopted standards in the industry is **IEEE 802.11**, a standard set by the **Institute of Electrical and Electronics Engineers (IEEE)**. The number "802.11" refers specifically to the category of standards for wireless local area networks (WLANs), and over time, it has become synonymous with wireless technology itself. You've likely encountered the term before, whether on a router or another wireless device.

As wireless technology has evolved, new substandards were introduced to address different types of wireless networks. The first significant substandards were **802.11a** and **802.11b**, which differed in the radio frequencies they used for data transmission. **802.11a** operates on the 5 GHz spectrum, offering faster speeds but shorter range, while **802.11b** uses the 2.4 GHz band, which provides greater range but slower speeds. Today, these differences are less important, as most modern devices support both frequency bands.

Subsequent standards brought improvements in performance. **802.11g** built upon **802.11b**, delivering faster speeds and a stronger signal. Then, **802.11n** introduced a breakthrough technology called **Multiple-Input Multiple-Output (MIMO)**. MIMO uses multiple antennas to transmit and receive more data simultaneously, significantly increasing the capacity of a **Wireless Access Point (WAP)**. This made it possible for more devices to connect to a network without causing slowdowns or dropped connections. Additionally, MIMO enables devices to utilize both the 2.4 GHz and 5 GHz bands at the same time, further improving performance.

Later standards like **802.11ac** and **802.11ax** built on MIMO and other technologies to push wireless speeds even higher. **802.11ac** delivered faster speeds, while **802.11ax**, also known as **Wi-Fi 6**, introduced even more advanced features for handling more devices, better efficiency, and faster speeds. **802.11ax**, released in 2019, remains the most recent widely used standard, providing enhanced capacity and improved performance in high-density environments.

The following table summarizes the key features of each of these major standards.

Standard	Signal type	Max range	Speed
802.11a	5 GHz	120 m	54 Mbps (megabits/second)
802.11b	2.4 GHz	140 m	11 Mbps
802.11g	2.4 GHz	140 m	54 Mbps
802.11n	2.4/5 GHz	250 m	600 Mbps
802.11ac	5 GHz	120 m	3466 Mbps (3.4 Gbps)
802.11ax	2.4/5/6 GHz	120 m	9608 Mb/s (9.6 Gbps)

Wireless Security

Another important feature of the IEEE 802.11 standards is the inclusion of built-in security measures. The designers of these standards aimed to address common wireless security vulnerabilities from the outset, rather than waiting to react to attacks after the fact. While these security features are not foolproof (as highlighted in the "Wireless Attacks" section on page 147), the proactive approach to security helped lay the foundation for wireless security protocols that have undergone multiple revisions and improvements over time.

Wireless authentication

One of the challenges of wireless networks is that it can be difficult to track who is accessing them. Since wireless signals are not confined by physical barriers like walls or doors, unauthorized users may be able to access the network from outside its intended coverage area. To address this, authentication techniques are required to ensure that only authorized users can connect. However, when you authenticate over a wireless network, your credentials could be intercepted by attackers. To protect your login information, it's crucial to encrypt your traffic.

There are two main methods of authenticating to a wireless network:

1. **Personal Mode (PSK - Pre-Shared Key)**: This is the most common authentication method used in home networks. In this mode, you connect to the network by entering a shared password or passphrase. The security of this method depends entirely on the strength of the password you choose. A weak password makes it much easier for attackers to break into the network. While Personal mode is simple to set up and use—requiring no additional equipment or management beyond the Wireless Access Point (WAP) itself—it can be vulnerable to attacks if the password is weak. This is also why many public Wi-Fi networks, like those in cafes or libraries, use this method, allowing guests to easily connect by sharing the password.
2. **Enterprise Mode (802.1X)**: This more advanced method uses an authentication database to validate access requests. When a device attempts to connect to the network, the WAP forwards the authentication request to the database. The database then verifies whether the device is authorized to access the network. These authentication requests are encrypted using the **Extensible Authentication Protocol (EAP)**, making them much harder for attackers to intercept. EAP also supports various authentication protocols, allowing flexibility in how users are authenticated.

One of the major advantages of **Enterprise mode** is that it provides a centralized authentication system, which can be used for both wireless and wired network access through the same WAP. This means users only need to authenticate once to gain access to all resources, simplifying the user experience. Additionally, Enterprise mode offers much stronger and more secure authentication methods, which are difficult to crack. However, the complexity and cost of implementing and managing this type of authentication make it more suitable for larger organizations rather than home networks or small businesses.

In summary, while **Personal mode** is easy and cost-effective, **Enterprise mode** offers higher security and centralized authentication but requires more management and infrastructure.

Wireless Encryption

A critical element of wireless security is protecting the data transmitted over the network from interception by malicious actors. Since wireless signals can be intercepted, attackers could potentially steal any data being exchanged between a device and the **Wireless Access Point (WAP)**. To safeguard the network, WAPs use various encryption techniques.

The first encryption method used in wireless networks was **Wired Equivalent Privacy (WEP)**, which was part of the original **802.11 standard**. WEP was designed to provide encryption comparable to that used in wired networks at the time. However, WEP failed to deliver adequate security because its encryption key was too short, making it vulnerable to attacks.

Recognizing WEP's shortcomings, the **Wi-Fi Alliance** developed a new encryption standard called **Wi-Fi Protected Access (WPA)**. WPA was meant to serve as a temporary solution to address WEP's flaws until a stronger encryption standard could be developed. WPA utilized the **Temporal Key Integrity Protocol (TKIP)**, which increased the size of the encryption key, making it harder to crack. Despite this improvement, there were still weaknesses in how WPA handled the encryption key, meaning an attacker could still potentially break the encryption.

The next evolution in wireless security was **WPA2**, which significantly improved on WPA. WPA2 introduced a new encryption algorithm called **Advanced Encryption Standard (AES)**, providing much stronger encryption. WPA2 also incorporated the **802.1X authentication protocol**, which was discussed earlier, to further enhance security. Today, WPA2 remains the gold standard for wireless security, offering encryption that is comparable to that of wired networks.

While WPA2 is highly secure, it's not flawless. However, it still offers robust encryption and authentication, making it very difficult for attackers to intercept wireless communications or gain unauthorized access to the network.

It's important to note that while modern WAPs support WPA2, many devices still support older, less secure protocols such as WEP and WPA. Therefore, it is crucial to check your WAP's settings to ensure it is not using outdated encryption methods that have known vulnerabilities.

Wireless Attacks

The most common attacks targeting wireless networks are **man-in-the-middle (MITM) attacks**. These attacks are particularly effective because wireless networks, by their nature, make it easier for an attacker to intercept communication between the **Wireless Access Point (WAP)** and the devices connected to the network. Since wireless signals travel through the air, they can be intercepted from a distance without direct physical access to the network infrastructure.

In addition to MITM attacks, there are other notable types of attacks that are prevalent in wireless networks:

1. **Wireless Sniffing**: This attack involves an adversary intercepting wireless signals to capture unencrypted data, such as login credentials or sensitive information being transmitted between devices. While strong encryption (such as WPA2 with AES) helps mitigate sniffing risks, networks using weak encryption methods like **WEP** remain highly vulnerable to this type of attack. A determined attacker can easily decrypt WEP traffic and access the data being transmitted.
2. **Denial of Service (DoS)**: Wireless networks are also vulnerable to DoS attacks, where the attacker floods the network with traffic or jams the wireless signal, causing legitimate devices to lose their connection or experience slow network speeds. Because wireless signals are transmitted through the air, it's relatively easy for an attacker to introduce interference or disrupt the communication, sometimes unintentionally using devices like microwave ovens or poorly shielded electronics. Intentional DoS attacks could involve more sophisticated tools to flood the network with excessive requests, overwhelming the WAP and rendering the network unusable.

To help illustrate how an attacker might carry out these attacks, here are a few specific examples:

- **MITM Attack (Evil Twin)**: An attacker can set up a rogue access point with the same name (SSID) as a legitimate network, often in public spaces like cafes or airports. When users unknowingly connect to this "evil twin," the attacker can intercept all data exchanged between the user's device and the internet, including passwords, emails, and browsing activities. This is especially dangerous if the attacker isn't using encryption, allowing them to read the transmitted data.
- **WEP Cracking**: If a network is still using WEP encryption, an attacker can use tools like **Aircrack-ng** to capture packets of data and then decrypt the traffic. Since WEP uses weak keys, attackers can easily crack the encryption and gain access to the network. Once inside, they can launch further attacks, steal sensitive data, or degrade network performance.
- **DoS with Jamming**: A simple way to perform a DoS attack on a wireless network is to use a **jammer**—a device that sends out signals on the same frequency as the network, effectively "drowning out" the legitimate wireless communication. This prevents devices from connecting to the WAP or causes disconnections, causing disruptions in service.

Understanding these attack vectors is crucial for securing your wireless network. By using strong encryption (like WPA2 or WPA3) and employing other security measures, such as regular network monitoring, firewalls, and intrusion detection systems, you can minimize the risks of these types of attacks.

Rogue Access Points

One way an attacker can set up a **man-in-the-middle (MITM)** attack is by impersonating a legitimate access point and tricking unsuspecting users into connecting to it. This type of attack is known as a **rogue access point**. Once a device connects to the rogue access point, the attacker can intercept and monitor any communication between the device and the network.

This attack is particularly easy to carry out because it doesn't require sophisticated or expensive tools. Often, it can be done using open-source software and the wireless card built into a standard laptop or computer. Essentially, the attacker sets up their machine to act as an access point, and any device that connects to it will send traffic to the attacker's machine as if it were a legitimate WAP.

To make the attack harder to detect, the attacker may configure their rogue access point to act as a bridge to a genuine WAP, routing traffic from the victim's device to the internet. This setup allows the victim to continue browsing websites and using online services without realizing that their communications are being monitored by the attacker, since the internet connection still appears functional.

A **variation of the MITM attack** is known as the **Evil Twin** attack. In this version, the attacker creates a rogue access point that mimics the name (SSID) of a legitimate, trusted wireless network. The attacker identifies the names of real networks in the area through a process called **wardriving**. Wardriving involves using a wireless card to scan for nearby networks, including hidden ones, and mapping their locations.

Once the attacker has identified a target network, they configure their device to create a rogue access point with the same SSID as the legitimate network. When unsuspecting users in the area see the familiar network name, they may connect to it, assuming it's the real network. Once connected, their data is intercepted and can be monitored or manipulated by the attacker.

The diagram below (which we can imagine or visualize) would typically show a victim's device trying to connect to the legitimate access point, but instead connecting to the rogue access point (Evil Twin), which intercepts all communications before routing them to the real network.

These types of attacks highlight the importance of **network authentication**, **strong encryption**, and **user awareness** to protect against MITM attacks and ensure that communications are not compromised by malicious actors.

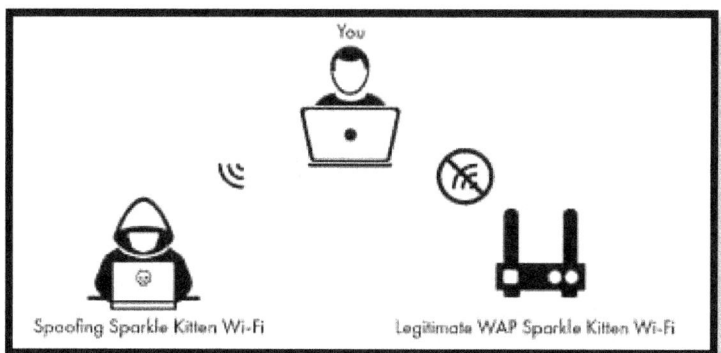

Fooling people into connecting to a fake access point is relatively easy, especially in places that offer guest Wi-Fi. A **black hat** (attacker) only needs to make their rogue network appear similar to one of the guest networks to lure unsuspecting users. This is especially effective in crowded areas, such as airports, where there are numerous guest network options. In such environments, users are often presented with a variety of Wi-Fi networks, including public networks from stores, cafes, and airports themselves, which creates a perfect opportunity for an attacker to hide in plain sight. This is why it's so risky to use public Wi-Fi in places like airports, as attackers can easily set up rogue access points that look identical to the legitimate ones.

The biggest risk with an **Evil Twin** attack is that many devices automatically store network information to make it easier to reconnect to previously used networks. This means that when a device encounters a familiar SSID (network name), it may automatically connect to it without checking if it's the real network or a fake one. This auto-connection happens because many devices periodically send out **association frames** looking for known SSIDs. When a rogue access point responds with the same SSID, the device connects to it, believing it's the legitimate network.

The danger here is that even though the device may look like it's connected to a trusted network, it's actually communicating with the attacker's fake access point, exposing sensitive information and data to potential interception.

To avoid falling victim to this type of attack, it's important to always verify the network you're connecting to. **Check the network name** (SSID) carefully and ensure it matches the expected one. Additionally, be cautious about enabling features like **automatic network connection** or **remembering networks** on your device, especially in public places. Always double-check your Wi-Fi settings to ensure you're connected to the correct network before transmitting any sensitive information.

Disassociation Attacks

As mentioned earlier, **affiliation** refers to the process of a device connecting to a **Wireless Access Point (WAP)**. When a device wants to connect, it sends an **association request frame**, a packet of data that asks the WAP to allow it to join the network. Once the WAP receives the frame, it begins the process of establishing communication with the device, including **authentication** if required.

In a **disassociation attack**, an attacker can exploit this process by obtaining a device's **MAC address** (the unique identifier for the device's network interface), copying it, and sending a **disassociation frame** to the WAP on behalf of the device. The disassociation frame essentially tells the WAP to disconnect the device. This is the opposite of an association frame, which connects a device to the network. Once the disassociation frame is received, the device is forcibly disconnected and must reconnect to the WAP.

An attacker can repeatedly send disassociation frames, preventing the device from maintaining a stable connection to the network. This is a form of **Denial of Service (DoS)** attack, where the victim's device is constantly disconnected from the network, rendering it unable to communicate.

A disassociation attack can have several consequences:

1. **Denial of Service (DoS)**: The most immediate impact is that the victim's device is continuously disconnected, disrupting their ability to use the network.
2. **Man-in-the-Middle Attack**: The attacker can use the disassociation attack to trick the victim's device into connecting to a rogue access point, which may be controlled by the attacker. This allows the attacker to intercept and manipulate the victim's network traffic, effectively executing a MITM attack.
3. **Cracking Encryption Keys**: In some cases, disassociation attacks can be used to capture encrypted data that is transmitted between the device and the WAP. This encrypted data can then be analyzed by the attacker in an attempt to crack the network's encryption key. If the attacker gathers enough encrypted frames, they may be able to use **brute-force** methods to guess the key and gain access to the network.

A common tactic in attacks against wireless encryption is to flood the network with a large number of **association** or **disassociation frames** to capture encrypted data as it is exchanged between the device and the WAP. Once the attacker has a sufficient amount of this encrypted data, they can attempt to break the encryption. The process of brute-forcing the encryption key becomes much easier and faster if weak encryption algorithms (such as **WEP**) are used. **WEP** is particularly vulnerable because its encryption key is relatively short, and cracking it requires much less encrypted data compared to modern encryption methods like **WPA2**.

The key takeaway is that weak encryption, such as WEP, is highly susceptible to attacks like disassociation and can be cracked with relatively minimal effort. Stronger encryption standards like WPA2, along with additional security measures, are essential to protect against these types of attacks and prevent unauthorized access to wireless networks.

Jamming

An attacker can disrupt a wireless network by introducing interference and jamming the signal, which prevents legitimate users from connecting. Wireless networks are particularly vulnerable to jamming due to their reliance on radio frequencies, which are also used by various other devices, including microwaves. Many of these devices, such as smartphones and wireless keyboards, are often located near the Wireless Access Point (WAP), increasing the likelihood of signal interference. In fact, it's easy to unintentionally create a jamming situation. Placing electronic devices close to powerful equipment—like servers or large kitchen appliances—can significantly degrade or completely disable a wireless network.

This problem is especially common with 2.4 GHz networks, as many household electronics operate within this frequency range. For example, positioning a 2.4 GHz WAP near another WAP can lead to interference. The 2.4 GHz spectrum is divided into twelve channels, but only three (1, 6, and 11) are non-overlapping. If two devices are on the same or overlapping channels, interference occurs, severely disrupting network performance for users.

While 5 GHz networks can also experience interference, they are more resistant to it due to the availability of 23 non-overlapping channels, reducing the risk of disruption from surrounding devices.

Setting Up a Wireless Network with Security in Mind

The best defense against attacks on your wireless network is to configure your wireless access point (WAP) with security in mind. By carefully positioning your devices, you can minimize the chances of an attacker exploiting vulnerabilities in your network. To do this successfully, you need a well-thought-out plan. One effective approach is to create a wireless network diagram—a visual map of the area where you will set up your network. This diagram should include details like the placement of WAPs, the desired coverage area, and the type of network you're building.

For instance, if you're setting up a wireless network to cover an entire office building, a diagram will help you assess how far each WAP's signal will reach and how many WAPs are needed to ensure full coverage. It will also allow you to strategically position the access points so that the signal is confined to the building, making it harder for attackers to access the network. With this setup, an intruder would need to bypass physical barriers, such as locked doors, before attempting a wireless attack, which adds an extra layer of security.

Additionally, a wireless network diagram can help prevent the placement of WAPs near equipment that might cause interference. The diagram ensures you're positioning devices in the most effective locations, reducing the likelihood of signal disruption. Below is an example of a wireless network diagram.

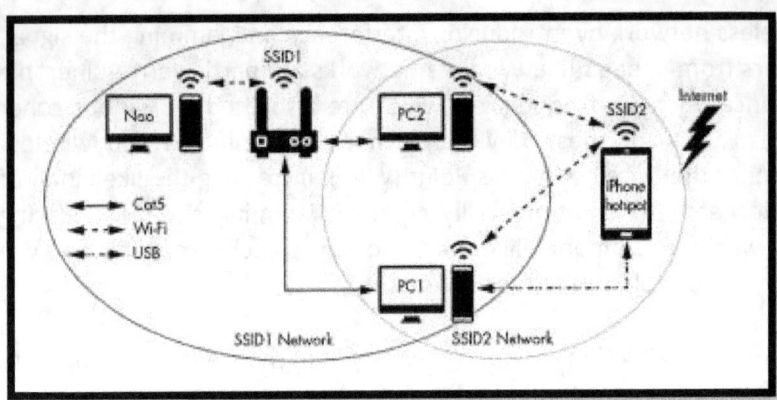

Using a wireless network diagram allows you to strategically configure your wireless access points (WAPs) and ensure they operate securely. It's crucial to verify that your WAPs are utilizing WPA2 encryption, paired with either 802.1X authentication or a strong passphrase, to safeguard your network. Additionally, it's recommended that WAPs be placed on a separate subnetwork from the rest of your internal network. This segmentation ensures that any communication from the wireless subnet to the main network must pass through extra access controls, similar to how a Demilitarized Zone (DMZ) operates, providing an additional layer of security.

Once your network is set up and confirmed to be secure, it's important to conduct regular site surveys. This involves walking through the coverage area to check for rogue access points or potential Evil Twin attacks. A wireless network sniffing tool can help detect any attackers attempting to spoof your network, as well as identify any hidden SSIDs that could be used by unauthorized devices to gain access.

In one well-documented case, an attacker posing as a janitor swapped out keyboards with identical ones that had small wireless transmitters and keylogger software installed. This allowed the attacker to capture keystrokes remotely. While this is an extreme example, it demonstrates how easily a malicious device can be inserted into your internal network, potentially giving an attacker unauthorized access.

The key takeaway is that wireless networks often require more stringent protection than wired networks, primarily because wireless signals can be easily intercepted. This doesn't mean wireless networks should be avoided entirely, but they must be managed with caution. Whenever possible, avoid transmitting sensitive data over wireless networks unless it is encrypted beforehand. That way, even if the wireless encryption fails, your data remains protected.

As a rule of thumb, public wireless networks—like those found in coffee shops or airports—should be avoided, as you can never be sure who might be intercepting the traffic. Always use WPA2 or later encryption, as older protocols like WPA and WEP are too vulnerable to be trusted for securing your connection. By following these security measures, you can enjoy the convenience of wireless networks without exposing yourself to unnecessary risks.

Exercise: Securing Your WAP

This exercise will guide you through enabling various security features on your wireless access point. While the specific configuration steps may vary depending on your WAP model, the focus here is on understanding the functions of these features, not on specific models. This knowledge will help you identify the right settings and security tools for your WAP, regardless of the brand. Let's begin by configuring your access point securely.

Setting up your access point.

Many wireless access points (WAPs) come with a setup wizard to help you configure them during the initial setup. To begin, power on the access point and allow it to fully boot up. Once it's ready, you should see indicator lights showing that the wireless connection is active.

Upon booting, most WAPs will automatically create a default wireless network. The name (SSID) of this network is typically printed on a label on the back of the device or can be found in the product documentation. Once you locate the network, you can connect to it either as an open access point or by entering the default credentials, which are also often provided on the device. If no default wireless network appears, you may need to connect directly to the WAP using an Ethernet cable.

After establishing a connection to the device or its default network, you'll need to use the setup wizard. To access this, you generally need to know the WAP's default IP address. This information is usually found on the device itself or in the product manual. The default IP is often **192.168.1.1**, but it may vary depending on the manufacturer. Once you have the IP address, type it into the address bar of your web browser and press **Enter**. This should direct your browser to the device, bringing up either the setup wizard or the administrative interface for configuration.

For example, the image below shows the main page for the ASUS wireless router setup wizard. From here, you can follow the on-screen instructions to complete the configuration process.

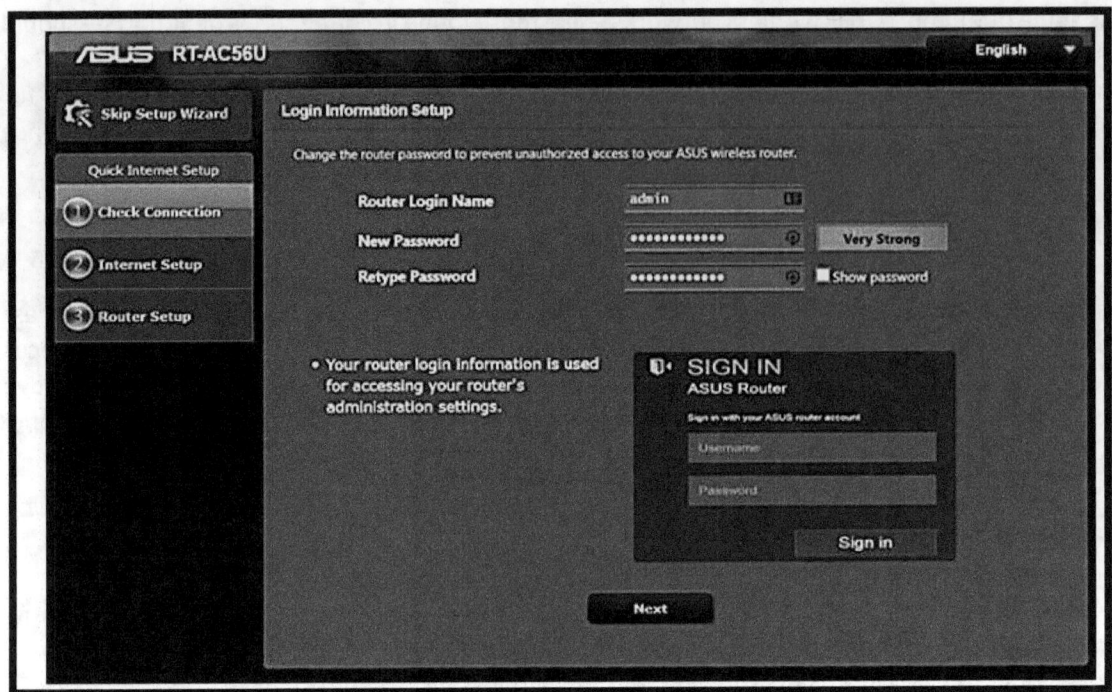

The setup wizard will typically prompt you to create a password for the administrator account. It's essential to choose a strong, secure password for this account, as it allows you to log in and modify the router's settings. Many routers, especially those provided by Internet Service Providers (ISPs), come with a default admin password. It's crucial to change this default password to something unique and secure to prevent unauthorized access. Even if the password is specific to that particular router model, it can still be easily found since it's often printed on the router itself.

Next, you'll be asked to set a **SSID** (Service Set Identifier), which is the name of your wireless network. By default, many routers use a generic SSID, but it's a good idea to assign a custom name to your network. This helps make it easier to identify, especially if you live in a densely populated area like an apartment complex where multiple networks are in range. Giving your network a unique name can also add a bit of personality— for example, I've named my network "Cat Party USA."

Once you've chosen an SSID, the next step is to configure the WAP's security settings. Be sure to enable encryption (preferably WPA2 or WPA3) to protect your network from unauthorized access. You can also adjust other security features, such as setting up a guest network or controlling the devices that can connect to your WAP. Properly configuring these settings is essential to keeping your wireless network secure.

Setting Up Wireless Security.

The first security setting you should review is the router's **wireless encryption standard**. Many modern routers come with **WPA2** enabled by default, and it may even be configured during the initial setup. However, to ensure the highest level of security, always verify that the correct encryption standard is being used and that it's configured properly.

To check and configure the encryption, navigate to your router's **security settings**. These settings are usually found within the wireless network configuration menu or a dedicated security section in the router's administrative interface. In the example below, you can see what this menu looks like on an ASUS router.

Make sure that **WPA2** (or ideally **WPA3**, if available) is selected. WPA2 is currently the most secure encryption standard for most routers, but if your router supports WPA3, it's recommended to use that for enhanced security. Once confirmed, ensure that the correct **passphrase** is set for the network, as this key is essential for keeping unauthorized users from connecting to your wireless network.

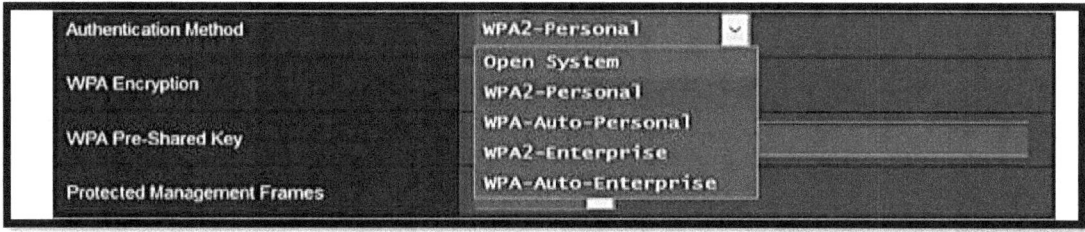

When configuring your router's security, one of the most important settings to consider is the **encryption method**. For residential networks, the most appropriate choice is typically **WPA2-Personal**. This option allows you to create a **pre-shared key (PSK)**, which is essentially a password used to secure access to your network. When setting the password, make sure to follow strong password practices to protect your network. It should be robust enough to resist brute-force attacks and other common password-cracking techniques, as others will be able to view the login menu.

You'll also need to select the **encryption standard**. The best option is **AES (Advanced Encryption Standard)**, which provides the strongest and most secure encryption available. AES is currently the recommended encryption standard for WPA2 and is widely regarded as highly effective in safeguarding your network.

Next, there are additional security features to configure. One such feature is **Wi-Fi Protected Setup (WPS)**, which aims to simplify the process of connecting devices to your WAP by allowing you to log in using a PIN or by pressing a physical button on the WAP. While this may seem convenient, **WPS has known vulnerabilities**, as the PIN can be brute-forced to gain unauthorized access. Due to its security risks, it is best to **disable WPS**.

You can typically find WPS settings in the **wireless network configuration** menu. In the example below, you can see where this option might appear in the router's setup interface. Disabling WPS ensures that your network is protected from these potential exploits and further hardens your wireless security.

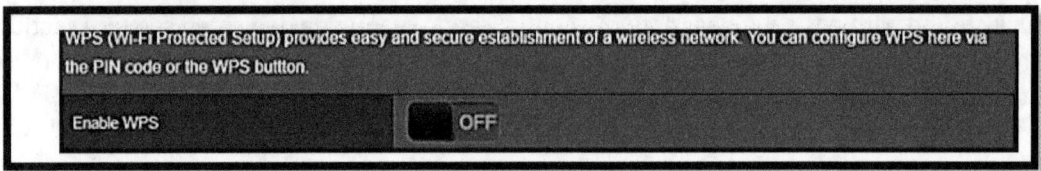

Another important security setting to review is your WAP's **remote access settings**. By default, some routers may allow remote access to the administrative interface via the internet (WAN), which can be a significant security risk. If this feature is enabled, an attacker could potentially gain access to your router's settings without needing to be physically present on your network.

To prevent this, ensure that **remote management** or **remote access** is disabled for your WAP. This will block external access to the router's admin panel via the internet, helping protect it from remote attacks. If remote management is necessary for your specific use case, make sure to configure it securely, using strong authentication and limiting access to trusted IP addresses only.

You can typically find the remote access settings in the **administrative interface** of your WAP. The graphic below shows an example of what this setting might look like on a router's configuration page. By disabling remote access, you significantly reduce the risk of unauthorized users attempting to modify your router's settings from the outside.

Another crucial remote access setting to review is how the connection to your WAP's administrative interface is secured. Avoid using **Telnet** and **HTTP**, as neither protocol encrypts the data transmitted between your browser and the router. This means that any sensitive actions, such as changing settings or entering passwords, can be intercepted by an attacker monitoring the network.

To ensure a secure connection, you should use **SSH** (Secure Shell) or **HTTPS**. **SSH** provides strong encryption, but it requires additional setup, as you must generate a unique encryption key for the device. For most users, the simpler option is **HTTPS** (Hypertext Transfer Protocol Secure), which encrypts the connection between your browser and the WAP's administrative interface. Enabling HTTPS ensures that any configuration changes you make through the web browser are transmitted securely, protecting your router from man-in-the-middle attacks and eavesdropping.

In summary, always opt for **HTTPS** (or **SSH**, if you're comfortable with the setup) to secure the connection to your WAP's settings page. This will ensure that your administrative access remains private and protected from external threats.

Enabling Filtering

Filtering is a powerful tool for controlling network traffic, allowing you to accept connections based on specific criteria while blocking all other devices or traffic. Depending on the model of your router, there are various filtering options available, each of which helps to strengthen your network's security. Let's explore some of the most common filtering methods.

One of the most widely used filtering options is **port filtering**, which lets you control traffic based on the port number. Port filtering is a great way to restrict certain protocols or services from being accessed over your network. For instance, you might choose to block **port 21**, which is used by FTP (File Transfer Protocol), a method of transferring files that is typically unencrypted and therefore vulnerable to interception. Similarly, **port 23**, used by the **Telnet** protocol, could be blocked as well, since Telnet is an outdated and insecure method of remote access.

However, caution is needed when applying port filtering, as blocking certain ports could inadvertently disrupt the operation of services or applications you need. For example, blocking a port that's required for a legitimate program or device could cause unintended connectivity issues.

The graphic below illustrates an example of port filtering settings. In this setup, the WAP allows you to configure whether ports should be blocked, and whether to use a **whitelist** (allowing only specific ports) or a **blacklist** (blocking specific ports). This flexibility allows you to fine-tune which traffic is allowed to access your network, based on your needs and security requirements.

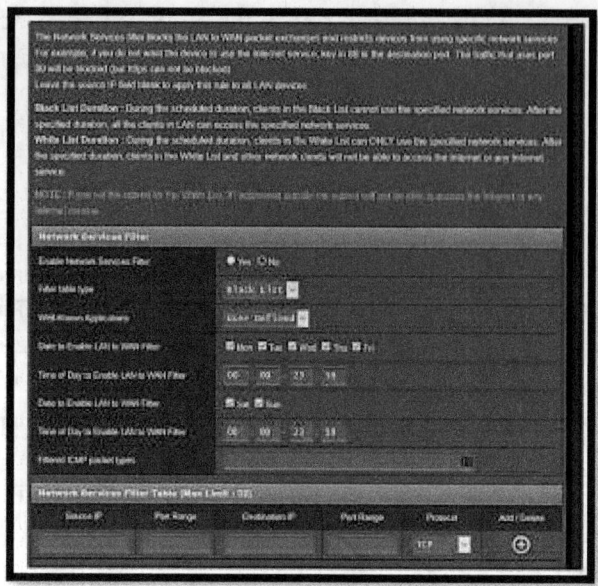

URL filtering is another valuable security tool that allows you to prevent the WAP from resolving specific URLs or even blocking certain terms within them. This means that when a user tries to access a website that contains one of these restricted URLs or terms, the WAP will block the request. URL filtering is commonly used for implementing **parental controls** or blocking access to undesired content, making it an effective way to control what can be accessed over your network.

However, URL filtering requires a high level of precision and can sometimes inadvertently block legitimate websites, so it's important to test the filter thoroughly. As with any filtering method, you may need to adjust and fine-tune the settings to avoid unnecessary restrictions or false positives.

Another widely used filtering method is **MAC address filtering**. In a Local Area Network (LAN), devices are identified by their **MAC addresses**, which help switches route traffic. MAC filtering allows you to control which devices are allowed to connect to the wireless network by creating a **whitelist** or **blacklist**. A **whitelist** is usually more effective since you are likely to know the MAC addresses of devices you want to permit access to the network, rather than trying to block every unauthorized device. If a device attempts to connect to the network but isn't on the whitelist, the WAP will deny the connection.

While MAC filtering is a great way to restrict access to your network, it has its limitations. It doesn't provide strong protection against attackers, as **MAC addresses are transmitted unencrypted** over the network. An attacker can use tools to **sniff** the network, capture the MAC address of a permitted device, and then **spoof** that address to gain unauthorized access. Since

MAC filtering doesn't differentiate between devices with the same MAC address, once an attacker obtains a whitelisted address, they can use it to bypass the filter.

This illustrates the importance of using **multiple layers of security** in your network. While MAC filtering might not prevent a determined attacker, it still adds an extra layer of defense. When used in conjunction with other security measures, such as strong encryption and authentication, it can contribute to the overall protection of your wireless network.

The image below shows an example of MAC filtering settings, where you can configure a whitelist or blacklist to control which devices can access your WAP.

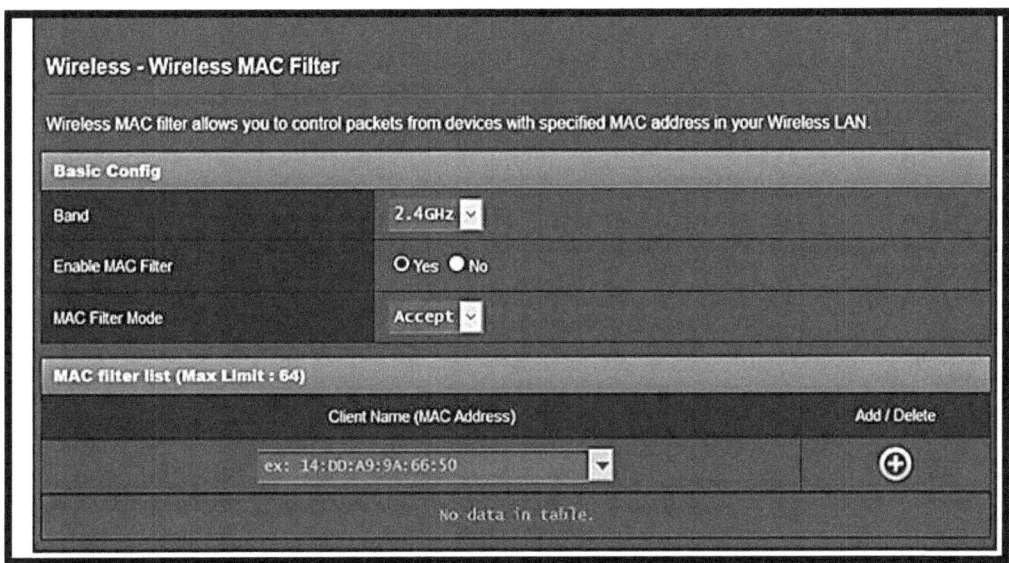

With these security settings in place, your WAP will be much better protected against both external attackers and unauthorized actions by legitimate users. While configuring all of these settings may seem like a time-consuming task, it's always better to take the extra time to secure your network than to risk leaving it vulnerable.

You don't necessarily need to use every single security feature available, but the more layers of protection you implement, the more difficult it becomes for attackers to breach your network. Each additional security measure, whether it's port filtering, MAC address filtering, or encryption, adds complexity for anyone trying to exploit weaknesses in your system. By stacking these layers, you're significantly reducing the likelihood of a successful attack.

Ultimately, a well-secured wireless network not only protects your data but also provides peace of mind, knowing you've taken the necessary steps to defend against potential threats.

CHAPTER TWELVE
PURSUING A CYBERSECURITY CAREER

Overview

In Chapter 11, you'll explore the diverse range of **cybersecurity career opportunities** available, along with the potential to earn a rewarding income. Whether you're interested in ethical hacking, network security, incident response, or cybersecurity consulting, there are numerous paths to consider. This chapter will provide insights into various roles in the field, the skills and certifications needed to excel, and the opportunities for growth within this rapidly expanding industry. Whether you're just starting out or looking to specialize further, cybersecurity offers a wealth of career possibilities to help you build a successful and lucrative profession.

Cybersecurity Career

In today's world, the demand for qualified **cybersecurity professionals** has reached unprecedented levels, creating a unique opportunity for anyone looking to build a career in this field. This surge in demand can largely be attributed to the increasing frequency of high-profile **ransomware attacks**, which have had significant real-world impacts, affecting businesses and individuals alike. Additionally, the **COVID-19 pandemic** has accelerated the shift to **remote work**, further amplifying the need for robust cybersecurity measures to protect distributed networks and data.

This trend shows no signs of slowing down. As remote work continues to rise and cyber threats become more sophisticated, the demand for skilled cybersecurity professionals is expected to keep growing. However, the supply of trained experts has not kept pace with the increasing need, leading to a **significant skills gap** in the industry. Job vacancies in cybersecurity are increasing at a faster rate than the available talent pool, creating a high-demand job market.

Given the scarcity of qualified professionals and the critical importance of their work, cybersecurity specialists are among the highest-paid in the **technology sector**. With competitive salaries, strong job security, and opportunities for growth, a career in cybersecurity offers not only a sense of purpose but also a lucrative and rewarding path.

Roles in Cybersecurity

Cybersecurity professionals have a wide range of responsibilities, which can vary depending on their specific role or area of focus. Regardless of the position, the core objective remains the same: to **protect data, networks, and systems** from unauthorized access, attacks, and compromises. In some roles, such as those within government or military agencies, cybersecurity specialists may even be tasked with offensive operations, such as **penetrating systems** or gathering intelligence by compromising adversarial data.

It's important to note that **cybersecurity** is not a one-size-fits-all career path. The field is broad, with numerous specialized roles and opportunities for growth. The industry is filled with various nuances, and professionals may choose to specialize in areas like **network security**, **incident response**, **penetration testing**, **cloud security**, and more. Because of this diversity, there is no single career trajectory or title that encompasses all aspects of cybersecurity.

Additionally, it's worth mentioning that job titles in the field of **information security** often use the term "**security**" instead of explicitly saying "cybersecurity" or "IT security." For example, you might come across titles like **Security Analyst**, **Security Engineer**, or **Security Consultant**, all of which can include a variety of responsibilities related to cybersecurity, even if the term "cybersecurity" isn't directly mentioned. This reflects the fact that the field is intertwined with broader **information security** practices, and the terminology can vary across organizations.

Experienced in the field of security engineering

Security engineers come in various specializations, but most are highly skilled technical experts who focus on **designing**, **implementing**, and **maintaining** information security systems for different types of organizations, including **corporate**, **government**, and **non-profit** sectors. Their primary role is to safeguard networks, data, and systems from potential security threats by building and managing robust security infrastructures.

In particular, **security engineers** in the **professional services** arms of technology vendors play a critical role in **ensuring the secure deployment** of software and security solutions at client sites. They help organizations properly configure and secure their software, ensuring that it meets the necessary security standards and is free from vulnerabilities before it's rolled out in production environments.

Security engineers often focus on a variety of tasks, such as:

- **Designing secure network infrastructures**
- **Implementing security protocols** (e.g., firewalls, VPNs, encryption)
- **Monitoring and responding** to security threats
- **Troubleshooting and debugging** security issues
- **Conducting vulnerability assessments** and **penetration testing**

Their expertise is vital in keeping organizations safe from cyber threats by proactively building systems that can withstand attacks, while also being able to react swiftly and effectively when an incident occurs. Whether working in-house for a company or as part of a vendor's professional services team, security engineers are at the forefront of cybersecurity efforts.

Security manager

Security managers are usually positioned in mid-level management roles within larger organizations, overseeing specific aspects of information security. For example, one security manager might be responsible for the company's security training program, while another may handle the monitoring of Internet-facing firewalls. While their primary role is to oversee and coordinate security operations, they typically do not perform hands-on technical tasks themselves; instead, these duties are often delegated to their team members.

Security director

Security directors are accountable for managing an organization's information security efforts. In smaller companies, the director often takes on the role of the Chief Information Security Officer (CISO). In larger organizations, multiple directors may oversee different components of the information security program, with each typically reporting to the CISO.

Chief information security officer (CISO)

The Chief Information Security Officer (CISO) plays a critical role in safeguarding an organization's information security. Often compared to the chief of staff in a military setting, the CISO oversees the strategic defense of the organization's data and systems. As a senior executive, the CISO holds a prominent position within the management hierarchy. The role requires a robust combination of leadership experience, extensive management skills, and in-depth expertise in information security.

Security analyst

Security analysts focus on proactively preventing information security breaches by thoroughly assessing both existing systems and emerging threats. They monitor potential vulnerabilities and evaluate new risks to ensure the organization's security remains robust and up to date.

Security Architect

Security architects are responsible for designing and overseeing the implementation of information security measures within an organization. This role requires a deep understanding of complex security infrastructures. Security specialists often collaborate across departments, contributing to projects such as designing security protocols for custom applications or providing guidance to networking teams on the development of the company's IT infrastructure.

Security administrator

Security administrators are skilled professionals responsible for implementing, configuring, managing, and troubleshooting an organization's information security measures. They play a key role in ensuring the security infrastructure runs smoothly and are often the primary point of contact for non-technical staff seeking assistance with security-related issues.

Security auditor

Security auditors are tasked with performing comprehensive security audits to ensure that policies, procedures, and technologies are operating as intended. Their primary goal is to verify that these security measures are effective in safeguarding the organization's data, systems, and networks.

Cryptographer

Cryptographers are expert professionals specializing in encryption techniques designed to protect sensitive data. Their primary role is to develop encryption systems that secure information. On the other hand, cryptanalysts are responsible for analyzing and breaking encrypted data and systems. Cryptographers are commonly employed in sectors such as government, military, and academia, where their expertise is in high demand compared to other roles in information security. In the U.S., government positions in cryptography typically require candidates to be U.S. citizens and possess an active security clearance.

Vulnerability assessment analyst

Vulnerability assessment analysts focus on thoroughly examining computer systems, databases, networks, and other parts of an organization's information infrastructure to identify potential security weaknesses. These professionals require explicit authorization to perform their work. While penetration testers, discussed in the next section, simulate external attacks, vulnerability assessors approach their tasks from within the system. They typically have authorized access to the systems they evaluate, enabling them to conduct in-depth assessments from the inside out.

Ethical hacker

Ethical hackers, also known as penetration testers or "pen-testers," are authorized to test systems and networks by simulating cyberattacks in order to identify and address security vulnerabilities. Their primary goal is to uncover weaknesses that can be fixed before malicious actors can exploit them. While many organizations employ ethical hackers directly, a significant number of professionals in this field work for consulting firms, offering their expertise to various clients.

Security researcher

Security researchers are professionals who specialize in identifying vulnerabilities in existing systems and evaluating potential security risks linked to new technologies and products. In their work, they often develop innovative security models and strategies. Ethically and legally, hacking into an organization without explicit authorization is illegal in many regions and goes against the principles upheld by security researchers and ethical hackers. Their work is rooted in the pursuit of improving security in a lawful and responsible manner.

Offensive hacker

Malicious hackers intentionally attempt to infiltrate networks with the goal of causing damage or stealing sensitive information. In the United States, it is illegal for private companies to engage in offensive actions, such as retaliating against hackers trying to breach their networks. All legitimate offensive hacking activities in the U.S. are carried out by government personnel, particularly within intelligence agencies and the military. For those interested in pursuing a career in offensive security beyond ethical hacking, opportunities in the government or military are the primary path. Many of these roles require security clearances.

Software security engineer

Software security engineers incorporate security measures directly into the design and development of software. They conduct thorough testing to ensure the software is free of vulnerabilities. In some cases, they may even be the ones who originally created the software, ensuring it is built with security in mind from the outset.

Software source code security auditor

Software source code security auditors meticulously examine the source code of programs to identify issues such as programming errors, vulnerabilities, policy violations, regulatory non-compliance, copyright infringements, and other potential risks. Addressing these concerns is essential to maintaining the security, integrity, and compliance of the software.

Security consultant

There is a wide range of security consultants available, offering expertise in various areas of cybersecurity. Many professionals, including myself, assist business leaders with security strategy, provide expert testimony, and play a key role in building and strengthening security organizations. While some consultants focus on hands-on activities like penetration testing, others specialize in developing or managing specialized security technologies and infrastructures. Information security roles can be found across a variety of industries, with security consulting being one of the key fields within this broader sector.

Security expert witness

Security expert witnesses are professionals with deep expertise in a particular area of security, who are called upon to provide testimony in legal cases. Trusted by judges, these experts offer their informed opinions on issues related to the case, helping to clarify complex security matters for the court.

Security specialist

The term "security specialist" encompasses a variety of roles within the field of information security. These positions generally require prior experience in cybersecurity or related areas, as they demand specialized knowledge and skills to address security challenges effectively.

Member of the incident response team

The incident response team is made up of key individuals tasked with managing and responding to security incidents. Their primary goal is to effectively contain and mitigate attacks, minimizing any potential damage. These team members often analyze incidents to determine their cause, sometimes concluding that no further action is required. Incident responders can be likened to cybersecurity firefighters: they manage high-risk situations and are occasionally called in to verify that there is no ongoing threat.

Expert in forensic analysis

Forensic analysts specialize in investigating digital events by examining data, computers, devices, and networks. They collect, analyze, and preserve evidence to determine what occurred, how it happened, and who is responsible. Similar to investigators from law enforcement or insurance companies who carefully inspect a property after a fire to uncover the cause and identify those at fault, forensic analysts methodically work to uncover the details of cyber incidents and hold the appropriate parties accountable.

Cybersecurity regulations expert

Cybersecurity regulation experts have in-depth knowledge of the various laws and regulations governing cybersecurity. Their primary role is to help organizations ensure they meet compliance requirements. While they often have experience in compliance-related fields, they are not necessarily lawyers. Instead, they provide guidance on how to navigate and adhere to the complex landscape of cybersecurity regulations.

Privacy regulations expert

Privacy regulation experts have a deep understanding of the laws and regulations related to privacy. They are instrumental in guiding organizations to ensure compliance with these privacy requirements. While many have experience handling various compliance issues, not all of them are lawyers. Their expertise helps organizations navigate the complex privacy landscape and mitigate risks associated with non-compliance.

Exploring Different Career Paths

When planning a career, it's important to carefully consider your long-term goals. If your ambition is to become a Chief Information Security Officer (CISO), gaining experience in a range of hands-on roles, pursuing an MBA, and seeking promotions and certifications in information security management will be key. On the other hand, if you aim to become a senior security architect, it would be more advantageous to build your career through roles in security analysis, design, and penetration testing, while earning technical degrees to deepen your expertise. Below are examples of potential career paths to help guide your journey.

Career path: Senior security architect

Security architects in the United States often earn salaries over $100,000, with some markets offering even higher compensation. This makes the role highly attractive to many professionals. While each person's career path may vary, a common route to becoming a senior security architect typically involves the following steps:

1. **Choose an educational path:**
   - Obtain a **bachelor's degree in computer science**.
   - Alternatively, earn a degree in another field and complete an entry-level cybersecurity certification, such as **Security+**.
   - Some individuals may choose to skip a formal degree and secure a technical role, demonstrating proficiency in relevant technologies.
2. **Gain hands-on experience:**
   - Start by seeking a position as a **network administrator** or **systems administrator** to build practical security experience.
3. **Enhance expertise with certifications:**
   - Consider earning specialized certifications, such as **Certified Ethical Hacker (CEH)**, to deepen your knowledge and skills.
4. **Build experience as a security administrator:**
   - Work as a **security administrator**, gaining experience with a variety of security systems and establishing a strong track record of effective security management over time.
5. **Obtain general security certifications:**

- o Earn certifications like **Certified Information Systems Security Professional (CISSP)** to bolster your credentials and showcase your broad security knowledge.
6. **Pursue a career in security architecture:**
    - o Take on roles in **security architecture** to gain valuable experience in designing and implementing security frameworks.
7. **Advance with specialized certifications:**
    - o Consider obtaining an advanced certification, such as **CISSP-ISSAP** (Information Systems Security Architecture Professional), to further specialize in security architecture.
8. **Reach senior-level security architect:**
    - o With significant experience and expertise, you can advance to the role of a **senior security architect**.

Becoming a senior security architect is a long-term goal that typically takes a decade or more of focused experience in relevant fields to achieve.

Career path: Chief Information Security Officer (CISO)

Chief Information Security Officers (CISOs) in the United States typically earn salaries of $150,000 or more, particularly in specialized industries. However, the role can be demanding and stressful, which may explain why many CISOs leave after just a few years. CISOs are responsible for safeguarding an organization's information security, often dealing with emergencies and crises. Their achievements may go unnoticed, while failures are subject to significant scrutiny. While each career path is unique, the following is a common trajectory for those aspiring to become a CISO:

1. **Start with a relevant degree:**
    - o Earn a **bachelor's degree** in a field such as **computer science, information technology,** or a closely related discipline.
2. **Gain hands-on technical experience:**
    - o Work in technical roles like **systems analyst, systems engineer, programmer,** or **network engineer** to build a solid foundation in IT.
3. **Transition into security roles:**
    - o Explore the field of **information security** by taking on positions such as **security engineer, security analyst,** or **security consultant**. This will provide broad exposure to various aspects of cybersecurity.
4. **Obtain key certifications:**
    - o Earn general **information security certifications** like **CISSP (Certified Information Systems Security Professional)** to enhance your expertise and credentials.
5. **Move into leadership roles:**

- Shift into management by leading a **security operations team**. As you gain more experience, aim to oversee multiple teams focusing on different facets of information security.
6. **Pursue further education:**
    - Consider earning a **master's degree** in areas such as **cybersecurity**, **information security management**, or **computer science**. Alternatively, an **MBA** can help develop your leadership and business acumen.
7. **Take on senior security leadership roles:**
    - Work your way up to positions like **divisional CISO** or serve as a CISO for a smaller company or nonprofit. This allows you to gain valuable leadership experience in the security space.
8. **Earn advanced security management certifications:**
    - Obtain an advanced **information security credential**, such as **CISSP-ISSMP** (Information Systems Security Management Professional), to deepen your expertise in security management.
9. **Achieve the CISO role in a larger organization:**
    - Finally, pursue the role of **Chief Information Security Officer** in a larger company, recognizing that this position requires a blend of extensive technical experience, leadership, and advanced education. Reaching this level may take many years, particularly in large corporations.

This career path typically combines **technical expertise**, **leadership experience**, and **continuous education**. Achieving the role of CISO, especially in a large organization, can take a decade or more of dedication and development.

Getting Started in Information Security

Many individuals in the field of information security begin their careers in other areas of information technology. For some, their journey into cybersecurity started while working in technical roles, where they became intrigued by the world of security. Others initially pursued technical professions unrelated to security but used those roles as a stepping stone to expand their skill set and transition into the cybersecurity field. Positions in risk analysis, systems engineering and development, and networking can serve as excellent starting points for building a career in cybersecurity.

For example:

- An **email administrator** will gain expertise in email security, secure network design, and server security.
- **Web developers** often acquire knowledge of web security and safe software architecture.
- **System and network administrators** develop key insights into the security of the systems and networks they manage, ensuring their functionality and protection.

Here are some **technical roles** that can provide foundational experience for transitioning into cybersecurity-related positions:

- **Programmer** (also known as a coder)
- **Software engineer**
- **Web developer**
- **Information systems support engineer** (technical support specialist)
- **Systems administrator**
- **Email administrator**
- **Network administrator**
- **Database administrator**
- **Website administrator**

Additionally, certain **non-technical roles** can offer valuable preparation for entering the information security field, particularly for positions that focus on the legal, regulatory, or risk management aspects of cybersecurity. Examples include:

- **Auditor**
- **Detective** (law enforcement)
- **Cybersecurity lawyer** (specializing in legal aspects of cybersecurity)
- **Attorney specializing in regulatory compliance**
- **Attorney specializing in privacy law**
- **Risk management analyst**

These diverse backgrounds—whether technical or non-technical—can provide the essential skills and perspectives needed to succeed in the rapidly evolving world of information security.

Exploring Popular Certifications

Cybersecurity certifications and course completion certificates can demonstrate to employers that you possess the necessary skills and expertise in the field, helping to advance your career. There is a broad range of information security certifications available, with some focusing on specific technologies or aspects of cybersecurity, while others provide a more comprehensive overview. It's important to recognize that certifying organizations are constantly revising their standards and curricula to stay current with the rapidly evolving cybersecurity landscape. Therefore, using an up-to-date study guide is crucial when preparing for certification exams.

CISSP

The CISSP certification, first introduced in 1994, covers a broad spectrum of security-related topics, each explored to varying depths. This certification highlights the importance of employees having a comprehensive understanding of different aspects of information security, particularly for those in senior management roles. Employers can be confident that their certified staff possess a well-rounded expertise in the field. Typically, professionals who pursue the CISSP certification have substantial experience in information security. While the exam can be taken without prior work experience, the certification is only awarded after meeting the required years of experience in the field. Individuals holding a CISSP certification often earn higher salaries compared to their uncertified peers or those with other certifications due to their deep knowledge and credentials.

Offered by (ISC)², the CISSP is widely respected for its broad applicability and vendor-neutral stance, making it a valuable and enduring certification in the cybersecurity industry. The exam is supported by various study materials and training programs and is available at multiple locations on different dates, making it more accessible than many other cybersecurity certifications. For those interested in specialized areas, such as information security architecture (CISSP-ISSAP), management (CISSP-ISSMP), or engineering (CISSP-ISSEP), there are additional options for further certification.

CISSP holders are required to adhere to a strict Code of Ethics and engage in ongoing professional development to maintain their credentials. These certifications must be renewed every three years. While the CISSP exam assesses a candidate's overall knowledge of security practices, it does not measure hands-on technical skills. Professionals interested in demonstrating expertise in specific technical areas, such as penetration testing, security administration, or auditing, may benefit more from pursuing specialized certifications focused on those domains or certifications tied to particular technologies and products.

CISM

The Certified Information Security Manager (CISM) certification, offered by the Information Systems Audit and Control Association (ISACA), has gained considerable recognition since its launch nearly two decades ago. As a credential from an organization with a strong focus on audit and control, CISM has a more specialized scope compared to the CISSP. It emphasizes the policies, processes, and technologies essential for managing and governing information security systems, especially within large organizations. Like the CISSP, the CISM certification requires candidates to have significant professional experience in the information security field.

While the CISSP and CISM differ in their focus—CISSP emphasizes technical aspects, while CISM is more centered on management and governance—there is a considerable overlap between the two. Both certifications are highly regarded in the cybersecurity industry and are recognized for their value in advancing professionals' careers.

CEH

The Certified Ethical Hacker (CEH) certification, offered by the International Council of E-Commerce Consultants (EC-Council), is designed for professionals with at least two years of experience who are dedicated to building their credentials as ethical hackers, or penetration testers. The CEH exam assesses candidates' abilities across a broad range of hacking techniques, such as reconnaissance, network penetration, privilege escalation, and data theft. The test covers practical skills in areas like malware exploitation, attack methods like SQL injection, cryptanalysis for breaking encryption, social engineering tactics to exploit human error, and strategies for evading detection and covering tracks.

Holders of the CEH certification are required to maintain their credentials through ongoing professional development. This requirement emphasizes the importance of staying up-to-date with the rapidly changing technologies and methods in the cybersecurity field.

Security+

The Security+ certification is highly regarded, especially for individuals who are beginning their careers in cybersecurity. Offered by CompTIA, a respected nonprofit organization focused on technology education, Security+ is a vendor-neutral credential that covers a broad range of cybersecurity topics. While there is no formal experience requirement to sit for the exam, it is recommended that candidates have some practical experience in the field, as this can significantly enhance their chances of success.

The Security+ exam provides a solid foundation in technical cybersecurity principles, making it an ideal certification for those pursuing entry-level roles in IT auditing, penetration testing, systems administration, network administration, and security administration. As such, CompTIA Security+ is a valuable certification for newcomers to the industry. Since 2011, individuals holding the Security+ certification have been required to complete continuing education courses to maintain their credentials, ensuring they stay current with evolving technologies and best practices in the field.

GSEC

The GSEC (Global Security Essentials) certification is an entry-level security credential offered by the SANS Institute, a well-respected provider of information security training. Unlike certifications such as CISM or CISSP, the GSEC focuses heavily on practical, hands-on material, which sets it apart in certain contexts. This focus on real-world application makes it particularly valuable in scenarios where practical knowledge is crucial, though it may be less desirable in other situations that prioritize broader theoretical knowledge.

Although the GSEC is marketed as an entry-level certification, it is often regarded as more challenging and comprehensive than the Security+ certification. To maintain their GSEC credentials, holders must demonstrate ongoing professional experience or continued education in the field of information security, ensuring they remain current with industry developments and best practices.

Verifiability

Employers can easily verify whether an individual holds the credentials they claim, thanks to the certification issuers of major information security credentials. Verification often involves checking the certification identification number, which is typically not shared by credential holders. To maintain your certification, it's important to regularly update your information in the issuer's database. Staying on top of updates is crucial to avoid losing your certification, as failure to submit continuing education credits or pay maintenance fees can result in forfeiting your credentials.

Ethics

The code of ethics for security certifications highlights the importance of adhering not only to laws and regulations but also to higher ethical standards that go beyond basic compliance. Understanding these ethical guidelines is essential for professionals in the field. When an individual loses their certification due to unethical conduct, it can severely damage the trust others place in them and lead to significant negative repercussions for their career in information security.

Overcoming a Criminal Record

A criminal history may not automatically disqualify someone from pursuing various cybersecurity careers, but it can present a significant obstacle when applying for specialized roles. For example, if an individual is unable to obtain a security clearance due to past convictions, they may be ineligible for certain government or government contractor positions. Employers typically assess the nature of past offenses, the time that has passed, and the age at which the crimes were committed when making hiring decisions.

Some information security companies may be open to hiring a reformed, former juvenile hacker, but they could be more cautious about hiring someone convicted of a violent crime as an adult. Likewise, individuals who have served their sentences for computer-related crimes committed years ago and maintained a clean record since then may be viewed more favorably by potential employers compared to those recently released from incarceration for similar offenses.

Conquering Bad Credit

For individuals who may not be well-versed in the security industry, the importance of a credit score might not be immediately apparent when considering job opportunities. However, in certain cases—especially for roles that require government work and security clearance—your credit score can play a significant role.

As part of the background check process for security clearance, employers often review an applicant's credit report. Financial stability is seen as a reflection of an individual's overall reliability and trustworthiness. The logic behind this is that those experiencing financial hardship could be more vulnerable to risks, such as the temptation to compromise sensitive information for financial gain. Consequently, a poor credit score may raise concerns during the clearance review.

If you're applying for a position that requires security clearance and know that your credit score is less than ideal—perhaps due to unforeseen circumstances like medical expenses or job loss—it's important to be proactive. Instead of waiting for the issue to be addressed during the clearance process, consider bringing it up early with the relevant parties. By providing context and showing that you are actively managing or resolving any financial issues, you can help alleviate potential concerns and improve your chances of a successful clearance evaluation.

Being transparent and taking the initiative to explain any negative marks on your credit report demonstrates qualities such as foresight and responsibility, which are highly valued for positions requiring security clearance. It also gives you the opportunity to showcase your financial management efforts, even in the face of challenges. This proactive approach can help prevent surprises during the clearance process and may ultimately increase your chances of securing the role.

Exploring Alternative Careers with a Focus on Cybersecurity

As the global focus on cybersecurity continues to grow, there are numerous opportunities for professionals across various industries to engage with cybersecurity experts and benefit from this expanding field. For instance, legal professionals may choose to specialize in areas like cybersecurity law or privacy compliance, helping businesses navigate complex regulations. Likewise, law enforcement officers can gain expertise in cybercrime investigations and digital forensics.

Cybersecurity is not only creating new career paths but also reshaping existing roles across a wide range of sectors. The growth of the cybersecurity field offers valuable opportunities for professionals of all backgrounds, regardless of their technical expertise. If you are interested in cybersecurity, there are many exciting avenues to explore and build a rewarding career.

Frequently Asked Questions

1. What are the job roles in cybersecurity?

Cybersecurity offers a wide range of job roles, catering to various skill sets and expertise levels. Some of the most common job titles include:

- **Security Analyst**: Monitors and protects an organization's network and systems from cyber threats.
- **Penetration Tester (Ethical Hacker)**: Simulates cyberattacks to identify vulnerabilities in an organization's systems.
- **Security Engineer**: Designs and implements security systems and protocols to protect an organization's infrastructure.
- **Incident Responder**: Investigates and mitigates security incidents or breaches.
- **Cybersecurity Architect**: Designs and builds secure IT infrastructures, ensuring robust security systems are in place.
- **Security Consultant**: Advises organizations on how to improve their cybersecurity strategies and policies.
- **Forensic Expert**: Specializes in investigating cybercrimes, often working with law enforcement agencies.
- **Chief Information Security Officer (CISO)**: Oversees an organization's entire cybersecurity strategy and operations at the executive level.
- **Cryptographer**: Focuses on developing encryption techniques to secure data and communications.

2. What do you understand by information security?

Information security (InfoSec) refers to the practices, policies, and technologies designed to protect sensitive data from unauthorized access, use, disclosure, modification, or destruction. It encompasses a wide range of activities, including protecting both digital and physical assets, ensuring data integrity, confidentiality, and availability. Information security involves risk management, setting up secure systems, and creating strong procedures to prevent data breaches and cyberattacks. It also covers aspects like compliance with regulations (e.g., GDPR, HIPAA) and ethical handling of information.

3. What are the different popular certifications in cybersecurity?

Several certifications are highly regarded in the cybersecurity industry, each catering to different roles and expertise levels. Some of the most popular ones include:

- **CISSP (Certified Information Systems Security Professional)**: A comprehensive certification for experienced cybersecurity professionals, focusing on information security management.
- **CISM (Certified Information Security Manager)**: A certification focusing on security management, governance, and risk management.
- **CompTIA Security+**: A foundational, vendor-neutral certification for those starting in cybersecurity, covering a broad range of topics.
- **CEH (Certified Ethical Hacker)**: Focuses on ethical hacking and penetration testing, certifying professionals to identify and fix vulnerabilities in systems.
- **CISA (Certified Information Systems Auditor)**: Specializes in auditing and assessing information systems for vulnerabilities and compliance.
- **GSEC (Global Security Essentials)**: An entry-level certification focusing on practical, hands-on skills in security.
- **CISSP-ISSAP, CISSP-ISSMP, and CISSP-ISSEP**: Specializations of the CISSP in areas such as architecture, management, and engineering.
- **CompTIA Cybersecurity Analyst (CySA+)**: A certification focused on detecting and responding to security threats and incidents.
- **Certified Cloud Security Professional (CCSP)**: A certification focused on cloud security, offering expertise in securing cloud environments.

4. How do you explore alternative careers in cybersecurity?

To explore alternative careers in cybersecurity, consider the following steps:

- **Identify Your Interests and Strengths**: Cybersecurity is a broad field, so figure out what areas intrigue you most, whether it's ethical hacking, risk management, security architecture, or compliance.
- **Research Different Roles**: Familiarize yourself with various job roles within cybersecurity (e.g., penetration tester, security consultant, forensic investigator, etc.), and understand the qualifications needed for each.
- **Take Introductory Courses**: Online platforms like Coursera, edX, or LinkedIn Learning offer courses in cybersecurity basics, which can help you determine which areas of the field appeal to you.
- **Obtain Relevant Certifications**: Start with foundational certifications like CompTIA Security+ if you're new to cybersecurity, or pursue specialized certifications based on the career path you're interested in.
- **Network with Industry Professionals**: Attend conferences, webinars, or local meetups to connect with cybersecurity professionals and learn more about the industry's diverse roles.
- **Look for Internship or Entry-Level Opportunities**: Gaining practical experience in the field through internships or entry-level positions will help you understand the skills needed for different roles and improve your chances of advancing your career.

5. How do you overcome a criminal record?

Overcoming a criminal record, particularly in cybersecurity or other security-sensitive jobs, can be challenging but not impossible. Here are some steps you can take:

- **Understand the Impact**: Recognize that certain crimes, especially those related to security, may make it difficult to get security clearances or positions in specific industries. However, the nature and recency of the offense will often play a significant role.
- **Demonstrate Rehabilitation**: If the offense is in the past, demonstrating rehabilitation is critical. This can include showing evidence of positive behavior changes, such as stable employment, involvement in community service, or personal development programs.
- **Be Transparent**: If asked about your criminal history during a job application or interview, be honest and upfront. It's better to address the issue proactively rather than let it be discovered later.
- **Explain Context**: Provide context for any offenses, particularly if they were committed at a young age or were the result of circumstances beyond your control, such as financial hardship or personal struggles.
- **Focus on Relevant Skills and Certifications**: If you're applying for a cybersecurity job, emphasize your certifications, skills, and ongoing commitment to ethical practices in the field. Cybersecurity employers often value technical expertise and ethical behavior.
- **Seek Employers with a Second-Chance Policy**: Some companies are more willing to hire individuals with a criminal record, especially if they can demonstrate a commitment to reform and a clean record since their conviction. Look for employers who prioritize diversity and second chances in hiring practices.
- **Consider Legal Advice**: In some cases, you may be able to have certain convictions expunged or reduced, depending on your local laws and the nature of the offense. Consulting with a legal professional could help you understand your options for clearing your record.

While a criminal record can present challenges, transparency, rehabilitation, and a focus on your skills and ethics can help you overcome these barriers in the cybersecurity field.

CHAPTER THIRTEEN
How to Defeat Black Hats

So far in this book, you've explored the basics of cybersecurity—understanding why hackers, or "black hats," target your data, the various methods adversaries use to attack your systems, and how to defend against specific types of threats. You've also learned about the risks present in different environments, such as your networks, social media platforms, email, and more.

However, as you've likely realized, effective security can't be reactive. Waiting for an attack to occur before trying to stop it is a losing strategy. It's similar to playing Whac-A-Mole: you might temporarily fix one issue, but without addressing the root causes, more problems will quickly surface.

To establish strong, long-lasting security, you need to build a proactive strategy from the ground up. This starts with creating a plan that details how you will set up, manage, and continually improve your security measures. In this section, you'll learn how to develop such a plan, incorporating everything you've learned so far.

Ultimately, you'll create a tailored security plan for a specific environment—whether it's a home, school, business, or another entity. By practicing the process of constructing a security strategy, you'll be able to apply your knowledge in real-world scenarios. By the end of this chapter, you'll be ready to start designing a security plan that can be used in any project, both at home and in the workplace.

What's the worst that can happen?

When developing a security plan or considering security more broadly, it's essential to start by envisioning the worst-case scenario. Security professionals are often seen as pessimists because they constantly focus on what could go wrong in any given situation, sometimes to an extent that may seem excessive. However, this mindset is invaluable for identifying potential vulnerabilities and understanding the risks your system faces. You can't address a problem unless you first recognize it. To start, it's important to distinguish between a *risk* and a *threat*.

At first glance, the terms "risk" and "threat" might seem interchangeable—they both refer to potential harm that could disrupt your system or organization. Both describe how your assets could be attacked or compromised. In reality, though, risks and threats are distinct concepts that require different approaches to manage effectively.

Risks

A *risk* is generally the result of your actions or decisions. It refers to the probability that something undesirable will happen due to the actions of an individual or organization. Take, for example, getting out of bed in the morning. There's a chance you might twist your ankle or step on a LEGO and hurt your foot. There's even a remote possibility that a grizzly bear might leap out of your closet and attack you the moment you stand up.

While you might dismiss the idea of a bear in your closet, especially if you don't live in bear territory, it's not entirely impossible—just highly unlikely. In cybersecurity, just like in daily life, no action is completely risk-free.

We assess risk by combining the likelihood of an event occurring with its potential impact. Let's revisit the "getting out of bed" example. What are the chances you'll step on a LEGO piece when you get up? If you have young children, the likelihood increases significantly. If they have LEGO sets, or if they play with them near your bed, the risk goes even higher.

Now, consider the *impact*. Sure, stepping on a LEGO might hurt, but the pain is temporary. It's a moderate-level danger, one that requires you to check the floor before getting out of bed but doesn't warrant banning LEGO sets from your home entirely.

To better understand and compare risks, it's helpful to use numerical ratings. While there are formal ways to quantify risk—such as evaluating the potential financial loss—you don't need to follow a strict standard. For example, you might use a scale of 1 to 5 to rate both the likelihood and the impact of an event. In the case of a grizzly bear in your closet, you'd probably rate the likelihood as 1 (because it's highly unlikely) and the impact as 5 (because a bear attack would be catastrophic). Multiplying these two ratings gives a total risk of 5.

Now, compare that to the LEGO example. If there are a lot of LEGO bricks in your home, the likelihood of stepping on one near your bed might be around 3. The impact is painful but not catastrophic, so you might rate it a 3 as well. This gives a total risk score of 9—almost twice as high as the risk of a grizzly bear attack.

The table below illustrates these calculations.

Risk	Likelihood	Impact	Total risk
Twisted ankle	3	4	12
Step on LEGO	3	3	9
Bear attack	1	5	5

Once you've rated the risks, the next step is deciding how to address them. When you identify a risk, it's crucial to act on it quickly. This is where the legal concept of "due diligence" comes in, which means taking reasonable precautions to prevent harm. In other words, if you know a risk exists, ignoring it could expose you to legal liability if the risk materializes.

There are several ways to manage risk:

1. **Avoid the Risk**: The simplest approach is to eliminate the activity that creates the risk. For example, if you avoid getting out of bed, you won't risk stepping on a LEGO piece.
2. **Transfer the Risk**: This involves shifting the responsibility for the risk to another entity, usually through insurance. For instance, if there's a chance your house could flood, you might buy flood insurance. If the flood happens, the insurance company takes on the financial burden.
3. **Mitigate the Risk**: This involves reducing either the likelihood of the risk occurring or its impact. In the LEGO scenario, you might check the area around your bed for loose bricks before going to sleep or enforce a rule that LEGO toys stay out of the bedroom to reduce the risk of stepping on them.
4. **Accept the Risk**: Sometimes, the risk is so low or its impact so minor that it's not worth taking any action to prevent or mitigate it. For example, the chance of a bear appearing in your bedroom is so minimal that no preventive measures are necessary.

Let's apply this to a cybersecurity example. Imagine the risk that one of your employees might click on a phishing email link. This is a significant risk for almost any organization, especially given the widespread use of email. If the employee falls victim to the phishing attack, the consequences could be severe, such as malware infections or stolen credentials.

Avoiding this risk entirely is unrealistic because most companies rely on email communication. Transferring the risk might involve purchasing cybersecurity insurance, but such policies typically don't cover the full range of damages that could occur. Accepting the risk is not a viable option either, since the potential fallout could be catastrophic and even put the company out of business.

In this case, the best strategy is to mitigate the risk. This could involve using spam filters to block suspicious emails and training employees to recognize phishing attempts. By taking these proactive steps, you reduce the chances of an employee falling victim to a phishing attack, while also minimizing the potential damage if it happens.

Managing risk in cybersecurity—or in any area—requires careful consideration of the likelihood, impact, and potential strategies for dealing with each risk. While risk management can be complex, thinking through these basic concepts will help you better understand and address the challenges you face.

Threats

A *threat* refers to any negative influence that could harm a system, individual, or organization. In simple terms, a threat is the force that drives bad things to happen. For example, when getting out of bed, the threat could be the factors that could cause you harm, like stepping on a LEGO or encountering a bear. While the threat in these cases is obvious, assessing the threat in other scenarios, such as twisting an ankle, can be more complicated. It depends on what caused the twist—was it a misplaced shoe, or was it just your own clumsiness? In the latter case, your own body (or the part of your brain responsible for movement) becomes the threat.

Threats come in many forms and don't always have to be malicious or intentional. For instance, buildings face the threat of fire or natural disasters, but these events aren't caused by an active, conscious agent. The term *threat actor* is used to refer to the person, group, or force responsible for causing the threat. While the distinction between a *threat* and a *threat actor* may seem subtle, it's crucial for effective threat management. Managing a general threat (such as fire or a storm) is different from managing a threat actor (like a hacker or an employee who clicks on a malicious link).

Take the example of managing the risk that employees will click on phishing links. The threat actor in this case might be the malicious individual who sent the phishing email. However, employees who click on the link are also threat actors, because their action triggered the risk. Since you can't eliminate all threat actors (after all, your employees are essential), the solution is to mitigate the threat through training, awareness, and technical measures like spam filters.

One way to manage threats more effectively is by categorizing them. By classifying threats, you can better understand how to neutralize them in your environment. One popular framework for categorizing cybersecurity threats is the STRIDE model, developed by Microsoft. STRIDE is an acronym that represents six common types of security threats:

- **Spoofing**: Impersonating another user or system.
- **Tampering**: Unauthorized changes or modifications to data or systems.
- **Repudiation**: Denying actions or events that occurred, making it hard to trace activity.
- **Information Disclosure**: Exposing sensitive or private data to unauthorized parties.
- **Denial of Service (DoS)**: Disrupting the availability of services or systems.
- **Privilege Escalation**: Gaining unauthorized higher-level access to systems or data.

Each of these categories represents a different type of threat that could potentially harm a system. By understanding and identifying these threats, you can better prepare your security strategy to defend against them.

Threat	Target
Spoofing	Authentication
Tampering	Integrity
Repudiation	Non-repudiation
Information disclosure	Confidentiality
Denial of service	Availability
Elevation of privileges	Authorization

By classifying attacks, you can gain a general sense of how they function or, at the very least, what their objectives might be. For instance, if I introduced a new attack called "Sparkle Kitten Bite," you might be unsure of how to respond. However, if I explained that "Sparkle Kitten Bite" is an elevation of privileges attack, you'd understand that its goal is likely to gain unauthorized access to accounts, potentially to execute commands within a privileged environment.

Controls

Categorizing threats and threat actors helps you choose the most effective control measures to prevent or reduce risks. By now, you're likely familiar with various controls designed to thwart different types of attacks. For instance, you know that a DoS attack can be mitigated by setting up redundant systems or filtering traffic before it reaches its target. Likewise, you understand that one of the most effective ways to prevent a brute-force attack is to create a password complex enough that even a computer would struggle to guess.

Just as threats are classified, controls are also grouped in categories to help you determine the most appropriate approach for your specific situation. In risk management, we typically categorize controls based on how they aim to protect a target from a threat. The five primary categories are: administrative, preventative, detective, compensatory, and corrective. The table below outlines these categories, along with their objectives and examples.

Category	Purpose	Example
Administrative	Provides guidance on how to conduct activities	Security awareness training, policy, procedure
Preventative	Attempts to stop unwanted activity before it happens	Firewall
Detective	Attempts to discover unwanted activity after it has happened or while it's happening	IDS, logging
Compensating	Adds additional security to make up for a weakness in another control	Encryption
Corrective	Fixes another control or flaw after it's discovered	Patch management, vulnerability management

Let's explore how to apply these controls in real-world scenarios. Preventative controls are straightforward in their purpose. For instance, a firewall blocks unwanted traffic by denying connections based on predefined rules, thus preventing malicious behavior before it can occur.

Detective controls, by contrast, are designed to identify harmful activity after it happens. A common example is reviewing login logs to determine if an attacker has gained unauthorized access to your system.

• **Compensating controls** work alongside other controls to enhance security. A great example is encryption: even if a primary control like authentication fails, encryption ensures that an attacker cannot read the data.

• **Corrective controls** are focused on addressing issues identified by other controls. For instance, if a security vulnerability is discovered, patching the affected system would be a corrective measure to fix the problem.

• **Administrative controls** provide guidance for implementing an organization's security strategy. For example, having a standardized process for configuring systems for new employees is an administrative control. By documenting and following consistent procedures, you ensure that security measures are properly applied and maintained. Administrative controls often dictate how other controls should be set up and kept in place.

Understanding risk, threats, and controls equips you to address the challenges your organization may face, particularly those posed by malicious actors. However, this knowledge alone isn't enough. You also need to perform due diligence—actively managing and addressing risks while maintaining your controls. This is where a risk management program becomes essential to ensure ongoing security and risk mitigation.

Risk Management Programs

Managing risk can be challenging because it involves balancing multiple aspects of cybersecurity simultaneously. Not only must you address existing threats, but you must also maintain the controls you've put in place to mitigate those threats. As a cybersecurity professional, you'll be required to communicate your organization's security posture to people with varying levels of technical knowledge. You'll need to explain why certain risks need to be addressed and how the controls you've chosen will mitigate them. This requires a thorough, ongoing understanding of your organization's security, which is no small task.

A robust risk management program is invaluable. Its purpose is to track your company's risks, the threats it faces, and the controls you've implemented to mitigate those risks. The program should be flexible enough to evolve as your environment changes. It should allow you to add or remove controls as new threats emerge or as previously identified risks are resolved. Additionally, the program should provide a framework for managing one-time risks, such as those associated with major system upgrades or new facility openings.

To manage all these activities, you'll need a specialized tool known as a **risk register**. This is essentially a system for documenting the risks you are actively monitoring. Think of it like an organizer, similar to the ones you might have used in school. It allows you to track the risk, how you're addressing it, and the controls you've implemented to mitigate it. The risk register also helps you monitor risks that haven't been addressed yet or controls that are still in the process of being deployed.

A risk register can be a complex software system that provides detailed status updates, or it can be as simple as a spreadsheet. Even a basic spreadsheet is better than not tracking risks at all. The primary goal of risk management is to track how you're handling risks, and this is often a legal requirement for due diligence. The example graphic below shows how a spreadsheet can be used to track risks. Let's break down each section of the register.

The first two columns list the organization's **risks** and **threats**. Remember that a risk is the potential for harm caused by your actions, whereas a threat is an external event that could cause harm. For example, in Sparkle Kitten Inc.'s case, the risk is that their email system could be compromised. The threat associated with this risk would be a phishing attack from a hacker.

Although risk registers may not always differentiate between hazards and threats, they are useful for tracking the various ways a risk could materialize. For example, **data loss from servers** is always a concern, but the register might list two different threats: one from **malware**, and the other from **user error**. Each has different likelihoods and potential impacts.

The **risk scores** help prioritize which risks need attention first. In the example, data loss due to malware is scored as the highest risk, meaning it should be addressed immediately, as its consequences would be the most severe. The next two columns describe how the risk is being managed and which controls have been put in place. In this case, **anti-malware software** is used to mitigate the risk of malware infection that could lead to data loss.

The following three columns track the status of the control. For example, the anti-malware software was installed on **May 20, 2020**, and **Cheryl** is the designated owner responsible for maintaining and monitoring the control. These columns also highlight any actions still required. For instance, although the organization decided to transfer the risk of kittens losing their fluffiness through **kitten insurance**, this control hasn't been implemented yet. **Ted** is responsible for purchasing the insurance and updating the register once it's in place.

Even though this spreadsheet is simple, it's a highly effective way to organize and manage your organization's risks. It gives you a clear overview of identified risks, their potential impact, and the status of the controls in place. You can easily see who is responsible for each control and which actions still need to be taken. The beauty of this approach is that you don't need deep technical expertise to get a clear picture of whether your organization is secure.

Putting it All Together

Let's apply everything you've learned from this book in a real-world example. Imagine you're a security analyst at a mid-sized company with 500 employees. Part of your daily duties involves monitoring notifications from both staff and security systems, like your firewall and intrusion detection system (IDS).

One morning, you receive an email from a concerned employee. They report having received a suspicious email and clicked on a link inside, which has made them worried about potential issues with their computer. To assess the situation, you run the email through quick phishing detection tools like VirusTotal and MX Toolbox. The email pretends to be a password reset request from Microsoft, but the sender's address is misspelled as M1cos0ft.com.

Upon examining the link, you recognize it might be malicious. The employee explains that clicking the link prompted them to download a password update program, which then ran on their computer. This behavior indicates a possible malware infection, so you immediately initiate a virus scan on the system.

While the scan runs, you check your firewall and IDS alerts for any signs of unusual activity. Sure enough, you spot new, potentially harmful traffic originating from the employee's machine. Not sure how to proceed, you escalate the issue to a senior security specialist on the team. After reviewing the alerts, the senior specialist concludes that the employee likely downloaded malware that's trying to spread ransomware across the network.

The senior specialist takes swift action, adjusting the IDS and firewall settings to block any attempts by the compromised machine to communicate with other systems. Meanwhile, your virus scan detects a known malware toolkit, which you isolate and remove. You also take the precaution of resetting the employee's machine to ensure no lingering threats remain.

Following the incident, you and your security team conduct a post-mortem review to understand what went wrong and how to prevent a similar occurrence in the future. The meeting, led by the CISO, reveals a gap in the company's ability to educate employees on identifying phishing emails—an issue that directly contributed to the ransomware attack.

The CISO adds this finding to the company's risk registry and begins exploring ways to implement training controls. The consensus is that using a specialized phishing training platform will be the most effective approach to addressing this vulnerability.

At the quarterly risk management meeting, the CISO presents this new risk and proposes purchasing a phishing training solution. The head of HR supports this plan, noting that the current employee training platform doesn't cover phishing awareness. The CFO also agrees, citing the low cost and significant potential benefits. The decision is made for the CISO to research several training solutions and report back within a month with a recommendation. The CISO updates the risk registry and assigns a team member to help with the project.

Though this scenario is fictional, it highlights how a company's security operations should work. In this case, simply responding to the employee's phishing report wasn't enough. The security analyst had to cross-reference multiple sources of information and consult with senior team members. Furthermore, security work didn't stop once the immediate threat was mitigated. The post-incident review allowed the company to identify weaknesses and take corrective action. Through collaboration with leadership, the CISO successfully advocated for a customized training platform. This example underscores why a risk management plan is essential—it ties together all aspects of security, identifies risks, and presents solutions in a clear, manageable way.

Exercise: Conducting a Risk Assessment

For this final exercise, choose a target and perform a risk assessment. A risk analysis helps identify all potential hazards to a target and evaluates the management strategy for each risk. Your target could be your home, school, workplace, or any environment where cybersecurity concerns exist. Once you've chosen your target, follow these steps:

1. **Identify assets**: List all assets in the area you're analyzing. For example, at home, you might include laptops, routers, and smart devices like gaming consoles or TVs. Write these down in a spreadsheet or on paper.
2. **List potential risks**: Identify how these assets might be attacked or damaged. Be realistic—while a rogue AI might take over your gaming console in a movie, that's highly unlikely in real life.
3. **Categorize risks using STRIDE**: Use the STRIDE methodology to categorize potential threats. For example, both your TV and game console might be vulnerable to Denial of Service (DoS) attacks.
4. **Evaluate the likelihood and impact**: Consider which threats appear most frequently in your analysis. The more examples you identify, the greater the likelihood of that threat occurring. Also, note the potential impact. For example, if a DoS attack targets your game console, it could prevent you from playing a new video game, which would be frustrating and have a significant impact.
5. **Create a risk registry**: List each risk in a registry, including the type of risk, the specific threat, and a risk score.
6. **Assess existing controls**: Consider the current security measures you have in place to mitigate these risks. For example, in the case of a DoS attack, you might assess the bandwidth your home network can handle, the security features of your console, and any safeguards your Internet Service Provider (ISP) offers.
7. **Document your control strategy**: Complete the risk register by noting how you plan to address each threat and which controls you have in place.

With a comprehensive risk register, you'll have a clear understanding of the risks your target faces and how to manage them. While some threats may be difficult to mitigate (such as a DoS attack), the risk register allows you to practice and refine your risk management approach.

Goodbye, and good luck.

Now that you've built a solid foundation in cybersecurity, you're ready to explore this dynamic field further. Whether you aim to become a cybersecurity professional or simply apply this knowledge to enhance your personal security, you're well-equipped to dive deeper into the topics that interest you.

Here are some final tips to guide you on your cybersecurity journey:

- **Think before you click**: Even the most seasoned experts can fall for phishing attempts when they're rushed. Cybersecurity requires patience—move slowly and carefully to avoid mistakes.
- **Make time for the process**: Security tasks might seem urgent, but rushing through them can lead to mistakes. Take a step back when needed and plan your next move carefully.
- **Trust your instincts**: If something doesn't feel right, don't assume someone else has already checked it. Trust your own judgment and double-check the setup.
- **Seek help when needed**: Cybersecurity isn't a solo endeavor. Reach out to others if you're unsure or need a second opinion—it's a team effort, and collaboration is key.
- **Keep learning**: The cybersecurity landscape evolves quickly. Stay informed and continue expanding your knowledge to keep ahead of new threats and trends.
- **Enjoy the journey**: While cybersecurity is serious business, don't forget to have fun along the way. The challenges can be exciting and rewarding, so embrace the journey!

By following these tips, you'll not only build a secure environment for yourself and your organization, but also enjoy the ever-evolving challenge that is cybersecurity.

CHAPTER FOURTEEN
Enhancing Your Cybersecurity

Improving your security doesn't always mean spending a lot of money. In fact, many effective measures are completely free and require minimal effort. Here are seven simple ways to strengthen your cybersecurity without a significant financial investment.

Understand that you are a target.

A key factor in staying cyber-safe is having the right attitude. People who recognize that hackers are actively trying to breach their devices—such as computers, smartphones, and other smart gadgets—tend to approach cybersecurity with more caution than those who don't fully grasp the threat.

Understanding the risks of today's digital world fosters a healthy skepticism, influencing not only how you protect yourself online but also how you respond to potential threats in everyday situations. This mindset can have a significant impact on your behavior, often in ways you're not even aware of.

For instance, if you believe you're a potential target for cybercriminals, you're less likely to fall for phishing attempts, like emails that appear to come from your bank, because you're more cautious and skeptical of unsolicited messages. But what if the email didn't come from your bank, but from your boss, asking you to ship a laptop to a specific address? Or what if it's a voice message that sounds like yo

ur boss, telling you to take the same action? Cybercriminals can now use deep fake technology to convincingly impersonate voices, making these scenarios even more dangerous.

Similarly, people who understand that their passwords and PINs are valuable targets are more likely to take steps to secure them, whereas those who believe that "cybercriminals wouldn't be interested in my information" may be more careless with their sensitive data.

Use security software.

Any electronic device, such as laptops, smartphones, tablets, etc., that stores sensitive information or connects to networks with other devices, needs security software. Affordable and widely used options typically include antivirus, firewall, antispam, and other protective tools.

For portable devices, it's important to activate tracking and remote wipe features, as well as install mobile-friendly security software right when you get the device. Many smartphones come with security software preinstalled by the carrier, so ensure that it's enabled and properly used.

Encrypt sensitive information.

Always ensure that sensitive data is encrypted. If you're unsure whether something requires encryption, it's better to be cautious and encrypt it. Many versions of Windows offer encryption by default, and there are also free encryption tools available. It's surprising how much sensitive information could have been protected if those who were targeted had simply used available encryption software.

Additionally, avoid sending important information unless it's encrypted. Never enter sensitive details on a website that doesn't use TLS encryption (sometimes mistakenly called SSL, even though SSL has been replaced by TLS). You can verify TLS encryption by checking for HTTPS in the website's URL. While encryption relies on complex mathematical algorithms, you don't need to fully understand them to effectively use and benefit from encryption.

Tip: Be aware that quantum computing — which leverages quantum physics to process data using qubits instead of binary bits (0 or 1) — could soon make many of today's encryption methods obsolete, exposing encrypted data to potential breaches. It's uncertain when quantum computing will reach "quantum supremacy," but experts have varying predictions. Keep an eye on vendor updates to ensure their products remain "quantum-safe."

Currently, two main types of encryption algorithms are widely used, in addition to emerging "quantum-safe" methods:

1. **Symmetric Encryption**: This method uses the same secret key for both encryption and decryption. It's commonly used in simpler encryption tools, and all you need to do is remember a password to decrypt your data.
2. **Asymmetric Encryption**: This uses two separate keys — one for encryption and another for decryption. This method is more secure but is vulnerable to quantum computing threats. In practice, asymmetric encryption is primarily used for securely exchanging data, such as sending a public key to encrypt information that only the recipient, who holds the corresponding private key, can decrypt.

Here's how asymmetric encryption works in practice:

- To send confidential data to John, you encrypt it using his public key. Only he can decrypt it with his private key.

- To send encrypted data to John, you encrypt it with your private key. John will use your public key to decrypt it and verify that you sent it, as only you have the private key that matches your public key.
- If you want to send information to John that only he can read and verify that it came from you, you encrypt the data with both your private key and his public key.

Because asymmetric encryption is processor-intensive, it's typically not used for entire conversations. Instead, it encrypts session keys that allow for symmetric encryption to take place during communication, with the session keys being securely exchanged through asymmetric encryption.

Back-Up Often

Make sure to back up your data frequently enough that if something goes wrong, you won't have to worry about losing too much information, especially if your last backup was days ago.

Tip: This is the general rule of thumb. If you're uncertain whether you're backing up often enough, it's likely that you're not. No matter how convenient it may seem, avoid keeping your backups connected to your computer or network. If your backups are attached in this way, there's a risk that ransomware or other types of malware could infect and damage them as well, rendering your backups useless. This is a real concern — many people who initially felt secure because they had recently backed up their devices became alarmed when they realized the backups had also been compromised by the malware.

It's important to store backups both onsite and offsite. Onsite backups offer quick recovery, while offsite backups ensure that you can still access your data even if something happens to the primary site, such as physical destruction or inaccessibility. Also, regularly test your backups to ensure they can be restored when needed. As many have learned the hard way, a backup is useless if you can't restore from it.

Don't share login credentials.

Everyone who uses a critical system should have their own login credentials. It's best not to share passwords for sensitive services like online banking, email, or social media with your children or significant other. Instead, create separate accounts for each individual.

Keep in mind that having individual logins not only makes it easier to trace the source of any issues that arise but also encourages a greater sense of responsibility within the household. This approach motivates everyone to take better care in securing their passwords.

Use proper authentication.

You've probably heard the common advice to use complex passwords for all your accounts, but don't overdo it. If having too many complicated passwords leads you to reuse them across multiple sensitive systems or write them down in insecure places, try using alternative methods for creating passwords. For example, combine words, numbers, and names in unique ways, such as *custard4tennis6Steinberg*.

For highly sensitive accounts, take advantage of stronger authentication methods, like multifactor authentication, when available.

For less important accounts, where security isn't a top concern — such as accounts that just allow a website to follow you but don't store anything valuable — you can use simpler, easy-to-remember passwords. There's no need to overcomplicate things for accounts that don't require high security. You can even reuse these passwords across such sites, but never for those where security is crucial.

Alternatively, consider using a password manager for convenience, but avoid storing your most critical passwords there. Keep these vital passwords in your memory to avoid relying entirely on one tool. If you need to leave passwords for someone else in case of an emergency, write them down on paper and store them securely in a fire- and water-resistant safe deposit box or safe.

Use Social Media Wisely.

Oversharing on social media has led to many problems, including the exposure of sensitive information, breaches of compliance regulations, and even aiding criminals in executing cyber and physical attacks. When posting online, double-check that your phone doesn't autocorrect or insert personal details without your knowledge. Also, be cautious about accidentally copying and pasting sensitive information into social media posts. These types of mistakes happen more often than you might think.

Separate internet access

Most modern Wi-Fi routers support multiple networks. If your router has this feature, take advantage of it. For instance, if you work from home, connect your laptop to one Wi-Fi network while your children use a different one for browsing and gaming. Check for the "Guest" option in your router's settings — this is typically where you can set up a second network. Many people use the Guest network not just for visitors but also for their children's internet-connected devices.

Use Public Wi-Fi Safely (or Don't Use It!)

While public Wi-Fi is a convenient tool that many people use frequently, it presents significant cybersecurity risks. If your phone allows you to create a personal hotspot, use that connection instead of relying on public Wi-Fi. However, personal hotspots aren't always an option, especially in areas with poor cellular signals, such as underground locations.

Cybersecurity experts who advise against using public Wi-Fi often face resistance, as it's not always practical to avoid it, much like advising people to abandon unsafe computers and revert to typewriters. If you must use public Wi-Fi, it's essential to know how to do so securely. Learn various techniques for protecting yourself from cyber threats before you connect, ensuring you're prepared to defend against potential risks.

Hire a Professional

Seeking expert advice can be a wise investment, particularly when starting or managing a small business. An information security specialist can help you develop and implement a solid cybersecurity plan. The modest cost of professional support is often well worth it, saving you time, money, and frustration in the long run.

Tip: Just as you would hire a lawyer if you were facing legal charges, a doctor for a serious injury, or an accountant if the IRS audits you, you should consider hiring a cybersecurity professional. The cybercriminals and hackers targeting you are highly skilled, and having an expert on your side is crucial to protecting your business.

CHAPTER FIFTEEN
Lessons from Major Cybersecurity Breaches

Gaining insight from the experiences of others can help individuals steer clear of unnecessary hardship. In this chapter, I focus on seven significant breaches that offer important lessons. I selected these breaches because they had a direct impact on either myself or a member of my family, and considering their scale, it's highly likely they affected you and your family as well.

Marriott

In November 2018, Marriott International disclosed a massive security breach in which hackers infiltrated the systems of the Starwood hotel brand as early as 2014. These intruders remained undetected until September 2018, almost two years after Marriott had acquired Starwood. Marriott estimated that the breach impacted up to 500 million customers, with compromised data ranging from basic details like names and contact information to more sensitive information such as passport numbers, travel histories, and frequent traveler numbers. Additionally, Marriott reported that up to 100 million credit card numbers, including expiration dates but not CVC codes, were exposed. However, the credit card data was stored in an encrypted database, and Marriott found no evidence suggesting the hackers could decrypt it.

Investigations suggested that the attack was orchestrated by a Chinese hacker group with ties to the Chinese government, aiming to collect intelligence on U.S. citizens. If these claims are accurate, the Marriott breach would become the largest known case of a nation-state-sponsored attack on civilian personal data.

In July 2019, the UK's Information Commissioner's Office (ICO) announced plans to fine Marriott $123 million for failing to adequately protect consumer data, as required by the European Union's General Data Protection Regulation (GDPR). Marriott indicated in an SEC filing that it intended to appeal the fine, which had not yet been formally imposed at the time of the announcement.

This incident highlights two key lessons:

1. **Thorough cybersecurity audits are essential when acquiring a company**: Any vulnerabilities or ongoing security breaches within the acquired company can lead to significant issues for the new owner. Moreover, regulators may hold the purchasing company responsible for any security lapses in the acquired firm. As noted by UK Information Commissioner Elizabeth Denham, the GDPR mandates that organizations must take accountability for the personal data they hold. This requires conducting rigorous due diligence during acquisitions and ensuring proper measures are in place to protect this data.

2. **Foreign governments highly value civilian data for intelligence purposes**: Nations, particularly those in competition with the U.S. and Western countries, are increasingly targeting civilian data. This information may be used for espionage, blackmail, or other purposes, such as leveraging financial stress to recruit informants. With storage costs low and advancements in quantum computing potentially breaking encryption in the future, governments may accumulate vast amounts of encrypted data, hoping to decrypt it later. As most data is not encrypted, any encrypted information may be seen as valuable, incentivizing efforts to collect it.

Target

In December 2013, Target revealed that hackers had breached its systems, compromising the payment card details of approximately 40 million customers. Over the following weeks, the company revised this estimate, and it was later determined that up to 110 million customers may have been affected. The stolen data included not only credit card information but also additional personal details, such as names, addresses, phone numbers, and email addresses.

The breach occurred when hackers exploited a vulnerability in the network of a third-party HVAC contractor that had access to Target's point-of-sale systems. The fallout from the attack led to the resignation of Target's CEO and CIO, and the breach ultimately cost the company an estimated $162 million.

Two key lessons emerge from the Target breach:

1. **Management accountability for cybersecurity**: When a company is hacked, its leadership is held responsible. The breach can damage professional reputations and derail careers.
2. **The security of third parties matters**: A company's cybersecurity is only as strong as its most vulnerable partner. In this case, an unsecured third party with access to Target's systems became the entry point for the attack. This highlights the importance of securing all parties that have access to your network. Even if you maintain good cybersecurity practices, allowing untrusted users or devices to connect to your network can lead to breaches, as malware from their systems can spread to yours.

Sony Pictures

In November 2014, a hacker publicly revealed sensitive data stolen from Sony Pictures, including copies of unreleased films, internal employee emails, compensation details, and personal information about staff and their families. The breach also involved the deletion of significant portions of Sony's IT infrastructure. Hackers had been infiltrating Sony's systems for up to a year, potentially exfiltrating as much as 100 gigabytes of data. Sony's cybersecurity measures seemed to fail to detect or adequately respond to the large-scale data transfer, and management appeared to dismiss many of the hackers' demands, mistaking them for spam emails.

The attack escalated when the hackers, claiming responsibility, threatened to carry out physical terrorist attacks on movie theaters screening Sony's upcoming film *The Interview*, a comedy about an assassination plot against North Korean leader Kim Jong-un. The threat was taken seriously due to the credibility established by the breach, leading major American theater chains to refuse to show the film. In response, Sony canceled the film's theatrical release, instead offering it for digital download and a limited number of screenings.

While some cybersecurity experts initially questioned the attribution, the U.S. government later blamed North Korea for the attack and its threats. In September 2018, the U.S. filed formal charges against a North Korean citizen, accusing him of orchestrating the hack while working for North Korea's intelligence agency.

Two key lessons from the Sony breach are:

1. **The need for proper data loss prevention (DLP) technology**: Depending on the technology Sony employed, this incident highlights either the importance of implementing effective data loss prevention measures or how cybersecurity tools can be ineffective if not used correctly.
2. **Nation-states may leverage cyberattacks for political purposes**: Governments may use cyberattacks to target companies or individuals they view as threats to their political or strategic objectives, as demonstrated by North Korea's actions against Sony.

U.S. Office of Personnel Management

In June 2015, the U.S. Office of Personnel Management (OPM), which manages federal employee records and personnel processes, announced that it had experienced a major data breach. Initially, the government believed that far fewer records had been compromised, but the total number eventually reached over 20 million. The stolen data included personally identifiable information (PII) such as Social Security numbers, home addresses, and birth dates, affecting both current and former government employees as well as individuals who had undergone background checks but were not hired.

At first, it was thought that sensitive SF-86 forms—used for background checks to grant security clearances—had not been accessed. However, later reports suggested that these forms were indeed compromised, potentially exposing a wealth of private information about individuals holding various security clearances. The breach is believed to be a combination of multiple incidents: one dating back to 2012 that was discovered in March 2014, and another that started in May 2014 but wasn't identified until April 2015.

Two major lessons from the OPM breach are:

1. **Government agencies are vulnerable to large-scale breaches**: Like private sector organizations, government institutions are not immune to significant cyberattacks. Even after experiencing a breach, they may remain vulnerable to future incidents. Additionally, these agencies may not detect breaches promptly and could initially downplay the severity of the situation.
2. **Breaches can affect people with no direct, recent ties to the organization**: The OPM breach impacted not only current and former employees but also individuals who had not interacted with the agency for years or who had applied for clearances long ago but were never hired. This highlights how breaches can extend far beyond the immediate organization and affect people who might not even remember their data was stored there.

Anthem

In February 2015, Anthem, the second-largest health insurer in the United States, disclosed that it had fallen victim to a cyberattack that compromised the personal information of approximately 80 million current and former clients. The stolen data included names, addresses, Social Security numbers, dates of birth, and employment histories. While medical records were not believed to have been targeted, the exposed data was still highly sensitive and posed a significant risk of identity theft for many individuals. The breach is considered one of the largest in the history of the U.S. healthcare industry, with the attack believed to have begun in 2014 after an employee at an Anthem subsidiary fell victim to a phishing email.

Two key lessons from the Anthem breach are:

1. **The healthcare industry is a growing target for cyberattacks**: The breach highlights the increasing vulnerability of the healthcare sector, a trend also seen in the rising number of ransomware attacks aimed at hospitals in recent years.
2. **Simple, classic techniques are often behind major breaches**: While high-profile attacks are often thought to require sophisticated methods, many serious breaches are the result of basic, classic tactics like phishing. Human error, such as falling for a phishing scam, remains a critical factor in most significant security incidents.

Colonial Pipeline and JBS SA

In May 2021, during the ongoing COVID-19 pandemic, two major organizations suffered significant ransomware attacks, both of which had wide-reaching societal consequences.

Colonial Pipeline Attack
On May 7, 2021, Colonial Pipeline, a major fuel pipeline operator responsible for transporting fuel to over half of the U.S. East Coast, was hit by a ransomware attack. The company's IT team quickly realized that the malware had the potential to severely disrupt the systems managing

pipeline operations. As a precautionary measure, Colonial Pipeline shut down its operations, leading to fuel shortages in various areas. Fuel prices, already on the rise, spiked further, and in some cases, airlines had to adjust their flight schedules due to difficulties in securing fuel.

Following the attack, Colonial Pipeline, under government pressure, paid nearly $4.5 million in Bitcoin to the cybercriminals, who then provided a decryption tool to restore the company's systems. The FBI was able to recover a portion of the ransom, though not all of it. In response to the attack, both the President of the United States and the Governor of Georgia declared states of emergency, and the Federal Motor Carrier Safety Administration took action to alleviate the fuel shortage. Later in 2021, the U.S. government offered a $10 million reward for information leading to the capture of those responsible. While law enforcement had strong suspicions regarding the perpetrators, the individuals behind the attack remained at large at the time of this report.

JBS

On May 30, just weeks after the Colonial Pipeline cyberattack, JBS S.A., a Brazilian meat processing giant supplying about 20% of the world's meat, suffered a ransomware attack. This disrupted beef and pork production in several countries, including the U.S., Canada, and Australia. The attack led to meat shortages in some regions and prompted the U.S. government to delay the release of data on wholesale beef and pork prices. JBS resumed operations on June 2 after paying an $11 million ransom in Bitcoin.

A significant takeaway from these attacks is that cybersecurity is vital for more than just protecting data and finances—it directly impacts our daily lives. People who faced long gas lines during the Colonial Pipeline breach or those who couldn't find meat at stores on a holiday weekend experienced firsthand how cyberattacks can disrupt everyday activities. As our dependence on technology grows, so does the potential for cyberattacks to affect our quality of life.

Until recently, there were several reasons to use public Wi-Fi, especially before 4G (the fourth generation of cellular networks) was widely available. Wi-Fi often provided faster connections than cellular networks, and mobile signals were unavailable in many areas or only accessible through phones and cellular tablets, not laptops. Additionally, mobile data plans were expensive, particularly for travelers outside their carrier's coverage area.

However, the situation has changed. With the widespread availability of 4G and the rollout of faster 5G networks, cellular connections now support most online activities, including business and leisure, without significant compromise in speed. Mobile data plans have also become more affordable, allowing users to share cellular connections with their devices. In many cases, using a cellular network instead of public Wi-Fi is both practical and safer.

Despite this, there are still instances where you might need to use public Wi-Fi, such as in underground facilities with no cellular service or when visiting locations where Wi-Fi is provided due to poor cellular coverage. If you find yourself in this situation, here are some important tips to protect your devices while using public Wi-Fi:

- **Be cautious about public Wi-Fi:** Avoid connecting to networks set up by potential hackers. Use a disposable device if you must connect to such networks, and ensure you aren't accessing any sensitive accounts.
- **Use your phone as a hotspot:** If you have an unlimited cellular data plan and a strong signal, turning your phone into a mobile hotspot is a safer alternative to using public Wi-Fi.
- **Turn off Wi-Fi when not in use:** Disable Wi-Fi to prevent your device from automatically connecting to potentially harmful networks. This also saves battery life and protects you from malicious networks posing as legitimate public Wi-Fi.
- **Avoid sensitive tasks over public Wi-Fi:** Refrain from banking, shopping, or accessing medical records while on public Wi-Fi. Avoid logging into anything that requires a password, especially in areas where others can watch you.
- **Don't reset passwords on public Wi-Fi:** It's safer to avoid resetting passwords in public places, whether or not you're on public Wi-Fi. Public areas may have cameras or other risks that make it unsafe to change sensitive information.
- **Use a VPN:** If you must use public Wi-Fi for sensitive activities, a VPN (Virtual Private Network) can add an extra layer of security. However, be aware that using a VPN might slow down your connection, and you should consider the legal implications of routing traffic through different countries.
- **Use encryption:** Always use HTTPS instead of HTTP on supported websites to protect the content of your communications. Avoid email services that don't encrypt messages during delivery. Encryption is even more important when using public Wi-Fi.
- **Disable resource sharing:** If your device shares resources, such as files or printers, make sure to disable these settings before connecting to public Wi-Fi. Check your device to ensure there are no shared resources left active.
- **Use security software:** Ensure that your device has up-to-date antivirus and firewall software when connecting to public Wi-Fi. For smartphones and tablets, use apps that secure your device.
- **Know the difference between public and shared Wi-Fi:** Not all public Wi-Fi is equally risky. A password-protected guest network at a business office is generally safer than an open network at a public library. However, even in a more secure environment, remain cautious as other users may still pose threats.

By following these precautions, you can better safeguard yourself and your devices when using public Wi-Fi networks.

CONCLUSION

As people spend more time online, it's essential to take precautions to protect oneself. Cybersecurity refers to the protective measures used to defend computer systems from unauthorized access or attacks, with the primary goal of safeguarding individuals' well-being, assets, and reputation. It's crucial to exercise caution when visiting unfamiliar websites and downloading content onto your devices. Always read the privacy policies of websites and seek advice from trusted adults, such as parents, when in doubt. Below are key guidelines to help ensure your online safety:

1. **Keep Personal Information Private:** Avoid sharing personal details online, such as your name, school, home address, phone number, social security number, birthdate, passwords, or other sensitive information. Cybercriminals can use this information to locate you or access your personal accounts. Be particularly cautious when sharing personal details on untrustworthy websites.
2. **Check for Secure Websites:** Ensure that websites you visit use "https://" in their URLs, indicating they are secure. A closed padlock icon next to the URL further confirms that the connection is encrypted. If you see an open lock, be wary as the site may be unsafe. Be cautious of counterfeit websites that may look like the legitimate ones you frequently visit. Always double-check the website's domain name (e.g., www.disney.com or www.facebook.com) and avoid sites with extra characters in the URL, like "www.disney1.com."
3. **Create Strong Passwords:** Many websites require strong passwords, often asking for a combination of uppercase and lowercase letters, numbers, and symbols. When creating passwords, aim for at least eight characters and avoid using easily guessable information, such as your name, pet's name, or birthdate. Instead, use complex combinations of letters, numbers, and symbols.
4. **Use a Password Manager:** If remembering multiple passwords is difficult, consider using a password manager. This tool securely stores your passwords, helping you avoid saving them in your web browser. Only save passwords in your browser if you have reliable antivirus software installed to protect your device.
5. **Think Twice Before Posting:** Anything shared online can be permanent and accessible indefinitely. Keep your social media presence positive and avoid sharing personal information about yourself or others. Don't post explicit images, and be mindful of the potential impact of your content, as it could reach a large audience.

By following these guidelines and being cautious online, you can better protect your privacy and ensure a safer digital experience.

INDEX

(

(IoT) security, 18

A

A Serious Matter, 31
Account Safety, 129
Addressing Power Problems, 167
Advanced, 13, 18, 45
Advantages and Disadvantages, 90
Adware, 39
Algorithms, 88
An Analysis of the Escalation of Cybercrime, 12
Analysis of Potential Attack Vectors, 17
Anticipated Developments in PKI, 95
APTs, 18
Artificial Intelligence (AI), 19
Assessing Your Existing Security Protocols, 233
Attacks on Web Services, 41
authentication, 162
Avoid conducting sensitive tasks, 136
Avoid installing software, 131
Avoid installing software from untrusted sources, 131
Avoid rooting your phone, 131
Avoiding Connection, 140

B

Backup solutions, 72
Biometric data, 162
Blended (opportunistic and targeted) attacks, 46
Blended malware, 40
Blockchain Technology, 19
Botnets and zombies, 28
Brute-force attacks, 47
Buffer overflow attacks, 48
Business data theft, 34

C

Captured in Transit, 31
Career path, 195, 196
CEH, 200
CEO fraud, 29
Challenges and Considerations, 87, 94, 97, 101, 105
Challenges and Opportunities, 14
Chief information security officer, 191
Chief information security officer (CISO), 191
Chief Information Security Officer (CISO), 196
CISM, 199
CISO, 191, 196
CISSP, 198
clicking on links, 138
communication protocols, 155
Compliance and Regulation, 18
COMPUTER SECURITY TECHNOLOGY, 143
Concerns about Network Security, 119
Concerns with Social Engineering, 125
CONCLUSION, 228
Conduct penetration tests, 166
Conquering Bad Credit, 202
Consider the consequences before you decide to share, 75
Consider using HTTPS, 166
Consider using one-time, 132
Consider your words before sharing them online, 76
credit card, 131, 132
credit card numbers, 131, 132
Cross-site scripting, 47
Cryptocurrency miners, 39
Cryptographer, 192
Cyber Bombs, 36
Cyber Bombs That Infiltrate Your Devices, 36
CYBERATTACKERS, 50
CYBERATTACKERS AND THEIR COLORED HATS, 50
Cyberattackers categories, 50
Cybersecurity Career, 189
CYBERSECURITY CONSIDERATIONS WHEN WORKING FROM HOME, 118
CYBERSECURITY FOR BUSINESSES, 147
CYBERSECURITY FOR BUSINESSES AND ORGANIZATIONS, 147
Cybersecurity Frameworks, 17
Cybersecurity Fundamentals, 9
Cybersecurity regulations expert, 194

Cybersecurity Threats and Trends, 18
Cyberwarriors, 58

D

Data destruction attacks, 28
Data exfiltration, 35
DDoS, 26
debit cards, 53
Defend your system from denial-of-service attacks, 165
Denial-of-service, 26
Denial-of-service (DoS) attacks, 26
Detecting, 72, 111
Develop standardized communication, 155
Direct financial fraud, 51
DoS, 26
Drive-by downloads, 43

E

Eavesdropping, 123
Effective Strategies for Incident Response, 106
Emerging Technologies, 19
Emerging Technologies in Cybersecurity, 19
Encrypting Data at Rest and in Transit, 96
Encrypting Data in Transit, 126
Encryption, 85, 86, 88, 89
Ensure efficient management of inbound access, 164
Ensure that personal items are not visible in the camera frame, 124
Ensure that your devices are always kept up to date, 135
Ensure the security of your video conferences, 124
Ensuring Cybersecurity, 123
Ensuring Data Security, 140
Ensuring Safety from Potential Hazards, 67
Ensuring the Protection of User Account Data, 130
Ensuring the Safety of Your External Accounts, 129
Ensuring the Security of Data Shared with Parties You've Interacted With, 138
Ensuring the security of employee data, 158
EtherPeek, 143
Ethical hacker, 192
Ethics, 201
Examining the Risks Addressed, 22

Examining the Risks Addressed by Cybersecurity Measures, 22
Exercise caution when using payment cards, 167
Experienced in the field of security engineering, 190
Expert in forensic analysis, 194
Exploring Alternative Careers, 202
Exploring Alternative Careers with a Focus on Cybersecurity, 202
Exploring Cybersecurity, 157
Exploring Defense Mechanisms, 17
Exploring the Monetization Strategies, 51
Exploring the Monetization Strategies of Cybercriminals, 51

F

Fake malware, 40
Fake malware on computers, 40
financial, 51, 52
Find out how backups are managed, 156
Firewall/router, 68
Frequently Asked Questions, 49, 82, 102, 126, 167, 203

G

GDPR, 18, 161
GETTING STARTED, 4
GETTING STARTED WITH CYBERSECURITY, 4
GETTING TO KNOW COMMON CYBER ATTACKS, 25
Google's highly advanced computers, 61
GSEC, 200

H

Hardware, 73, 140
Highlighting Maintenance Challenges, 44
high-risk locations, 136
HIPAA, 19, 162
Human error, 123

I

Identifying Indicators, 113
Identifying Signs of Compromise, 114
Implement and uphold social media policies, 152

Implement policies for employees, 163
Implement policies for employees to bring their own devices (BYOD), 163
Implementing Effective Cybersecurity, 2
Implementing Effective Cybersecurity Measures, 2
Implementing employee policies, 150
Importance of Cybersecurity Measures, 14
incident response, 194
INCIDENT RESPONSE BASICS, 104
Incident Response Lifecycle, 104
Information Assurance Fundamentals, 9
Injection attacks, 47
Insurance, 19, 74, 157
Interception, 31
Internet of Things, 18, 65
INTRODUCTION, 1, 83
Introduction to Cybersecurity Considerations, 118
Introduction to Incident Response, 104
IOCs, 113
ISO/IEC, 17
Issues caused by human activity in the environment, 57

K

Keep a close eye on your accounts, 133
Keep track of employees, 153
Key concepts, 16
Key concepts and terminologies, 16

L

Laws regarding the disclosure of breaches, 161
LC4, 144
Learning, 74
Limit the access of administrators, 149
Lock your PC, 135

M

Make sure to access your accounts in secure locations, 136
Make sure to respond promptly to any fraud alerts, 137
Malformed URL attacks, 48
Malicious software targeting, 41
Malicious software targeting mobile devices, 41
Malvertising, 42
Malware, 36
management, 164
Managing a Remote Workforce, 153
Metasploit, 144
Methods for Securing Data during Transmission, 96

N

Natural disasters, 57
Network and Security Concepts, 9
Network Infrastructure Poisoning, 42
NIST, 17
NMAP, 144
Not All Dangers Come From Attackers, 55

O

Offensive hacker, 193
opportunistic and targeted, 46
Opportunistic attacks, 45
Overcoming a Criminal Record, 201
Overview, 50, 83, 88, 118, 129, 143, 147

P

Pandemics, 57
Password theft, 43
passwords, 138
Perimeter defense, 67
Persistent, 13, 18
Personal data theft, 33
Pharming, 31
Phishing, 29
phone number, 138
Phony security subscription, 41
Phony security subscription renewal notifications, 41
physical, 71
PKI Components, 91
Privacy, 195
Profiting off illegal trading of securities, 52
Protecting against These Attackers, 62
PROTECTION AGAINST CYBER ATTACKS, 63
Provide each individual with their own set of login credentials, 149
Public Key Infrastructure (PKI), 91
PURSUING A CYBERSECURITY CAREER, 189

Q

QualysGuard, 143

R

Ransomware, 37, 54
Recovering, 72
Regularly monitor access device lists, 137
regulations expert, 195
Remember to log out once you're done, 134
Report any suspicious activity as soon as possible, 133
Responding, 72
Review the most recent login information, 137
Risk Identification, 66
Rootkits, 47

S

Scareware, 38
Secure Communication Protocols Types, 98
Securing Data at Parties You Haven't Interacted With, 139
SECURING YOUR ACCOUNTS, 129
Security administrator, 192
Security analyst, 191
Security architect, 191
Security auditor, 192
Security consultant, 193
Security director, 191
security engineer, 193
Security expert witness, 194
Security manager, 191
Security researcher, 193
Security software, 70
Security specialist, 194
Security+, 200
Senior security architect, 195
sensitive information, 131, 137
Separate Internet access for personal devices, 163
Session hijacking, 48
Smishing, 30
social engineering, 137, 157
social engineering tactics, 157
Social Security numbers, 60
Software, 193
Spyware, 45

SQL, 48
SQL injection, 48
State-Sponsored Cyber Warfare, 13
Stealing credit cards, 53
Stealing goods, 53
Strategies for Exploitation and Financial Gain, 12
SuperScan, 144

T

Tampering with Other People's Belongings, 31
Targeted attacks, 46
The CIA Triad, 22
The General Data Protection, 18
The General Data Protection Regulation (GDPR), 18
The Health Insurance Portability, 19
The Health Insurance Portability and Accountability Act, 19
The Health Insurance Portability and Accountability Act (HIPAA), 19
The Importance of Secure Communication Protocols in Cybersecurity, 99
The objective of cybersecurity, 22
The Origins, 12
The Significance of PKI in Cybersecurity, 93
The Value of Transitioning, 8
The Value of Transitioning from a Non-Technical Background, 8
The vulnerability of cybersecurity, 55
The World without Cybersecurity, 19
Theft, 123
Threat, 41, 64
Threats, 11, 13, 14, 16, 18, 55
Tips for maintaining your privacy, 77
Tracking the location of mobile devices, 61
transactions, 130
Trojans, 37
trustworthy individuals, 130

U

Unauthorized access, 35
Understanding Endpoints, 66
Understanding Your Current Cybersecurity Posture, 63
unencrypted connection, 137
Use a familiar network, 155

Use a separate browser solely for tasks that require a higher level of security, 135
Use alerts, 136
Use payment services that eliminate the need, 131
Use suitable devices, 136
Using Smart Devices with Safety in Mind, 81

V

Verifiability, 201
Viruses, 12, 36
Vishing, 30
VPN, 166
Vulnerability assessment analyst, 192

W

What are the common security risks associated with remote-worker networks?, 119
What Is Cybersecurity?, 4
What steps can be taken to mitigate these risks?, 120
Wi-Fi, 136
Worms, 12, 37

Y

Your mobile devices, 64
Your networking tool, 65
Your work environment, 65

Z

Zero-day malware, 40